An Introduction to the Collected Works of C. G. Jung

An Introduction to the Collected Works of C. G. Jung

Psyche as Spirit

Clifford Mayes

ROWMAN & LITTLEFIELD
Lanham • Boulder • New York • London

Published by Rowman & Littlefield
A wholly owned subsidiary of
The Rowman & Littlefield Publishing Group, Inc.
4501 Forbes Boulevard, Suite 200, Lanham, Maryland 20706
www.rowman.com

Unit A, Whitacre Mews, 26-34 Stannary Street, London SE11 4AB,
United Kingdom

British Library Cataloguing in Publication Information Available

Library of Congress Cataloging-in-Publication Data
Names: Mayes, Clifford, author.
Title: An introduction to the collected works of C.G. Jung : psyche as spirit / Clifford
    Mayes, Brigham Young University.
Description: Lanham : Rowman & Littlefield, [2017] | Includes bibliographical references
    and index.
Identifiers: LCCN 2016000796 (print) | LCCN 2016008725 (ebook) | ISBN
    9781442262126 (cloth : alk. paper) | ISBN 9781442262133 (pbk. : alk. paper) | ISBN
    9781442262140 (electronic)
Subjects: LCSH: Jung, C. G. (Carl Gustav), 1875-1961. | Jungian psychology.
Classification: LCC BF109.J8 M348 2017 (print) | LCC BF109.J8 (ebook) | DDC 150.19/
    54092—dc23
LC record available at http://lccn.loc.gov/2016000796

Printed in the United States of America

Contents

Acknowledgments

I am grateful to Molly White, associate editor for psychology and psychotherapy at Rowman & Littlefield, and Alden Perkins, senior production editor at Rowman & Littlefield, for their superb help in guiding this project to completion. They are the gold standard of editors.

My research assistant, Alex Newton, consistently goes the extra mile for me, and he does so with a keen intelligence as well as a delightful sense of humor.

I wish to offer Dr. Pamela Blackwell, a Jungian-oriented therapist of rare insight and skill, a very special thanks for our intensive and extensive conversations about Jungian psychology over the last two decades. They have been highly important in my ever-evolving view of Jung the man and the psychology he engendered in its classical, developmental, and postmodern forms.

I'm thankful to those colleagues who reviewed this book and offered their invaluable feedback, including among others Eugene Geist (Ohio University) and Susan Rowland (Pacifica Graduate Institute).

I alone am responsible for any errors or shortcomings in this book.

To Father David Mayer, SVD, PhD, I am thankful for spiritual guidance and encouragement in my research and, indeed, in my life over the last thirty years. *Cor ad cor loquitur.*

I am grateful to Genpo Roshi Merzel, Abbott of the Big Heart Sangha, who helped me over years of sitting at the Kanzeon Zen Center in Salt Lake City to arrive at inner places that allow me to appreciate many things, not least of all the realm of the archetypes, more deeply. I am also grateful to my Tai Chi teacher, Dr. Art Barrett, for his similarly profound instruction over the last two decades.

The precious friendship of professors Robert Bullough, Joe Matthews, and Vance Randall sustained me through various moments and passages of personal doubt and even defeat in the last decade and helped me regroup and stay on track.

Above all, I am grateful to my daughter, Elizabeth, and to my wife, Evelyn, for being the two beams of inexpressibly lovely light from heaven that clarify my path and gladden my heart.

My daughter's courageous lifestyle choices, her passionate commitment to social justice, her enormous poetic gifts, and her compassion and humility render her heroic in her father's adoring eyes and thankful to God for the honor of being her father.

In my wife, Evelyn, I have been blessed beyond measure. As I read aloud the *Eshet Chayil* before saying the *Kiddush* every Friday night in my imperfect Hebrew, I feel that its author must have seen my wife in vision when he wrote: "Her worth is far above rubies. The heart of her husband trusts in her and nothing shall he lack. She is robed in strength and dignity. She opens her mouth with wisdom. Her tongue is guided by kindness. Her children come forward and bless her. Her husband too and he praises her." It is to her that I dedicate this book.

Introduction

I first read Jung in 1971, when I was a junior in English literature at the University of California. It was a ragtag, used-bookstore copy, fiercely underlined in red and mercilessly dog-eared, of *Man and His Symbols.* Jung's introduction to that volume bore down on me like lightning out of suddenly cracked-open space.

Here was something that answered my dedication to the world of symbols, which I had not found in my parents' agnosticism, organized religion, or the existentialist ethos that ruled the day in academia. For I believed then, and even more so now, that the symbolic domain takes precedence, subjectively, over the "objective" empirical world—in those things that matter most, that is.

Reading more and more deeply into Jung—a project that started then and has not stopped to this day—what I found gathered under one tent in Jung's *Collected Works* were psyche, culture, art, and spirit, which the physician-scholar Jung had brought together in the opening decades of the twentieth century. He had done so in a way that shed light on one's personal issues in all their specificity, to be sure, but also in terms of universal themes and images spanning all times and places. A portrait of psyche that viewed the individual human being *sub specie eternitatis* as a creature of eternity, must, I felt, be inherently spiritual.

Today, I find that two things continue to be true in my ongoing engagement with Jung's works and lend bearings to my journey.

The first is simple awe at how the Eternal manifests itself uniquely in each person's life as well as across the spectrum of spiritual traditions. The second is an ever-deepening appreciation of the power of Jung's view of psyche to honor this uniqueness in what he maintained must be each individual's pilgrimage to the Timeless within, and to accomplish this with reference to the universal symbols, figures, myths, and motifs that announce both the exasperating limits and perpetual possibilities of the human condition. In Jung's work, the general and the specific wed.

This inevitably individual trek to the Eternal both *in* and *as* one's center is known in Jungian psychology as the process of "individuation." It is a cornerstone of Jung's *Collected Works.* As does Hinduism, Jung called this Center in each of us the "Self"—with the capital *S* added by later Jungians to distinguish it from the mere "ego." It is our primary life task to courageously engage and uniquely absorb the universal Center in and as our own center, and then to bear witness to that union with the inner-Eternal in compassionate action in the world.

Forty-four years after I first opened a copy of *Man and His Symbols* at eighteen years old, I am still engrossed by Jung. His writings have deeply influenced my personal life and shaped my work as a professor of educational psychology whose goal has been to approach the mysteries of what it means to teach and to learn by sailing on the ship of Jungian psychology to the various shores of those enigmatic processes. I am told that these journeys have resulted in something called "Jungian pedagogy."

Naturally, my understanding of Jung has been greatly affected over the years by second-, third-, and even fourth-generation Jungian and post-Jungian research, as well as by personal scholarly conversations with other Jungian scholars and practitioners. Whether by phone, talks over dinner, e-mails, or at conferences, these conversations always deepen my own understanding of Jung's work, even when—indeed, *especially* when—my conversant and I disagree.

For it is one of the more felicitous facts about Jungian scholarship that Jungians tend to be a very agreeable lot despite the various groups into which we have formed. Such differences are a sign of life, not strife, if handled well. We all seem, in my estimation, to have a shared sense of "something far more deeply interfused" in the human experience, as Wordsworth put it at the end of *The Prelude* in 1850, just twenty-five years before Jung was born. Indeed, the sense of *something far more deeply interfused* in the human experience is a good start at a working definition of a central concept in Jungian psychology: the archetype. We will discuss it in depth throughout this book.

I see the process of individuation and the discovery of the Self as being a spiritual goal, and our central one in this life. I believe that this is what Jung and his inner circle of disciples intended, although how we might comprehend and enact that extremely variable, highly charged idea "spirituality" in our lives is a moveable feast.

I favor the notion of existentialist theologian Paul Tillich (1987) that continuously exploring and always deepening one's "ultimate concerns" regarding this life, and what may or may not lie beyond it, while growing in passion and compassion, *are* one's spirituality. By this standard, I have found that many people not involved with any kind of organized religion are very spiritual and some people who are members of an organized religion are not.

There are Jungians who feel it is an error to say that Jung was himself, or intended his work to be read as, in any sense "spiritual." I mention them throughout the book and direct the reader to some of their major works so that you can follow those lines of thought if you wish. Although I obviously do not hold to these interpretations of Jung in their entirety, I certainly see value in many of them and have learned much from them.

Still, I and many Jungians feel it is abundantly clear that Jung's intent was not merely to cast light on the individual's *psychological* functioning but, more importantly, on his or her psycho*spiritual* dynamics, seeing the specific human being against the backdrop of eternity—*sub specie eternitatis* again—bound by time but wishing to bound beyond time.

At the same time, Jungian psychology is quite practical—like its hearty Swiss founder. Jung was not only arguably the most brilliant psychiatrist of the twentieth century, but also an accomplished student of ancient languages and literature, and a born mystic.

He was, additionally, a skilled chef (his last words are said to have been: "Let's have a really good wine for dinner tonight!"), a worker in stone (he built the medieval tower in which he did much of his writing), an avid sailor (who was often seen from the shore of Lake Zürich in his small red boat), occasionally a military physician (he relished donning his officer's uniform and marching down the streets in local parades), an intrepid adventurer (sometimes to the brink of being fatally foolish) in dangerous jungles and deserts, an artist (he opulently illustrated some of his own writings), an avid motorist (he loved driving his American-made cars but was not fond of fixing them), and a sexually vital man (sometimes too vital, having what amounted to a second wife in Toni Wolff, a woman who, like his lifelong wife, Emma, was an individual of substantial gifts and complex sensibilities that he fostered in her and, also like Emma, was an author of some importance in the large body of Jungian literature that even then was beginning to form around his work).

His looming, rangy, country-bred physique usually overshadowed everyone in whatever room he occupied. His rustic table manners could be an embarrassment, even to his four children as they sat at breakfast listening to him slurp steaming coffee and watching the yokes of poached eggs dripping from the toast which he used instead of a spoon, yellowing Papa's moustache. Exquisitely spiritual and supremely attuned emotionally yet also eminently pragmatic and stubbornly individualistic—these words portray both the man and the psychology he founded.

For Jung proclaimed, against every prevailing intellectual tide of his day, that optimal growth requires a living link between one's ego—the domain of consciousness that negotiates the daily psychosocial world of one's will, work, and sexuality—with one's timeless core, the Self. A second-generation Jungian, Edward Edinger, would later call this synergistic tie the "ego-Self axis" (1973). Establishing that axis was a task typically best done in the second half of life, the first half being primarily concerned with the construction and consolidation of the ego.

Generally from about the age of thirty-five to forty on, warned Jung, an ego with no connection to the Self becomes dull and dry as well as arrogant and superficial—out of touch with anything higher in life than itself. This was no less true of the individual whose involvement in a religious organization was not heartfelt but merely formal and obligatory—just a façade. In such cases—and Jung, whose father was a Protestant pastor, had seen plenty of them growing up—membership in a church was the worst type of hypocrisy, a falsely pious, darkly paternalistic means of legitimating an oppressive political and cultural order. Our spiritual commitments—whatever they may be—must be at the very center of our existence, Jung insisted, a matter of total and unapologetically subjective risk and commitment. True spirituality has little, if anything, to do with just signing our name on an institution's dotted line.

Although Jung's work has become increasingly known since the 1970s, the decade after his death on June 6, 1961, it is still not recognized, studied, or utilized nearly enough. Jung's stance and voice pose a radical challenge to Western psychology in its naïve fixation both in his day and even more so in ours (as he predicted) on statistical models, quasi-scientific methodologies, social "functionality," and conformity to the hegemonic projects of the ever-expanding corporate state.

Nevertheless, he introduced concepts, terms, and techniques into academic and clinical psychology as well as into popular consciousness that are still not usually acknowledged as having come from him: the *lie-detector test*, which, however, he did not devise for criminological purposes but to uncover the presence of psychological complexes in patients; the recognition of the phenomenon of *countertransference* by the doctor onto the patient in therapy; the ideas of *introversion and extraversion*; a categorization of *personality types*, which have become popularized in all sorts of personality quizzes; the term *synchronicity*, which was often present in his own paranormally saturated life; the assertion that every male has an *inner feminine* and every female an *inner masculine*, although this idea has been justly problematized by the LGBT community, but was a radical one when Jung introduced it and liberating for my generation; the notion of *projection*, and the clinical definition of one's *shadow*. What is more, Jung took *dream analysis* to depths and heights that few psychotherapists today even remotely know about, much less know how to deploy to more skillfully serve their patients. He also indirectly played a role in the formation of *Alcoholics Anonymous*.

As a scholar, Jung revisioned and rehabilitated the *alchemical tradition* in his exhaustive examination of alchemical texts in their original languages, especially those in the medieval and Renaissance Christian tradition, showing that alchemy was not merely primitive chemistry as it had previously been assessed by historians of science but was in essence a protopsychological system. His were also some of the earliest scholarly studies of gnosticism, both Judeo-Christian and pre-Judeo-Christian, from a modern psychological perspective. Indeed, one of the most important gnostic scrolls that was literally unearthed in the twentieth century is named after him: the *Jung Codex.* Many New Age philosophies claim Jung as their patron saint—though Jung would certainly be appalled by the intellectually slippery and emotionally sloppy nature of many of those "philosophies."

I have divided this book into six chapters. Chapter 1 discusses some of the fundamental philosophical assumptions, drawn from the work of Immanuel Kant, that Jung made in his inquiries into the nature of psyche, showing how dramatically these differed from those of psychoanalysis. Unlike most psychodynamic theorists of his day, Jung was keenly aware of and writes throughout the *Collected Works* about the epistemological underpinnings of his own approach to psyche in what he called analytical psychology to distinguish it from psychoanalysis.

Chapter 2 looks at the origins of depth psychology at the turn of the twentieth century. Jung's internship as a physician was under the illustrious Eugen Bleuler at the Burghölzli Clinic, the psychiatric hospital attached to the University of Zürich. There he added to his already existing familiarity with Freud's approach to psychopathology.

However, it was around 1912 that Jung would experience what the historian of depth psychology Henri Ellenberger (1970) has called a "creative illness." According to Ellenberger, this was typical of many of the great figures in depth psychology before they found their own ways of understanding and working with the psyche. In 1912 at thirty-seven years old—and thus probably in his own midlife crisis—Jung began to break his relatively brief association of about six years with Freud to return to his own path, claiming with increasing force and volubility that it is the discovery of the *Imago Dei,* the image of God, within ourselves and the establishment of a vital connection between it and the ego that ultimately constitutes psychological health, especially in the second half of life.

In chapter 2 I also discuss certain developments in psychoanalysis in the second half of the twentieth century. These are especially important for the purposes of this book because of their potential in bringing post-Freudian and post-Jungian psychology into fruitful contact.

These developments are also significant historically because they are tied to the rise of "transpersonal psychology" in the 1960s, which, genealogically related to Jungian psychology, is discussed in chapter 1. In the work of the post-Freudians Heinz Kohut, D. W. Winnicott, and Donald Fairbairn, the classical psychoanalytic model of the topology and dynamics of the psyche remains intact. However, for these theorists it is no longer the sexual impulse that primarily powers psyche but the need to be an integral personality in life-giving relationship with others. Sexuality revolves around that center—but it is not the center.

Happily there are now post-Freudians and post-Jungians who no longer see their two approaches to the depths of psyche as antithetical but as cross-fertilizing, in that both schools of psychology envisage the core of psyche as being something that is ethically compelling, not sexually consuming. This reconciliation hopefully portends a reuniting of the two major schools of depth psychology, which were sadly and unnecessarily torn apart because of the politics of Freud and Jung's falling out.

Chapter 3 deals with Jung's view of psychological development in the first half of life. Although Jung agreed with much that Freud had to say about this stage of life, he offered concepts and terms that refined and extended, and in crucial ways challenged, Freud's model. These alternative ideas about what the ego is and what it might become are the subject of this chapter.

Also discussed in chapter 3 is how Jung was the first psychologist to name and explore the midlife crisis—that crucial middle point and passage in the lifespan where the ego, having planted its flag in the world of will, work, romantic love, and sometimes family, now looks around at everything that for good and ill it has set in place and asks, "Is this all there is?"

Chapter 4 deals with psychospiritual development in the second half of life. It is here that Jung made his most significant contributions. Jung was a pioneer in modern Western psychology in privileging spirituality. However, he was also a pioneer because he declared—the first modern psychologist to do so—that the second half of life was important in its own right, had its own quandaries and potentials, and was not just a compulsive playing out of psychodynamic issues from life's first half, especially its first five or so years. The first half of life focuses on the establishment of the ego, but the second half should be concerned with the discovery of the Self. Accordingly, it is here that the *anima* and *animus,* the archetypes, and the collective unconscious are discussed.

In chapter 5, I explore in more detail the nature of the ego-Self axis as well as other key Jungian concepts such as paradox and the transcendent function, *enantiodromia,* the *numinous*, the *temenos,* and Jung's theory of personality types.

In chapter 6, I review the major terms in Jungian psychology that have been examined in the book. Jung's total engagement with psyche—in interior vision, therapeutic practice, and scholarly work—supported his lifelong conviction based on profoundly spiritual experiences (as revealed to the public in the 2009 release of his opulently illustrated private journal *The Red Book*) that psyche is ultimately a *mystery*, perhaps *the* mystery. As such, it far exceeds the power of any theoretical model to capture.

What Jung's personal and professional inquiries and explorations yielded, therefore, was not a "model of psyche"—much less one to which he was trying to enlist the reader. Rather, what one finds in *The Collected Works* is a rich array of terms, perspectives, formulations, figures, hints, and, above all, symbols that allow us to *approach* psyche, not *theorize* it—for, finally, Jung was more a "poet" than a "scientist" (Rowland, 2005; Shamdasani, 2003). These I call his *psychospiritual lexicon.*

Each item in Jung's lexicon—"the archetypes," "the collective uncon-scious," "*anima* and *animus,*" "the transcendent function," "individuation," "the Self," "projection," and so on—is a vector of approach to the landscapes of psyche, interweaving with the other vectors of approach, but each vector also a unique angle of arrival. It is this psychospiritual lexicon that is revisit-ed in chapter 6.

Now, any "presentation" of Jung's thought is necessarily an "interpreta-tion" of it. This is not only inevitable but fruitful if an author's views are the result of rigorous engagement with Jung's writings and the scholarship sur-rounding it. At the same time, the author must be as aware as possible of his assumptions and commitments and upfront with his readers about them so that readers may judge for themselves how grounded the presentation is and how useful the interpretations are.

Existentialist theology, especially in the writings of the Jewish existen-tialist theologian Martin Buber and the Christian existentialist theologian Paul Tillich, has influenced me deeply. I have also been informed by Jewish and Christian gnosticism, which are discussed in this book, but not because they are important to me but because they were important to Jung throughout his writings and are key to his interpretation of alchemy—which was the culminating labor of his career—as psychologically of the highest signifi-cance. But existentialist theology was probably also important to Jung, as is implied in his characterization of himself as on the far left of Protestantism and in his many psychospiritual analyses of Judaism and Christianity (and of Eastern religion, too).

I have provided an extensive but not laborious bibliography that should help the reader pursue a particular direction of Jungian scholarship for further research for a class or simply out of the desire to know more about Jungian psychology. That is also why I have chosen to footnote various topics in Jungian psychology and related points of interest more than is typical of an introductory text. I do not suppose that the reader will refer to all of the footnotes, but I hope that he or she will consult them when happening upon an area that answers to special purposes or interests.

On a stylistic note: I will use the third person singular "he" throughout the book as the general personal pronoun. After trying in my books and articles over the last thirty years to work with "he and/or she," "he/she" and "(s)he" constructions in order to avoid sexism grammatically or subtextually, I decided that it was too grammatically and rhetorically unwieldy and had inelegant effects on my writing.

Moreover, this book represents my best attempt—after over forty years of studying Jung and Jungians, practicing Jungian psychology in many of its forms and fields, and living it in my own life—to write an accessible yet, I trust, nuanced introduction to Jung's work. Its aim is to enable the reader to more confidently and insightfully read Jung, his first "disciples," and the several generations of Jungians who have followed. I deeply hope that it will inspire the reader to delve into Jung's *Collected Works*. I will be very happy if readers find, and make their own, some of the many treasures I have found there. I will be even happier if the reader finds gems that I, in my limitations, may have missed along the way.

In conclusion, Jung's life was not, as his strangely vituperative critics would have it, one that he shrewdly strategized in order to become the object of a cult worship; nor was his life, as many of his naïve admirers would have it, an iconic tale of a twentieth-century saint bedecked in exotic psychological garb—his words almost scriptural in status. He was, in my view, simply the greatest thinker in the field of psychology of the last century—his writings as relevant now as they were then, and maybe even more so.

What stands out for me most in the life and work of Carl Gustav Jung (forty-four years after I first opened that used-bookstore copy of *Man and His Symbols*) is his massive courage—intellectual, emotional, and ethical—in bucking the arrogantly materialistic and sexually fixated assumptions of academic and clinical psychology of his day. From 1912 on, when he was still a relatively young doctor, he never wavered from the outrageous insistence that at the center of the psyche is each individual's unique identity as a spiritual being—but dressed in mortal clothes, moving on mortal soil. For such a being, no durable and deep ways of existing here and now can be found without him also discovering the Timeless within, and then witnessing to his communion with it by empathetic action in and for the world.

Chapter One

Modeling Psyche

The Problem of "The Disciplines"

Any academic discipline—whether in the arts, sciences, social sciences, or humanities—rests on various assumptions about what is "really real," or at least what "really counts" in the human experience. It also makes assumptions about what "slice" of that is important or worthwhile to study and the best way to do so. What a discipline claims to have discovered or created at a given time in its "domain" makes up its current *body of knowledge and products,* and the way it has done so makes up its current *methodologies and practices.*

Thus, the knowledge and methodologies that comprise a discipline are determined by the discipline's original assumptions about "how things are" and "what matters." Then, the discipline's "findings" double back to reinforce the assumptions that launched the whole enterprise in the first place. There is clearly a circularity in disciplinary "knowledge." It is "self-referential." This is even true in mathematics, as the great philosopher of mathematical logic Ludwig Wittgenstein (1953) felt compelled to concede.

What is more, the foundational assumptions out of which the discipline's enterprise originally arose are *themselves* not fixed or certain but have changed in the history of that discipline—and will continue to do so (Gadamer, 1980). To make matters shakier, the so-called slice of Being that a discipline has fenced off to train its focus upon may not ultimately exist as a slice of *anything* that exists in some absolute way but may merely be a projection of the discipline's own assumptions. Or it *may* exist but in a different way than the discipline is capable of imagining.

Typically these problematic assumptions are made explicit by "experts" in that field, who have been institutionally and culturally authorized to do such things. Usually those assumptions go unquestioned. Only rarely are the constructs and procedures that comprise a discipline held up for critique by workers within that discipline. Even rarer is when a discipline so radically challenges its own assumptions that a revolution occurs in that discipline in a historically pivotal moment of disciplinary self-redefinition (Kuhn, 1970).

Rather, an aspiring "expert" is typically just acculturated into a currently "legitimate" community of discourse that is overseen by its already-certified experts. The price of admission into that field is that one demonstrates a high level of competency within the parameters that define, while also thereby limiting, the scope of that discourse (Foucault, 1972). The rhetorical theorist Kenneth Burke (1989) summed it up nicely: "Every way of seeing is also a way of not seeing."

Questions regarding what should comprise a discipline's body of knowledge and which methods of inquiry and judgment are valid are handled by people who have been "duly credentialed" to determine such things. When there is general agreement among the experts who head the field, there is what is called "intersubjective agreement among a community of experts" and the discipline is more or less unified (Jansen & Peshkin, 1992). But this is rarely the case in any discipline. Usually there is some sort of civil warfare going on within a discipline, inevitably involving academic politics to decide which experts' views shall prevail.

In a word, disciplinary knowledge is dicey. A specialized discourse, however useful (or use*less*) it may prove to be, generally amounts to just a "best guess" about something from a specific angle of approach, and it is valid only "until further notice" (Giddens, 1990).

The question of "disciplinary knowledge" leaves us standing before the Enigma of Being itself, which refuses to yield its jealously guarded mysteries to our disciplinary investigations. We do well to remember Hamlet's advice to his best friend: "There are more things in heaven and earth, Horatio, / Than are dreamt of in your philosophy"—or than are theorized about in our disciplines.

THE USES AND MISUSES OF MODELS OF MIND

It is for these reasons that Jung wanted to avoid *reifying*—that is, treating something as somehow *really* real—the models of mind that dominated the academic and clinical power structures in psychology during his day, and even more so in ours.

Take, for example, Freud's term "ego." We reify that term if we assert that it refers to something that absolutely and unconditionally exists in and of itself. For in that case "ego" would be something that is absolutely real. It would have "ontological status," in philosophical terms. It would not just be a word/concept that we use to try to talk about something we do not fully grasp, and, given our human limitations, never will. Indeed, the very idea of "having a self" and what standards we may employ in judging the "sanity" of that self have arisen and evolved in various historical contexts and differ from each other, sometimes greatly, from culture to culture and from time to time (Foucault, 1961; Giddens, 1991).

There is therefore a humble wisdom in a letter Jung wrote to a friend in January 1929.

> Can't you conceive of a physicist who thinks and speaks of atoms, yet is convinced that those are merely his own abstractions? That would be my case. I haven't the faintest idea what "psyche" is in itself, yet, when I come to think and speak of it, I must speak of my abstractions, concepts, views, figures, knowing that they are our specific illusions. That is what I call "non-concretization." (Jung, 1973, p. 11)

Freud and Jung differed radically in their philosophy of psychology. Jung emphasized the primacy of the individual and the irreducibility of that individual's subjective experiences. These can never be totally accounted for by general rules of psychic functioning, however useful those rules might be. Instead, he stressed the ultimate unknowability of psyche. Everyone is unique, a *terra incognita*. This attitude stands in stark contrast to Freud's attempt at scientific explanations of what the psyche "is" and how it "really" operates. Jung's tentativeness about the enigma of the psyche was one of the major reasons for his break with Freud around 1913.

In his "scientism," Freud was clearly a product of eighteenth-century Enlightenment rationalism and nineteenth-century naturalism, which operated in the fond hope that reason could discover sovereign truth in natural laws (Becker, 1966; Rieff, 1961). Freud did what Jung refused to do—*concretize* his terms and constructs.

Freud insisted with an almost evangelical fervor that there *was* an ego, *was* a subconscious, *was* a superego, instead of them being simply useful words for building a contingent, necessarily incomplete *model* of the psyche—that "best guess until further notice." In the rationalist spirit of the nineteenth-century natural sciences, Freud was confident that he had come upon natural laws, just as Marx felt he had uncovered immutable, universal economic laws; and Darwin, biological ones. In this, Freud, Marx, and Darwin had the same historically conditioned mindset of the eighteenth and nineteenth centuries.

Throughout his writings, Jung warns against such sweeping claims for *any* model of the psyche. Indeed, he warned against "models" of psyche in general. He knew that the human mind, with its inherent and inescapable limitations, is not able to lift itself by its own bootstraps into the pure realm of absolute knowledge. This was all the more true regarding psychological models, where mind was both the tool of investigation and the thing being investigated. This epistemological situation, turning in and in upon itself in an especially dizzying way, gave rise to a whole new set of conceptual conundrums that made theorizing about psyche a very tenuous affair.

Thus, as we proceed throughout this book, it is important that the reader keep in mind that *Jung, in his understanding of psyche and the terms and constructs he devised to convey that understanding, was not positing a model of mind*—although certain models may usefully be inferred by various interpreters of Jung for both theoretical and practical purposes. *Rather, Jung was offering a kind of "dictionary" of terms and constructs that were the results of both his prodigious studying as well as his personal and clinical experiences.*

Jung's hope was that the reader of this "lexicon" could use its items in such a way that it would offer that person a variety of psychospiritual possibilities to explore. These the reader could employ to further his own unique journey to a very personal center, where, paradoxically, the universal Center resides. In this way, the particular and the universal could be wedded in acts of individuation. It is in this spirit that I present the basic elements of Jung's "lexicon" in this book.

"ULTIMACY" AND PSYCHE

Clearly, then, Jung believed that all of one's propositions can ultimately be traced back to a basic assumption or set of assumptions, but these are conditioned by personal and cultural factors as well as the historically determined range of intellectual possibilities into which one has been born. One is perfectly at liberty to *proclaim* one's basic assumptions to be ultimately true. However, one cannot *prove* those foundational assumptions to enjoy that status for the simple reason that they would be the point of origin of any concepts and methods one might use *in* that proof—the perfect example of *petitio principii,* which is to assume the truth of what one then sets out to prove as true by using those very assumptions to do so. It is "begging the question."

This unprovable but necessary point of origin—whatever it might be for a single individual, discipline, ideology, or culture—is the touchstone we all unavoidably use in deciding whether something is sensible or foolish, correct or deviant, worthy of notice or negligible—true or false. It is what the Protestant theologian Paul Tillich (1987), his focus also squarely on the individual, called a person's sense of "ultimacy." One's sense of ultimacy is valid, according to Tillich, to the degree that one has pursued it rigorously and courageously—in good faith.

Whether or not we are aware of it, we all have a set of ultimate convictions, "fiduciary commitments" as they are also called, that consciously or unconsciously guide us in our thinking and acting. Claims to ultimacy are, of course, especially evident when it comes to religions and their charismatic founding figures, whose originating revelation or teachings believers then scrupulously guard, carefully elaborate in doctrines, and solemnly encode in rituals practiced by the community of believers (Berger, 1967).

Whatever form the foundational commitment may take, ultimacy carries us beyond the realm of propositional truth and into the realm of what must be called faith, for our primary existential stances cannot be proven. They precede proofs and, as we have seen, they are often enough the launching pads from which various "programs of proof" then take flight. Our basic commitments are a matter of the intensity of the believer's investment in them. This is why throughout his writings Jung states that he makes no judgment as to the ontological or metaphysical validity of a person's spiritual experiences and assertions.

In fact, however, Jung does seem to make such judgments from time to time (Rowland, 2005; Shamdasani, 2005). This apparent contradiction in Jung's writing is due to various factors. One of them has to do with the politics of academic discourse.

Especially earlier in his writings, Jung exhibited caution in affirming what might be seen as a spiritual orientation or even a spiritual tone. This would have caused his work to simply be dismissed in the academy of his day. On the other hand, he undoubtedly felt the increasing need to give some sort of expression to his own crescendo of mystical experiences, which were presented after his death in *The Red Book* (2009). This he managed to do in his public writings—but in camouflaged terms. It is best when confronting the mixed messages we sometimes receive from Jung regarding spirituality to understand it as resulting from these and other factors. Failing to appreciate the complexity of this issue, the interpreter of Jung falls into one of two errors.

The first is to focus on sections in Jung that seem quite agnostic and marshal them to argue that his intentions were merely existentialist (Brooke, 1991). The second is to focus on those passages in Jung that are undeniably spiritual in their intent and use them to turn Jung into an object of hero worship, his words almost scriptural in status (van der Post, 1975). In fact, there were various reasons for Jung's sometimes incongruous notices about spirituality in his writings.

For instance, we cannot rule out the possibility that Jung was not immune to doubt. We may be witnessing some evidence of this in his conflicting statements about the ontological status of spirituality, especially considering that his views on the topic matured as he aged in the direction of ever more openly spiritual declarations.

Furthermore, there is the fact that Jung quite legitimately believed in two things at once: the indispensability of spiritual vitality for a healthy psyche, on one hand, but the impossibility of proving the "truth" of any given spiritual commitment, on the other hand. The contrasting views of spirituality that we sometimes find in Jung reflect his attempt to hold these two notions in a creative tension.

Jung advised that even though a person may feel that through divine revelation he knows ultimate reality, what he is reporting is a subjective experience that, however compelling for him and however sincere his testimony of it, can never be so firmly established that others are under any sort of obligation to credit it for themselves.

This does not mean that the belief is wrong. It may be wrong. It may be right. It may be right and wrong in different ways. Indeed, on a certain plane of being, "right" and "wrong" as we know it may not even be relevant terms. We simply cannot know in any way that would be convincing to everyone. And even if it *were* convincing to everyone, that might simply mean that everyone is caught in shared illusions—a central point in Buddhism (Suzuki, 1964).

What we do know, however, said Jung the psychiatrist, is that without *feeling* that one is in contact with something ultimate, one will be far less integrated, efficacious, and humane than if he did. This is why Jung advised the therapist not to try to talk a patient out of his faith if the patient had one that was life-giving to him (Jung, 1978, p. 52, fn. 16).

At any rate, key in Jung's writings is his Kantian assumption that all we perceive and think we do so through epistemological filters that are inborn in us (Nagy, 1991; Pauson, 1988). Indeed, in the final analysis, our minds *are* those filters. In this sense, *all of our knowledge is psychological* since everything we know or feel is filtered through our psyches, and we can never be confident that the filters that comprise psyche really capture or even correspond to ontological or metaphysical truth. Our words and concepts are finally just that: words and concepts. They are at best only provisionally and partially true "truth" with a lower-case *t*, as it were, and not absolutely true, "Truth" with a capital *T*.

"ESSE IN INTELLECTU" AND "ESSE IN ANIMA"

Jung leaned heavily on Immanuel Kant's (1781/1997) distinction between *esse in intellectu* (Being in the mind, in intellect) and *esse in res* (Being in the thing [itself]) (Jung, 1971, pp. 44ff). The *esse in intellectu* is something as it is rationally conceived using what Kant called our "mathetic" faculty, derived from the word "math."

The mathetic faculty is one of our inborn epistemological filters. It causes us to see things in terms of the *a priori* categories of space and time. Through them we perceive, interpret, speculate about, and act on our individual and shared life-worlds by means of syllogistic reasoning and disciplinary conventions. They produce the models we devise to make sense out of and shape our world. On the other hand, the *esse in res* is something as it really is in itself, Kant's *Ding-an-sich*, something's absolute nature. However, our mathetic and discursive tools and rules may or may not correspond to things as they really are. We can never totally know. There would thus seem to be a fatal gap between the human being and the Ground of Being.

But all is not lost, said Jung. There *is* something that we *can* know with certainty. It is the *esse in anima*—Latin for "the thing in the soul." This phrase refers to our engagement with something or someone with our entire being as we stand face to face with it, reach out to it, touch it, internalize it, and then weave the images and ideas born of that encounter into the ever richer interior tapestry of experience. All of this includes our reason but goes beyond it. It encompasses our organic, psychosocial, historical, and spiritual dimensions. It extends to the depths and heights of our sense of who we are, or who we may become, both individually and in relationship with others, for it is in relationship that we know ourselves as individuals. We intersubjectively define our being by being *with* each other.

The *esse in anima* is within the individual, but in an even deeper sense it *is* the individual—one who is in authentic communion with other similarly constituted individuals.[1] This is living soulfully—as the very word *anima* suggests. As we live in and by the *esse in anima,* we engage the things, events, and people in our lives with the impassioned entirety of our being. In this fashion, we both know and forge our being fully, and out of that fullness are able to be creative—in faithfulness *to* that being. This alone endues life with passion and purpose.

Because of its complex, holistic, transrational nature, the *esse in anima* is experienced and expressed in symbolic, intuitive terms, using what Kant called our "poetic" faculty. Our poetic faculty stands in vivid contrast to our mathetic faculty. And despite how our culture is mathetically obsessed, we must never lose sight of the fact that our poetic faculty is no less important. It is our other epistemological filter. If we do not employ both the mathetic and poetic faculty, we grow either pathologically static on the mathetic side in

---

1. The reader of Heidegger will recognize here a correspondence to the twentieth-century German philosopher's idea of *Dasein*—the individual in his existential authenticity and phenomenological vibrancy—and *Mit-Dasein*—the individual in rich relationship with other *Daseins* (Heidegger, 1964).

merely what can be logically proven, or we become pathologically awash on the poetic side in every swelling emotion.[2]

As we will see in greater depth as we go on, it was Jung's constant contention that depth psychology is, or at least should be, nothing less than the study of the soul, its self-disclosure and organic evolution in its *own* imagistic terms—principally in dreams, religion, myth, meditation, imagination, and art (Jung, 1954b; 1966b). Indeed, even a relatively undramatic "psychoneurosis must be understood, ultimately, as the suffering of a soul which has not discovered its meaning"—a meaning it finds by means of symbols (Jung, 1970b, pp. 330ff).[3] In chapter 5, we will look more closely at the crucial role of the symbol in Jungian psychology as an incarnation of the *esse in anima* and how one moves into dialogue with it in order to achieve a more attuned and creative life.

For now it is enough to grasp that "between *intellectus and res* [between intellect and an actually existing concrete or abstract 'thing'], there is *esse in anima*, [which] makes the whole ontological argument superfluous" (Jung, 1971, p. 45). The "ontological argument"—the question of whether or not the *intellectus* can in some form adequately capture the *res*—becomes unnecessary in light of the inescapable fact that all we can know of reality, indeed all we *need* to know, is its significance *to us* in our ongoing life project of becoming more whole, clear, powerful, and sensitive, both within ourselves and in our relationships with others. Jung's view of the idea of the *esse in anima* is one of his most signal contributions to the philosophy of psychology.

This dichotomy of *intellectus* and *res* and the impossibility of certain ontological knowledge does not mean, however, that theorizing is unimportant. Jung was, after all, one of the great thinkers of the twentieth century. It is simply to recognize that the best we can do is to constantly be honing our little-*t* truths while always humbly recognizing their only partial validity. In that process, we may come up with other theoretical models that we hope are bringing us closer to Truth with a capital *T*. But we must never fall captive to the arrogant, dangerous delusion that we could ever know Truth with such finality that we have the right to try to impose it on another.

---

2. As I have argued in other studies in educational psychology (Mayes, in press, 2016; Mayes, 2007; Mayes, 2009b), the principal malady that besets education in the United States today is its obsession with the mathetic domain—not to mention how poorly it actually teaches it as disconnected items to be memorized and reproduced on high-stakes standardized tests. The poetic domain has been all but banished from the classroom (Mayes, 2007). But this is the domain where intuition, emotion, and generativity reside! Imprison and then exterminate the poetic domain from education and learning quickly turns into a joyless, soulless affair that only prepares students to endure drudgery and uncritically obey authority. Class by class, day by day, term by term, year by year, this both neuroticizes students and makes them politically slavish—a point Jung also strenuously argued (Jung, 1969a, p. 181).

3. See also Jacobi (1974); Jaffé (1975); Ulanov (1999, 2001).

WAS JUNG "RELIGIOUS" IN HIS APPROACH TO PSYCHE?

Where does this leave religions, with their special claims to truth? Jung, the son of a Protestant minister and someone who characterized himself as on the very far left of Protestantism (Jung, 1984, p. 215) replied that if one is fortunate enough to believe in a "revealed truth" because one's heart authentically finds both purpose and passion therein and not just out of familial or cultural allegiances, one can only be grateful for the comfort of that belief, cherishing one's truth privately and with a community of believers.[4] However, this was not the case with Jung, nor, Jung suspected, was it the case for most people in our disillusioned times, who could no longer subscribe to any religious dogma. If they were to find the Divine, it would have to be by cutting out their own paths to it, one by one.

Thus, the believer and his community should understand that what is at stake here is faith, not certainty. For believers in a "one true faith" have historically proven themselves too prone to hammering their beliefs into a tool to emotionally or politically bludgeon others into submission. Jung was an enemy of dogmatism, what he called "doctrinarism," in any form: political, psychological, or spiritual (1969a, p. 86). The witness to two world wars, he was acutely aware of the atrocities committed under the banner of political and religious absolutism.

Jung had great respect for religion and drew deftly from its symbolism to probe the psychospiritual depths of the individual (1970b). Indeed, this was one of his major contributions and distinguishing features. However, he saw each religion in relative terms, as a culturally founded, historically morphing, mythopoetic system that uniquely, but never absolutely, bodied forth the Timeless. Specific religions "are merely the changing leaves and blossoms on the stem of the eternal tree" (1984, p. 215). It was finding the Eternal within that mattered, not the route one took to get there.

There are those who argue that Jung's orientation and purposes were not in some sense of the term "spiritual" and that his approach to psychotherapy is a variation on existentialist psychotherapy, which views belief in something that transcends the limitations of this life as often a neurotic formation, a false "immortality project," to avoid having to come to grips with the finality of death, ending the individual's existential trajectory (May & Yalom, 1995).

However, it is clear that Jung did believe that a life lived in hopeful response to "the lure of the transcendent" is not only possible but necessary for the individual, who must respond in his own way to this call issued by the cosmos (Huebner, 1999). It is not only *not* neurotic to follow the inner path

---

4. For the idea of Jung being on the far left of Protestantism, see Goldbrunner (1964); Kelsey (1984); Sanford (1993); and Stein (1982).

to the transcendent, it is crucial that one do so—key to psychological health. But Jung adamantly refused to waste his time in the futile exercise of defining what that transcendence might consist of—something that, in any case, would run contrary to his purpose of inciting the individual to follow his own path to the Divine within. "God," like the "unconscious," was just another construct in search of the Unknown (1969a, p. 68).

Toward the end of his life, he uttered the famous statement that he did not need to believe there was a God because he *knew* there was. Still, Jung was far from religious in any conventional sense. Jung's apprehension of the Divine is gnostic (Hoeller, 1982), the gnostic notion being that any definition of divinity falls far short of *the actual experience of divinity* (1954a, p. 289). This experience leads to a personally convincing *knowledge* of divinity, but this knowledge will vary from individual to individual. And so it was for Jung himself. But even for Jungians who have focused on the question of Jung and spirituality, it is very difficult to pin down Jung's own brand of it. But it is a mistake to maintain that he did not have one—especially, as noted previously, in light of the 2009 publication of *The Red Book*.

Thus, one is on firm ground asserting Jung felt that access to the Eternal is found only in the innermost operations of the individual's psychospiritual dynamics, indeed that those interior motions might *be* the Divine engaging man. When the individual rigorously attends to his depths, especially as he shapes and is shaped by the symbols that circulate in those depths, "psyche" has the potential of becoming a new kind of "sacrament" (Dourley, 1981).[5] This was not an abstract theological point for Jung. It was a practical psychotherapeutic one, and pivotal. For without a patient finding the transcendent within, there could be no "cure."

MODEL AND MYSTERY

To sum up: unlike Freud with his linguistic absolutism (equating a word with an ontological reality), Jung cautioned that the terms that we use in psychology, or in any discipline, are ultimately just theoretical constructs. They are semantic instruments that we craft and then labor with to dig more deeply into the primal yet also transcendent mystery.

Hence, Jung warned, we must approach his terms and constructs, figures and tropes, regarding the enigmas of psychospiritual energy—its unknown origins and its countless travails, transformations, and triumphs—as simply an approach to psyche and spirit, not psyche and spirit themselves, and certainly not any given individual's *experience* of psyche and spirit.

---

5. For this view of Jung's spirituality, see Chapman (1988); Dourley (1981); Edinger (1992); Martin (1985); Sanford (1993); Stein (1984); Ulanov (1999).

Every individual has the potential to be on his own private journey to the inner Divine. Jung meant his maps and postulations to be useful to the traveler each in his own way. But Jung cautioned that his psychospiritual "lexicon" was primarily meant to suggest some of the general stages and directions in a person's trek to his psychospiritual core. It was there, and only there, that the Divine must reside, and it must be found individually by the seeker.

As the Zen saying goes: "The finger pointing at the moon is not the moon."

Chapter Two

Freudian, Post-Freudian, and Transpersonal Theory

From Ego to Cosmos

Jung had been forming his views of psyche since his days as an undergraduate college student in a series of addresses he gave to his fraternity, the Zofingia, between 1896 and 1899 at Basel University. In *The Zofingia Lectures*, Jung argued against the glib, fashionable rationalism of his peers and covered topics from theology and spiritism to philosophy and (of course) psychology. Naturally, his inquiries grew more concentrated during his early years as a medical student and young psychiatrist, his radical vision of psyche percolating in him with growing intensity (Shamdasani, 2003, 2005).

Jungian psychology also arose as both a critique and extension of Freudian theory into psychodynamic realms that Freud either did not credit as being real or that he was apprehensive about probing into, for they seemed to Freud to smack of the occult (Jung, 1965). Freud sensed, even insisted, in conversations with Jung during their heyday together, that such things would threaten the rationalist worldview—the philosophical foundation upon which Freud's model of psyche toweringly arose.

Thus, although it is correct not to overemphasize Freud's effect on Jung, it must be recognized that what Jung garnered about psychodynamic functioning in his relationship with his senior colleague, Freud, was not insignificant. Jung's high-profile involvement in psychoanalytic theory over the relatively few but formative years of his and Freud's close association was important to the young psychiatrist, emotionally and intellectually.

Without overdoing Freud's influence on Jung's gestation of his own vision of psyche throughout his life, it would be historically and theoretically inaccurate to approach classical Jungian psychology without looking at some of its roots in psychoanalytic theory. So it is to an overview of classical Freudian psychology and its later iterations by post-Freudians over the last half century that we now turn.

Such a survey is also important because it will be seen that post-Freudian psychology, moving beyond Freud's monolithic insistence upon sex as the center of psychodynamics, portrays the innermost sanctum of psyche as being dedicated to one's broader existential commitments—especially as they were formed, or malformed, in the earliest interpersonal relationships between the individual and his primary caregivers. This has resulted in a vision of the center of psychodynamics that is theoretically and practically compatible with both classical and post-Jungian psychology.

The chapter then concludes with a presentation of what is called *transpersonal* psychology—of which Jung's work is one of the primary cornerstones, and perhaps the most important one. We will look at the later work of Abraham Maslow, the inventor of the famous hierarchy of needs paradigm, to see how his lesser-known, post-hierarchy psychology was instrumental in forging a bridge between certain aspects of post-Freudian theory and transpersonal psychology. He thereby extended depth psychology in the twentieth century from the realm of "I" to the reaches of "cosmos," with psychological health now seen as lying in the honoring and wedding of both "I" and the Transcendent.

CLASSICAL FREUDIAN THEORY

Toward the end of the nineteenth century and in the opening years of the twentieth, Freud introduced the first systematic depth psychology onto the Western intellectual and medical scene. Psychoanalysis was a theory of the psyche that went far more deeply into human psychic functioning than the simplistic stimulus-response, rat-in-a-maze behaviorism of Pavlov and Watson—the major alternative to Freudian psychology at the turn of the century—could even begin to imagine.

The popular notion that Freud "invented" depth psychology, however, is not wholly accurate. Explorations into the depths of the psyche—indeed, the assertion that there even *was* a subconscious—had been going on for at least 150 years before Freud (Ellenberger, 1970). Freud's great contribution was not so much that he *discovered* psychodynamic areas and impulses that lay outside conscious awareness as that he *systematized* the previous approaches to them, for they often had a rather hit-and-miss, folk-medicine orientation.

By the early decades of the twentieth century, Freud had devised a map of the psyche and crafted a psychotherapeutic system that was replete with an impressive array of terms, many of which are now mainstays of popular speech: repression, sublimation, libido, id, ego, superego, oral and anal fixations, narcissism, latency, and so on.

Especially since the closing decades of the twentieth century, classical Freudian psychology has been strongly criticized for its insistence that what powers the psyche is the sexual drive (Eagle, 1993). Freud is sometimes forgiven his exaggerated emphasis on sexuality on the grounds that his medical practice, research, and writing were carried on in the context of prudish Vienna of the late nineteenth and early twentieth centuries. It is understandable, even inevitable (so this line of reasoning goes), that many of the patients who came to Freud's consulting room would be suffering from a spectrum of psychological and somatic maladies caused by the damming—and damning—of the natural flow and healthy play of sexual energy. By this view, Freud was only reporting his own personal and clinical experiences and succumbing to the all-too-human tendency to overgeneralize on the basis of them. It is also possible that Freud was sexually disturbed himself and that his theories reflect that disturbance—and obsession (Homans, 1989).

However, it is not clear that Freud's Vienna suffered from such severe sexual repression. Some historians of psychology, especially Ellenberger (1970), have argued that Vienna was much less prudish and much more illicitly and licitly sexual than is generally supposed in discussions of the origins of psychoanalysis (see also Jansz & Drunen, 2004; O'Boyle, 2006).

Classical Freudians—dwindling in number though they be—may still insist that although wrong in some particulars, Freud was essentially right in isolating sexual desire as the key to understanding the psyche. However, the legacy of Freud today resides most robustly in the *post*-Freudian schools of psychology: self-psychology, ego-psychology, and selfobject psychology (Eagle, 1993).

These theories and therapies still accept the general "topological survey map" that Freud proposed for the terrain of the psyche and the way psychic energy flows through it. They also still use some of the same terms that Freud introduced. However, they differ radically in one crucial respect: they do not see sexuality as the sole, or even just the central driving energy that impels the psyche. Rather, these theorists contend that *what primarily powers psyche is the need to form a rich and durable ego-structure that allows the individual to relate to others sensitively in love and meaningfully in work.* This is the engine that drives conscious and subconscious psychodynamics.

Post-Freudians remind us that we have many needs, ranging from the simple one to belong to groups of people who care for us, to the desire to do satisfying work in life, to the search to find a partner to share life's journey, to the impulse to discover for ourselves if there is a Divinity to which we might have access and, if so, what our relation to that Divinity could or should be.[1] To reduce all of these aspects of the total human experience to mere sexuality is simplistic and leads to despair since it does not answer to the breadth or height of our desires, tensions, fears, or potentials.

Basics of Classical Freudian Theory[2]

Freud's genius is not to be dismissed, however. He created a potent model about *how* the psyche is structured and functions, even though his analysis of *what* powers the psyche was lopsidedly sexual. In fact, if we look closely at his writings we see that as early as 1912 he had begun to move tentatively in the direction of self-psychology. There were, he allowed, "various points in favor of the hypothesis of a primordial differentiation between sexual instincts and other instincts, ego instincts" (Freud, 1957, p. 106).

Freud took the term *ego* from the Latin word for "I." The ego is who I am in the world. It is not a static entity. It is better pictured as the ongoing flux of memories and predictions, limitations and dispositions, weaknesses and strengths, dreads and hopes that make up a conscious awareness of ourselves and our environment from moment to moment. The ego is that part of the psyche which enables us to have an ongoing sense of a cohesive identity as we register in consciousness and deal in action with the natural and social worlds. This we must do in order to survive. The ego thus works in the service of what Freud called *the reality principle*.

When it is operating well, the ego is able to satisfy the requirements of the reality principle by striking a functional balance between the two other layers of the psyche in Freud's three-tiered architecting of mind. These two layers are the *superego*, which is the layer "above" the ego, and the *id*, which is the layer "below" the ego. Our social roles and duties constitute the upper tier of the psyche. It is the site of all the moral, and often punishingly moralistic, demands we make on ourselves and others. Its rafters easily swell with a chorus of unseen, condemning voices that chatter at us inside our heads so persistently and mercilessly. The majority of the scripts that run inside our

---

1. From the beginning of psychoanalytic theory, there has been a small but vocal group of Freudian (and now post-Freudian) theorists and therapists who have said that the search for a connection with the Eternal is of great, perhaps primary, psychodynamic moment and that the sexual impulse is either ancillary to the need for transcendent connectedness, or that the goal of the sexual impulse is to be refined ("sublimated") into the love of one's fellows and the Divine. The first of these psychoanalytic theorists was a member of Freud's inner circle who, significantly, was also in particular communication with Jung—the Protestant minister and psychoanalyst Oskar Pfister. Pfister, also a professional teacher, applied his version of psychoanalysis to educational issues (1922). Rizzuto (1979) and Meissner (1984) have explored the interaction of psyche and spirit from psychoanalytic perspectives from a monotheistic angle as have more recently Washburn (1995) and Epstein (1995) from a Buddhistic one.

2. Elements of the following summary of Freudian and post-Freudian psychology first appeared in my 2009 article "The Psychoanalytic View of Education, 1922-2002" and is reproduced here with the kind permission of *The Journal of Curriculum Studies* (2009b).

heads throughout the day are negative and self-condemning (Conger & Galambos, 1997).

The superego holds a tight rein on our feral, mostly sexual desires. These desires exist in that bottom tier of the psyche that Freud called the *id*, which knows nothing but *the pleasure principle* and the energy of *libido*. The ego exists in and as the middle tier of consciousness. From that intermediary position, the ego is constantly brokering more or less workable agreements between the desiring whispers of the pleasure-seeking id and the demanding shouts of the ethically exacting superego. If the ego is doing its job well, then the individual can get some measure of pleasure but will do it in socially productive and acceptable ways. This is the Freudian ideal, the great goal of psychoanalysis—the ability "to love and to work," as Freud famously put it.

To sum up, the Freudian model of the psyche consists of the id (which is amoral and even immoral), the ego (which strives to follow *mores* and thus to be "moral" but also to get libidinal gratification), and the superego (which is "moral" to the point of being hypercritical). When tensions among these three constituents of psyche cannot be successfully managed, they get repressed. However, the goal of therapy is not to produce a tension-free, unrepressed life. This is a gross misinterpretation of Freud that began to predominate around the 1960s (Homans, 1989; Mayes, 2009b; Rieff, 1961).

A completely unrepressed, tension-free life is impossible, said Freud, since the elements of our psyche must always be at odds with each other to some degree. Even in the best of circumstances, there will be a tug-and-pull between our feral, sexual needs and our roles as members of a culture with all of its rules and regulations. This is simply the human condition. The human being is fated to be a conflicted creature, and therefore to some extent a neurotic one.

The goal of therapy is to keep this neuroticism under control so that it is not so grave as to seriously impair the individual's social and sexual functionality. But repression, the mechanism that keeps psychic energy from breaking out at any of its levels and disrupting the whole system, is not always successful. Fugitive psychic energy will sometimes press to the surface in the form of a *neurotic symptom*—what Freud called a *reaction formation*. It is at this point that a person may need therapy, depending upon the severity of the formation.

If a patient in therapy projects some of her core issues onto the therapist, it is often the case that these images refer to her relationship with her parents. This is not surprising since the therapist is also an authority figure—a kind of parental figure—and one, moreover, who is being given special access into very private regions of her psyche, where family-of-origin issues still swirl with a mighty force.

If the patient had a difficult relationship with her father, for instance, she might see in the therapist certain of her father's characteristics, especially the ones that were difficult for her to deal with—whether or not the therapist actually has those characteristics. This process of the patient projecting her relationship with important people from her past onto the therapist in the present can provide the therapist with useful information about issues that need to be dealt with in the course of therapy. Freud called this process *transference* since the patient is transferring things from her past onto the therapist (Freud, 1990).[3]

An example of this transference is the female patient above who thinks that she sees judgment and ridicule in her male therapist's eyes whenever she talks about her desire to go to graduate school. This is exactly what she got from her father. He never credited her as having any real intelligence whenever she tried to engage him in discussions about a big story in the news or a book she was reading.

She "sees" the same dismissiveness in the therapist now when she discusses her plans to get a doctorate. As a matter of fact, the therapist happens to think she is very bright and would do well in a PhD program in history, which she has been talking about with him the last several sessions. He is nothing but sincere when he enthusiastically encourages her to go ahead with those plans.

But what she "hears" in the therapist's words of support are lies. ("Of course he *would* say that. I'm paying him $100 an hour, for crying out loud!") His smiles of approval she misconstrues as *really* being just his thinly veiled bemusement that she would ever consider in her wildest dreams something as intellectually ambitious as a doctorate in history. ("He probably *really* thinks I should just work at a temp agency for the rest of my life and call it good.")

The patient has transferred her father onto her therapist to such an extent that she can scarcely see the therapist at all, only images of her father that she has covered the therapist in. A wise therapist will, as noted, become aware of this in his patient and use it as crucial information about the issues that are besetting her and, in light of what they have already discussed about her past, will begin to form a good idea about where those issues originate.

But the transference is not a one-way street. The therapist is not a god. He has his own psychodynamic issues. One expects that he will already have dealt with them more profoundly and extensively than the patient has, of course. But one never resolves *all* of one's psychodynamic issues. As Freud indicated in the title of one of his essays, therapy is both "terminal and interminable." Although one may adequately deal with an issue or even an array of them, one never resolves *all* of one's issues in the course of a lifetime. They are too multifaceted and deep-rooted for that.

---

3. For more on transference, see Aichhorn (1990); Cooper (1990); Greenson (1990); Jacoby (1984); Kirsch (1995); Orr (1988); Schwartz-Salant (1995); Woodman (1995).

Since depth psychotherapy is such an emotionally high-risk endeavor, the therapist can easily get caught up in the whirlwind of the process and begin to project his own issues back onto the patient in response to her projections onto him. This is called *the countertransference* (a term devised not by Freud but Jung).

Because of the specter of countertransference in any really transformative therapeutic process, it is necessary that the therapist himself be engaged in continual self-examination because countertransferential projections onto the patient may do the patient emotional harm and can even lead the psychotherapist to sexually act out his countertransference on the patient—the person who had promised to assist in liberating her now just becoming another one of those who have colonized her psychosexually.

Thus, to turn the tables: if a male patient comes to a female psychotherapist because he had inadequate mothering as a child and is projecting his mother needs onto his female partner in a way that threatens their relationship, it will accomplish little if the therapist then also, in a counterprojection, takes on the role of a mother and simply enables the man to replay the problem in the consulting room and not deal with it in his life.

A female therapist in this instance *might* strategically assume the role of a mother with the patient in order to "re-parent" the patient and also to get a clearer sense of the nature of the patient's projection onto her. However, this is something that the female psychotherapist needs to do in extreme clarity and relatively briefly lest she become just another mother substitute for the patient. The same is true in cases where a female patient is dealing with father issues with a male psychotherapist.

Generally speaking, however, the conflict between the id and the super-ego does not require therapy and more or less successfully resolves itself by a natural process that Freud called *sublimation.* In sublimation the psyche strategically allows forbidden energy to express itself in a symbolic, socially acceptable form. Thus the id gets some form of gratification while the ego is still conforming to social norms, thereby mollifying the superego.

Instead of playing with its own feces, for instance, the child would learn to shape figures in clay and might ultimately become an architect or sculptor. The infant who had been inadequately breastfed might sublimate the frustrated desire for the nipple into smoking cigarettes as an adult. And instead of physically and emotionally merging with his mother—the object of the famous Oedipus complex—the young boy would learn to sublimate that need into sexual desire for a wife, thereby directing primal passions into the socially approved and socially cohesive vessel of marriage.

However, when sublimation fails—when, that is, the id's desires cannot be adequately satisfied in socially normative ways—the psyche, to prevent the person from literally acting out exactly what the id wants, has no alternative, if it is to go on functioning in a socially functional fashion, but to banish those desires from conscious awareness. By the classical Freudian view, this is the only device the individual can "go on" in the world without engaging in rape, murder, theft, or other socially catastrophic practices.

This painful, messy psychological process of violently shoving down and banishing desires from conscious awareness is what Freud called *repression.* The place to which repressed energies were banished Freud called the *subconscious.* The subconscious was thus a kind of garbage heap at the base of the psyche—or a dark prison house that held all those horrible revelations into our brute nature that we must exile into the perturbed dungeon of black forgetfulness lest they flood and destroy us.

Sadly but inevitably, felt Freud, repression was just the price that the human animal had to pay in order to live harmoniously with others in society. For if everyone acted on their feral urges, the result would be chaos and bloodshed, the destruction of society, and this would spell extinction for one and all. We are not only sexual animals. We are also social animals who rely on each other in order to survive. The human animal therefore had no choice: when sublimation failed, the individual had to curb his brute nature by repression if he were to live peacefully and productively with his fellow beings in those social roles and rules that made his survival as a communal creature possible. When repression and sublimation failed, the path led to the consulting room.

There therapy would deploy all its clinical tools and techniques to make the person "normal" and "functional" again—maybe for the first time in his life. Although psychoanalysis is sometimes seen as a program to promote sexual indulgence, this was never its founder's intention. Rather, the finally Victorian Freud (despite his marital indiscretions) was quite conventional in his insistence upon the primacy of social order, the central role of the family in maintaining it, and the use of psychoanalysis to repair ruptures whenever the order of things had failed. The historian Phillip Rieff (1961) is correct in claiming that Freud had "the mind of the moralist."

In the last phase of his writing and practice, Freud considerably expanded the notion of the id, or *libido,* calling it *Eros* and depicting it as a sort of generalized life instinct within the individual, still deeply involved with sexuality but not completely reducible to it. It was constantly doing battle with a death instinct that he called *Thanatos. Thanatos* was the desire of every creature to return to an undifferentiated state of eternal rest in the primal ground of being. Freud called this "natural law" the *Nirvana principle.* In the perpetual war between *Eros* and *Thanatos*, death must inevitably triumph, for it always has the last word. "The goal of all life is death," Freud concluded on a grim note of biological determinism in *Beyond the Pleasure Principle*, for "the inanimate was there before the animate" (Freud, 1957, p. 160).

POST-FREUDIAN THEORY AND THERAPY[4]

Now let us proceed to three of the most important psychoanalytic theorists who followed Freud. Although they differ in important ways, they are similar in that they often disagree with classical psychoanalytic theory and make substantial modifications to it.

First, they reject Freud's "hydraulic" or "plumbing" model of the psyche, with its picture of the subconscious as unrelenting, blind instincts. Like toxic gases in a cramping container, these are always threatening to explode and break through their ego-container at one or several points in the form of a neurotic symptom, or even shatter it in a psychotic break. Many post-Freudians now see the instinct model as an outdated metaphor of the human organism from nineteenth-century biology. Even those few recent theorists who preserve a model of psyche that relies upon the idea of warring instincts within the individual picture those instincts as including but not limited to sex.

Second, the post-Freudian theorists whom we will look at see the need to enter into authentic relationship with others as the primary human motivation, and to do so in such a way as to establish one's own identity as an integral being. Sex may figure into this need for relationship but usually it does not—or at least, it is not of primary importance in most relationships.

Third, many post-Freudians see psychological health not as the containment of primordial impulses but as the pursuit of ethically and, arguably, spiritually significant purposes in one's lifeworld (Meissner, 1984; Rizzuto, 1979).

Heinz Kohut (1913–1981)

Heinz Kohut is the father of "self-psychology" (Kohut, 1978). For Kohut it is the fostering of a stable and integral *self* that is the overriding psychodynamic purpose. Sexual issues will certainly come to play in defining and maintaining this self, as will many other issues, but they will all be oriented to the life goal of the founding, maintenance, and evolution of the self (Eagle, 1993). The goal is what Kohut called a state of *healthy narcissism*—not to be confused in this phrase with the negative connotations that surround the word "narcissism" in common usage. The person who does not live in the desired state of healthy narcissism suffers from a *narcissistic wound*.

The infrastructure of a person's sense of self can be traced back to his earliest relationships with primary caregivers—or *selfobjects*, so called because they are the objects of the infant's earliest attention and affection. Through them the infant learns about the world and itself. The selfobject is

---

4. Parts of this summary of the post-Freudian theorists examined below have been drawn from my (2007) study *Inside Education: Depth Psychology in Teaching and Learning.*

not, in the final analysis, *actually* the other person. Rather it is the *image* of that person that the infant—and later the adult—has internalized or, in psychoanalytic parlance, has *introjected* (Kohut, 1978).

Typically the infant's most influential selfobject is its mother. The infant's psyche is so dramatically shaped by its interaction with its mother because it is symbiotically fused with her at this primal stage.[5] Indeed in the infant's earliest experience the mother is indistinguishable from itself according to many psychoanalytic theorists. This idea has come under fire from some quarters, however, where it is believed that the child has a sense of its mother as a distinct person, and not just an extension of itself, virtually from the first moments of conscious awareness—perhaps even *in utero* (Wade, 1996).

At any rate, if the mother's interaction with the infant communicates love and acceptance, the infant learns that it is loveable and accepted and that the world is essentially trustworthy and beneficent. The infant comes to see itself as essentially a good, stable, and integrated being. In this way, the child's *primary narcissism* finds confirmation and gratification in its union with the loving mother. This happens in two ways (Kohut, 1978).

The first is in the *mirroring transference.* This consists in the infant seeing itself through the mirror of its mother's responses to it. The second is in the *idealizing transference.* The infant, enshrining the mother as not only the apex of reality but indeed *as* reality, finds its own ideals in its merger with this godly figure. The "idealized parental imago . . . is gazed at in awe, admired, looked up to, and [is that] which one wants to become" (Kohut, 1978, p. 430). The idealizing transference is the root of the child's ability to form and develop a value system.

The opposite of this kind of value-enabling mother is the one who communicates to the infant in her interactions with it that she is unhappy that it has come into the world, anxious about it, or even repelled by it. This lays the foundation for a variety of psychic disorders in the developing infant that come to tragic bloom in the adult—especially the *narcissistic personality disorders.* For what the infant now sees in the "mirror" of the mother is its own undesirability, inadequacy, and lack of unity. It thereby learns—in a catastrophic failure of the mirroring and idealizing transference—that the world is neither welcome nor welcoming but rejecting, cold, perilous, and confusing; a place that is either valueless or whose values are unattainable or irrelevant to the child's personally desolating experiences (Kohut, 1978).

The narcissistic personality disorders are distorted attempts to experience the primary mirroring and idealizing that a person never experienced as an infant—or never experienced enough (Kohut, 1978, pp. 440, 478). These

---

5. See Melanie Klein (1932/1975) for her crucial work in psychoanalytic theory and practice regarding the nursing child's relationship with the mother.

manifestations of isolation are called *secondary narcissism*. Healthy human development originates in *primary narcissism*. But when primary narcissistic needs are not met, the many problems of secondary narcissism are bound to occur.

In his later work especially, Kohut's focus is on the relationship between healthy narcissism and productivity. He explores "the ways by which a number of complex and autonomous achievements of the mature personality [are] derived from transformations of narcissism—i.e., created by the ego's capacity to tame narcissistic cathexes [releases of psychic energy] and to employ them for its highest aims" (1978, p. 460). Humor, empathy, wisdom, and creativity are the fruits of the successful transformation of primary narcissism into mature, healthy narcissism.

D. W. Winnicott (1896–1971)

From the extraordinarily rich body of work of British child psychotherapist D. W. Winnicott, we will look only at three of the most salient concepts: *holding environments*, *good-enough mothering*, and *transitional objects*.

Like Kohut, Winnicott sees the roots of psychic health or illness in the infant's relationship with its mother. Ideally, the mother will provide a good *holding environment* for the infant. This involves the physical act of lovingly holding the infant, of course, but more broadly it implies the mother providing the child with physical and emotional contexts that are supportive of its needs and beneficial to its growth—an environment, in short, that *holds* the child so that it can mature in safety:

> A wide extension of "holding" allows this one term to describe all that a mother does in the physical care of her baby, even including putting the baby down when a moment has come for the impersonal experience of contact with suitable non-human materials. In giving consideration to these matters, it is necessary to postulate a state of the mother who is (temporarily) identified with her baby so that she knows without thinking about it more or less what the baby needs. She does this, in health, without losing her own identity. (Winnicott, 1988, p. 259)

Note Winnicott's insistence that the mother should provide not only adequate holding for the child but that she should do so "without losing her own identity." Good mothering does not mean *perfect* mothering, in which the mother must always be available to the infant, meeting its every need almost before it arises. A so-called perfect mother would have to forgo her own identity and needs—her boundaries.

Ironically, such *perfect* treatment of the infant, far from actually *being* perfect, is disempowering for the infant and stunts its psychic growth, for it does not allow it to experience those moments of opposition—in healthy and monitored doses, of course—that it must know in order for it to begin to mature. A mother who psychically fuses with her infant to such an extent that she forfeits her own healthy sense of boundaries will present to the infant a distorted example of what relationship means.

On the other hand, *good-enough mothering* prevents burnout in the mother by providing for her own identity and allowing occasional mistakes. "Good-enough mothering gives opportunity for the steady development of personal processes in the baby" (1988, p. 456)—processes that will feed positively upon the mother's realistic humanity and not her neurotic perfectionism.

Good-enough mothering accommodates the mother's necessarily increasing separateness from the child as it begins to mature—a process best embodied and symbolized in weaning. With increasing separation, the infant, and then the older child, comes to register the existentially inescapable lesson that there is a grand divide between the world of Me and Not-Me—the Not-Me world first presenting itself to the child's awareness in the form of the withdrawing and sometimes even absent mother. To negotiate the space between the world of Me and Not-Me, the infant will come to rely upon a *transitional object* to fill that gap.

To take a prime example of a transitional object, consider the infant's own thumb. It replaces the mother's breast when the infant wishes to nurse but mother is not available for feeding. Often this is the child's first transitional object. Through a basic exercising of the infant's still rudimentary imagination, the thumb comes to replace the absent breast. The thumb is no longer just a thumb to the infant, although the child does not mistake it for a nipple either.

Rather, the thumb becomes a transitional object—a psychologically living symbol whose significance lies in the fact that the child's imagination infuses it with the power to satisfy at least some of its needs. In the same way, a favorite blanket becomes the child's substitute for the mother when she is away. Through creative fantasy, the child turns the blanket into a transitional object that is now not a blanket or a mother but a "poetic" fusion of both.

The thumb stands for an external or Not-Me object, is symbolical of it as we would say. The external object being sufficiently available, it can be used as substitute. This transition is itself allowed to take place slowly and gradually, in the infant's own time. Transitional objects (such as pieces of cloth, dolls, teddy bears, toys, and so on) are provided or are adopted, which (when the infant is resting from the arduous process of sorting out the world and the self) are cuddled or pushed away without being classified as thumb or breast symbols (1988, p. 436).

The transitional space is the place and the transitional object is the thing where the interior world of "I" and the exterior world of "Other" can come into fruitful contact in the form of a symbol. As the child develops, it chooses more complex transitional objects to use symbolically to express and deal with the existential gap between inner needs and outer reality.

In a sense, therefore, all of our philosophical and artistic products, our concepts and images, may be seen, in Winnicott's terms, as highly evolved transitional objects through which we handle our fundamental existential urge to interpret and interact with an external reality that ultimately extends to the limits of the cosmos, and perhaps beyond. Religion may also thus be seen as a transitional object between a human being or a group of them and the universe.

This idea points us toward viewing culture in more broadly existential, not just specifically political, terms—as a *collective transitional object*. Culture, by this view, is the manifestation of how a group of historically founded and formed people have jointly experienced the universe, and how they are presently evolving in that experience. Culture is a transitional object that also translates that communal, cosmic experience into the daily world of means and modes of interaction. And finally, culture emerges as a symbolic means, a "final transitional object," as it were, for the individual to have and to hold in order to feel a sense of unity with it in facing the reality of death. As Peter Berger, the sociologist of religion, has written:

> Every human society is, in the last resort, men banded together in the face of death. The power of religion depends, in the last resort, upon the credibility of the banners it puts in the hands of men as they stand before death, or more accurately, as they walk, inevitably, toward it. (1967, p. 52)

W. R. D. Fairbairn (1889–1964)

Fairbairn's (1992) work radically reframes psychoanalytic theory and practice. It has particularly important implications for the treatment of psychoses. Fairbairn's basic idea is that "libido is not pleasure-seeking but object-relation-seeking" (Eagle, 1993, p. 75). It is not primal sexual or power drives that energize the psyche but the need to enter into human relationships that emotionally and ethically do so.

In a statement that turns classical psychoanalysis on its head, Fairbairn proclaimed that "it must always be borne in mind . . . that it is not the libidinal attitude which determines the object-relationship but the object-relationship which determines the libidinal attitude" (Fairbairn, 1992, p. 34). Instead of animalistic drives as the origin of psychic conflict, transformation, and growth, Fairbairn sees the formation of ever deeper and richer ego structures as the primal psychic need. Integrating these unfolding ego-structures into a satisfying and productive holistic identity is the basic psychotherapeutic goal and one that, in Fairbairn's view, is a lifelong process.

Also of great interest—and which I have examined (2007, 2009b) as being especially applicable to educational theory—is Fairbairn's insistence that overintellectualization can represent "a general tendency on the part of individuals with a schizoid component to heap up their values in an inner world" (1992, p. 8).

There are many people who lead a life of the mind, what are called "symbolic analysts" in the sociology of labor. But most of them balance their scholarly work with rich and vibrant relationships with friends and family. They spend a good deal of time with them engaged in all sorts of activities, from hiking to going to movies to just sitting around a barbeque and having a few beers on a Sunday afternoon. Fairbairn is not talking about them. He is referring to those individuals who would always rather be buried in a book or hidden in a lonely lab than be with another person. "This high libidinization of the thought process," wrote Fairbairn, is characteristic of people who "are often more inclined to develop intellectual systems of an elaborate kind than to develop emotional relations with others on a human basis." Indeed, such individuals are inclined "to make libidinal objects of the systems which they have created in lieu of the pleasure of human contact" (1992, p. 21). Intellectualization, "a very characteristic schizoid feature," can be misused as an

> extremely powerful defense technique [which often operates] as a very formidable resistance in psychoanalytical therapy. Intellectualization implies an overvaluation of the thought-processes; and this overvaluation of thought is related to the difficulty which the individual with a schizoid tendency experiences with making emotional contacts with other people. (1992, p. 20)

THE POST-FREUDIAN TURN

Post-Freudian theory has unhooked psychoanalytic theory from the short leash of sexuality, allowing it to explore the origins of psychic energy in the desire for nurturing relationships, meaningful work, and a sense of universal connectedness. Sex is a powerful human impulse, but post-Freudians have reminded us that it is no more powerful than the desire to relate and create. Indeed, Kohut, Winnicott, and Fairbairn have argued that sexuality is often an outgrowth of these more primary needs, not their origin.

The formation and expansion of a capable, empathic, and vibrant self, then, are both the source and goal of psychic energy in the post-Freudian view. When these goals cannot be attained, the individual becomes ill and his identity impaired—sometimes even imperiled, and, in the most severe psychotic cases, obliterated.[6] But what, finally, is death except the loss of iden-

---

6. See Bateson (1972); Grof (1988); Laing (1967); and Watts (1969) for studies of psychosis from transpersonal perspectives some of which see psychosis as sometimes a potentially creative "emergence" from one level of consciousness to another.

tity? Most neuroses are ultimately about the anxiety about death, "nothingness," as existentialist philosophy and existentialist psychotherapy assert (May & Yalom, 1995; Sartre, 1956). This explains the acuteness of the pain experienced in a neurosis. Still, for all its agonies, neurosis is only a partial rupture of one's identity, leaving one more or less still functional. The terrors of psychosis, which is the blowing apart of one's identity into a chaos of disconnected fragments, are far greater.

Selfobject psychology renders a fascinating portrait of the complexity and even nobility of the ego in search of itself in its most creative outpourings. It also paints a doleful portrait of the damage done when that central existential need is thwarted and distorted. Selfobject psychology takes us into new galaxies of existential and therapeutic possibilities, light-years beyond Freud's bubbling planet of volcanic sexuality. It honors the individual as a soul searching for wholeness, relatedness, and even self-transcending purpose. It is "man's search for meaning" (Frankl, 1967).

FROM EGO-PSYCHOLOGY TO TRANSPERSONAL PSYCHOLOGY

Selfobject psychology has admirably refined and broadened the scope of the psychoanalytic vision. And in the later work of Abraham Maslow we find, in turn, an extension of selfobject psychology in the bridge he built between ego-based psychologies and those that move beyond merely the personal realm. His work invites ego-based psychologies to incline towards the *trans*personal realm, there to locate the organizing center of psyche.

Maslow (1908–1970), although a "humanist" psychologist—a school rooted in existentialist philosophy and not a strictly psychoanalytic one— nevertheless believed along with the selfobject psychologists that the formation and care of a vibrant, empowered self was the goal of psychological development—the apex of his famous pyramidal hierarchy of needs model.

As his work evolved, however, Maslow came to feel that creating a viable ego—the Western cultural ideal in the twentieth century (Taylor, 1992)— was, although necessary, not adequate in accounting for the more cosmic aspect of psyche. The need for the individual to establish contact with something transcendent had been a running theme in the Western literary and philosophical tradition but was mostly lost on academic and medical psychology in the first half of the twentieth century. Coming from one of the chief founders of the self-actualization movement of the early 1960s, this assertion of a center in psyche that goes beyond self-actualization was heady stuff.

Maslow's earlier model of the psyche is well known. It posited a pyramid of needs, starting at the base with physiological needs and then ascending to safety needs, followed by belongingness needs, esteem needs, cognitive needs, aesthetic needs, and culminating, like selfobject theory, in self-actualization needs. However, what is less generally known is that around the mid-1960s Maslow began to feel that his model was wanting.

Above self-actualization needs, Maslow started to perceive the inherent human need to transcend ego, to forge a link with "the naturalistically transcendent, spiritual, and axiological" (Maslow, 1968, pp. iii–iv). He called this "religion with a little 'r.'" One experiences it in moments of epiphany, to which he gave the name "peak experiences."

Maslow asserted that a complete picture of the human psyche must not only include issues from one's *personal* history but also acknowledge *transpersonal* realities that inform both cosmos and psyche—realities that are perennial, universal, and that incarnate in the *conjoined* psyche and spirit. This would take place in the *psychospiritual* domain. Maslow publicly speculated in his seminal *Towards a Psychology of Being* that such a psychology would be "centred in the cosmos" and, without neglecting the personal realm, would go "beyond humanness, identity, self-actualization, and the like."

The task of engaging in psychospiritual theorizing and creating psychospiritual therapies in this new key was becoming clear to Maslow, because "without the transpersonal, we get sick, violent, and nihilistic, or else hopeless and apathetic" (1968, p. iiif). Various theorists and therapists from mainline psychology took Maslow's injunctions to heart. An increasing number of them—though still relatively few—started to explore those areas in one's innermost zones where spirit and psyche meld, where the Eternal is found by the individual and where it burgeons within him.

Building upon but moving beyond selfobject psychology, psychoanalytic theorists such as Michael Washburn (1995), Michael Epstein (1995), and James Grotstein (2000) have accordingly made compelling cases for a recasting of psychoanalytic theory and practice in transpersonal terms, which it is doing to some extent although one could wish for a more general resonance to the psychospiritual domain in psychoanalytic theory.

It is important to stress here that *transpersonal psychology does not view spirituality and religion as necessarily the same or even similar things*. Each of us knows someone who characterizes himself as being very religious but whom we do not consider very spiritual, just as we all know someone we believe quite spiritual although that person has no religious affiliation and subscribes to no particular dogma, and even avoids such things. The transpersonal psychiatrist Bruce Scotton states it succinctly:

> [T]he words *transpersonal* and *spiritual* refer to levels of functioning of human consciousness that are potentially available in all cultures, with widely varying content and context. . . . Transpersonal psychiatry and psychology address that universal aspect of human consciousness that is transpersonal

experience and do not propound the belief of any one religion. (Scotton, Chinnen, & Battista, 1996, pp. 4f)

ENTER CARL GUSTAV JUNG

It is generally acknowledged that Jung's researches were among the earliest, and arguably remain the most important, in the modern Western psychological tradition to venture into the transpersonal contents and dynamics of the psyche. They came well before Maslow's pronouncements. They showed up as early as 1912, in fact, when Jung's *Symbols of Transformation,* his first major work in psychodynamic theory that probes the transpersonal domain (although it did so in a still tentative and rambling way), appeared. It shocked Freud. He saw the handwriting on the wall. In Jung's "disobedient" approach to analyzing a young woman's psychotic break, Freud clearly sensed that his successor was abandoning the psychoanalytic kingdom.

In the current biographical literature on Jung, Bair (2003) is representative of the common view that Jung had a complete nervous breakdown at this point, perhaps even a psychotic one, because he was left without any bearings just after the break with Freud, whose theories he had completely embraced but now suddenly renounced to his extreme emotional and professional harm. But Shamdasani (2005) lays out the much more convincing view, consistent with what we know of Jung's life and thought before Freud, that this was a time when Jung underwent that creative crisis so typical of the great innovators in depth psychology. During this period of creative crisis, these early explorers of the inner world clarified and claimed their own personally true apprehension of the mystery of psyche, finally resolving not to conform to an already delineated one (Ellenberg, 1970).

Thus, Jung's period of storm-and-stress was not one in which, deprived of his Freudian moorings, he sank into an almost total disorientation and fracturing, a broken man bereft of a vision. Instead it was one when, *finding* his vision again, he painfully shook off the paternalistic Freud's dogma because it was not consonant with his own deepest understanding of what the psyche is and because it did not honor his own psychospiritual, even mystical, experiences throughout his life (Jung, 1965).

Jung emerged from this creative illness with the essential elements of his psychological views and approach to therapy in hand. They flowered out of insights from both his medical practice and astonishing inner experiences.[7] He named his burgeoning school of thought and vision "analytical psychology"—to distinguish it from psychoanalysis.

Having explored some of psychodynamic theory's influences on analytical psychology, let us now set out on some of the roads that analytical psychology has carved out for us to explore.

---

7. On his mother's side, Emilie Preiswerk, Jung came from a long line of gifted psychics, seers, and others adept in such arts. Paranormal experiences were common in Jung's household when he was growing up and in the home he and his wife, Emma, created. Jung wrote his medical dissertation about a female medium. The dissertation was titled *An die Sogennante Okultische Phänomena, On So-Called Occult Phenomena.* As it turns out, the female medium was his cousin, who may have been in love with him, which fact might, of course, have colored what she did and said in her trances, and which Jung may have been observing and interpreting with something less than clinical detachment (Bair, 2003).

Chapter Three

The Ego and Its Relation to the Shadow

The First Half of Life

Jung offered one of the first modern transpersonal psychologies. However, he also wrote a great deal on the psychology of the ego, and an entire volume of his *Collected Works* is about Freud and psychoanalysis (1961).

Jung felt that Freud's sexual theory was useful but limited. So also, thought Jung, was the theory of Alfred Adler, another of Freud's original inner circle who, like Jung, broke ranks and wound up creating his own school of psychology (Adler, 1930). Adler maintained that the need to be an efficacious member of society and to ascend to higher levels of influence in it was the primary psychological motivator. Jung (1971) agreed about the importance of the culturally sanctioned gratification of the sexual impulse as well as social empowerment (1971), particularly in the first half of life. But there was more to psyche than just sex and power.

JUNG AND FREUD ON THE MORAL IMPULSE

Morality: Archetypal and Teleological

One area of major disagreement between Jung and Freud was about the nature of the moral impulse in the individual, which manifests itself early in the child's development and is key to its ego formation (Coles, 1990; Piaget, 1997). Jung rejected Freud's notion that morality was merely internalized social norms in the shape of the superego, its only function to rein in animal instincts to ensure social coherence. "Morality is not imposed from outside," said Jung, for "we have it in ourselves from the start—not the law but our moral nature" (Jung, 1966c, p. 27).

Whereas Freud saw the operation of the psyche as mired in biology, Jung was always looking for psyche's higher possibilities. Jung described this difference by characterizing Freud's approach as "reductive" and his as "constructive":

> The reductive standpoint is the distinguishing feature of Freudian interpretation. It always leads back to the primitive and elementary. The constructive standpoint, on the other hand, tries to synthesize, to build up, to direct one's gaze forward. It is less pessimistic than the other, which is always on the lookout for the morbid and thus tries to break down something complicated into something simple. (1954a, p. 105)

Freud's approach to psyche was *biological*. He looked for the primal, indeed, the primate substratum of psyche. Jung's approach was *teleological*. He looked for a higher purpose in psyche. Freud looked backward, Jung forward.[1] As Jung caustically noted, "Before Freud, nothing was allowed to be sexual; now everything is nothing but sexual" (1954a, p. 84). And so it was with the idea of morality. Freud saw morality as a control mechanism, its mission to check sexuality and the excessive aggressions that might grow out of it. Jung took a more creative view of the moral impulse as an adventure in principled self-construction. In this, Jung was again influenced by Kant.

Jung relied on Kant's notion of "moral intuition" and its "categorical imperatives" which, like the epistemological filters discussed in the previous chapter, are innate. "Moral intuition" provides us with a shared sense of what is right and wrong in certain basic respects. Jung believed that what he in Kantian fashion called "the moral sense" was "archetypal" (1966c, p. 27)—a term which we will examine in depth in what follows since it is a centerpiece of Jungian psychology (Nagy, 1991, p. 22).

At this point in our discussion, an *archetype* can simply be understood as that which is innate in the psyche and furnishes an individual with typical ways of seeing, being, and acting in the world regardless of the culture or historical epoch into which he was born. An archetype bears a striking resemblance to Kant's epistemological filters. Although Jung believed that the moral impulse was archetypal, he was a great student of cultures who fully appreciated the fact that how morality—or *any* archetype—is defined, embodied, and enacted will, of course, vary from culture to culture. Indeed, this idea is pivotal in Jungian psychology.

Jung's point was simply that a culture, to be cohesive, necessarily organizes itself around certain values. These provide the culture with a widely agreed upon set of criteria that enable its members to determine what conduct is obligatory, what forbidden, and what simply acceptable. This is an archetypal reality, readily observable in even a cursory comparative survey of

---

1. See also Homans (1995) and Jadot (1991).

cultures ancient and modern. These criteria determine the "average expectable," or *norm*-al, ways of seeing, being, and acting.

The educational psychologist Jerome Bruner (1996) makes the archetypal point that these values are found in their original form—have their *locus classicus*—in the sacred stories, the foundational myths, upon which a culture originated in the misty beginnings of its history. The modern ethicist Alasdair MacIntyre has observed that mythology as a moral exemplum is at the heart of a culture and is its primary mode of education into "virtue" (1985). In its myths a culture's value system is most clearly discernible.

In brief, a culture revolves around a set of values, however disparate those values might be from culture to culture, although there is a remarkable general consistency in them across cultures (Fay, 2000; Giddens, 1991). These core values are distillations of the ethical messages inherent in the culture's founding stories, its archetypal narratives. Thus, the moral sense is archetypal, narratively specific, and not philosophically abstract. The distillation and elaboration of moral principles into abstract philosophical systems comes later as a secondary, cognitive process. It is based upon a primary, poetic process. Jung therefore honored tradition and feared the disorienting consequences of its loss in a culture (1966a).

On the other hand, he did not see the ethical life as consisting of rigid adherence to a fixed body of rules. Having grown up in a Protestant home with a minister for a father, Jung had seen too many pious self-deceptions and outright hypocrisies in his family and community to believe the ethical life could ever be just formulaic.

An unflinching individualist, Jung never strayed from his conviction that "morality . . . rests entirely on the moral sense *of the individual* and the freedom necessary for this" (1966c, p. 153; emphasis added). Because Jung was such an immovable advocate of individual freedom, responsibility, and development, there is a political subtext running throughout his work advocating for democracy as the best guarantor of individual rights. Jung loathed any form of political collectivism.[2] Throughout *The Collected Works*, Jung calls the reader's attention to how "special attention must be paid to this delicate plant 'individuality' if it is not to be completely smothered" (1966c, p. 153).

Jung saw psychotherapy as first and foremost an ethical endeavor and in this sense took a "moral approach" to the therapeutic enterprise (Beebe, 1986; Fierz, 1991). For Jung a paramount therapeutic goal was to liberate the patient from psychological compulsion and confusion so that he could now make his choices in ethical liberty and spiritual centeredness. Examining

---

2. For the important question in Jungian studies of Jung's politics, see Odajnyk (1976, pp. 183, 186). See also Clift (1993, p. 46); Fierz (1991, p. 285); Mattoon (1998); and Weisstub (2000, p. 145).

one's own issues as courageously as one could was necessary because one could not see a situation clearly enough to ethically evaluate it well if one was viewing it through the storm clouds of neurosis. Furthermore, if one had not looked at one's own interior darkness, one was all too prone to project it onto another person and then charge that person with a moral flaw that was really one's own (Jung, 1969b, p. 208).

Going beyond Freud's medical model, Jung boldly declared that what transpires in the consulting room between a therapist and patient is of the highest ethical moment. Throughout his writings, Jung asserts that the great moral summons to us all—but one that relatively few really rise to because of the enormity of the task (1967, pp. 116f)—is to embark on the hard and often dangerous journey of exploring one's psyche to its very foundations. The journey is worth the effort, however, for it leads to realism, humility, and compassion—the preconditions of humanely assessing and sensitively acting in any situation (Bockus, 1990, p. 56).

In every psychological problem, Jung saw the possibility for an individual to use the dilemma as an opportunity for catapulting himself to higher psychospiritual ground. "Infallibly, in the last resort, it is the moral factor that decides between health and sickness" (Jung as cited in Pauson, 1988, p. 53).

The Two Hermeneutics

Freud and Jung exemplify what the French philosopher Paul Ricoeur (1991) has called the two different modes of interpretation, what in philosophy is called *hermeneutics*. The first mode operates from a position of doubt and sees the human being as a voracious, power-hungry animal. This is Freud's hermeneutics of suspicion. The second mode is from a position of hope that sees the human being as improvable—living, moving, and having his being within the context of eternity. This is Jung's hermeneutics of hope. Jung saw the ethical impulse as valid and necessary for growth in a rich psychospiritual life. This parallels the idea in existentialist philosophy and psychology of "living in good faith"—making one's courageously discovered, freely chosen "ultimate concerns" the litmus test of one's actions (May & Yalom, 1995; Tillich, 1987).

Indeed, some see Jung's psychology as existentialist (Brooke, 1991). Although this is an interesting suggestion that captures elements of Jung, it overlooks the simultaneously spiritual nature of his writings. If Jung *is* an existentialist, it is more in the tradition of Judeo-Christian existentialism, as in the works of Paul Tillich and Martin Buber, than in the atheistic existentialism of Sartre and Camus. Atheism is simply too inconsistent with the preponderance of what Jung wrote and has become untenable in light of

Jung's mystical experiences as revealed in 2009 with the appearance of *The Red Book* (Dourley, 1981; Ulanov, 1985).

THE EGO ACCORDING TO JUNG

Jung characterizes the ego as

> the complex factor to which all conscious contents are related. It forms, as it were, the center of the field of consciousness; and, insofar as this comprises the empirical personality, the ego is the center of all personal acts of consciousness. The relation of a psychic content to the ego forms the criterion of its consciousness, for no content can be conscious unless it is represented to a subject. (Jung, 1969b, p. 3)

From this we gather first of all that the ego is a "complex"—another one of the terms coined by Jung that are widely used today although few people, even in academic and clinical psychology, know who the author was. Although "having a complex" has negative connotations in the popular understanding of the term, this was not Jung's view. As he wrote, having a complex

> only means that something discordant, unassimilated, and antagonistic exists, perhaps as an obstacle, but also as an incentive to greater effort, and so, perhaps, to new possibilities of achievement. In this sense, then, complexes are nodal points of psychological life which we would not wish to do without; indeed, they should not be missing, for otherwise psychic life should come to a standstill.(1971, p. 529)

The ego as a complex is an assemblage of sensations, perceptions, emotions, attitudes, memories, and ideas—always in some degree of flux—which when healthy "constitutes the center of my field of consciousness and appears to possess a high degree of continuity and identity" (Jung, 1971, p. 425). The ego, our "empirical personality," is the sense we have of our identity "holding together"—even though some measure of tension is always necessary as a spur to growth and is, in any case, inevitable given the complexity of life. But optimally the ego is a relatively constant, unique, and efficacious field of conscious awareness in that ceaseless movement which Heraclitus said characterizes everything.

At the same time, it is necessary to recognize that the ego, although *relatively* constant, is not fixed. One's conscious awareness varies—often from moment to moment—depending upon the physical environment; the social environment, particularly one's positioning and intentions within it; one's shifting awareness of one's physiological/emotional state; and the sense one is making of this particular situation at this particular moment (Solso, 1998).

When we believe that sense of coherence is in jeopardy, we say that we are "falling apart." We fear that the functional unity of the sensations, impulses, ideas, and associations that make up our conscious awareness is coming unglued. It becomes increasingly difficult to navigate the daily world with competence and confidence.

However, if one is nevertheless still able to "go on being" in the world (Winnicott, 1992), then one is simply suffering from a neurosis, which, although painful, is not dangerously debilitating. But where there are psychic eruptions and fractures so serious that they shatter any sense of existential cohesion and dramatically compromise the ability to function in the world, then we are moving into the realm of psychosis. Neurosis and psychosis indicate differing degrees of ego-disintegration (Comer, 1998).

THE PERSONA

The ego is more than just a self-enclosed field of present awareness. It also includes ongoing stances and strategies for operating in the world *with others* and how the ego experiences others' stances and strategies in interacting with *it*. The ego is not just a *psychological* phenomenon. It is a *psychosocial* one (Vygotsky, 1986). The sociologist Erving Goffman (1997) uses the term "face-work" to speak about the various masks that the ego puts on throughout the day, and throughout a lifetime, in order to navigate the maze of interpersonal situations in which we play those social roles that make up so much of our lives. Jung called these masks *personas*, drawing the term from the ancient Greek drama's assortment of masks an actor held up to his face to indicate the part he was playing (1966c, p. 174).

The term *persona* has also taken on a negative connotation in popular parlance. "That's just his *persona,*" we hear, as if having personas were a shady affair, evidence of being unreal with oneself or others. But Jung noted that it would be ruinous, individually and collectively, if everyone always said exactly what he was thinking or feeling. The delicacy and flux of interpersonal relationships and the complex social contexts and conditions within which they take place make it inevitable that we all play various roles in the course of a day, sometimes in the course of an hour, even a minute. This is not necessarily because we are being unreal. Most often, it is simply because "being together" in the world is a convoluted dance.

Personas, however, do become a problem, warned Jung, if an individual wears them excessively in order to hide from relationship or to avoid facing truths about himself that need to be surfaced and worked through. Personas also detract from authenticity when one so entirely identifies with a social role that there is no individual left behind the mask. This is a form of death and eventually breeds terror in the person who has so overly identified with his social roles that he wakes up one morning to find that *he* is no longer there. He is out of touch with himself. In fact, he has committed psychological suicide.

Celebrities, constantly in the public eye, likely struggle to shed their personas more than most. Consider the movie star who seems to have everything. But alone in his mansion at night, he knows that he has allowed himself to be turned into a glitzy, empty image by his agent and studio. He has relinquished his identity and bartered away his talent for success in a few movies that made him fabulously wealthy but that he knows are artistic trash. He can no longer be certain if other people now show him affection because it is genuine or because they want something from him.

He might even turn to drugs to try to dull the pain of no longer being an "I"—a vibrant *subject* defining himself in creativity and passion in real communion with other such individuals—but instead an "It"—an *object* who no longer exists in health and authenticity *for* himself and *as* himself (Buber, 1965). "Living" in an identity-bereft, ethically fatal submission to the toxic demands and desires of others, he has become an existential ghost. And one day, you might read about his suicide in *People* magazine while waiting to check out at the supermarket stand. But his suicide merely confirms an existential death that, in fact, had already occurred well before the overdose.

In short, the persona is a necessary psychosocial tool—a human instrumentality, proof of Aristotle's notion that we are social animals who must find ways to live civilly and productively with each other. We must be careful, however, that the instrument does not come to possess us, does not become a vacuum that sucks our identity, and does not render us social *objects* instead of transcendent *subjects* evolving in responsible freedom, creative identity, and unfeigned compassion. For the primary "existential project" in each of our lives is to create a personal narrative that is filled with meaning and set against the backdrop of the Timeless (Ricoeur, 1976). This is one way of understanding Jung's term *individuation*. It is a central item in the Jungian vocabulary, and we will look at it in depth in the following chapters.

THE SHADOW

Jung's above definition of the ego is also intriguing in his observation that "the relation of a psychic content to the ego forms the criterion of its consciousness." Jung disliked what he called "power language"—fancy phrases and complex sentences. He was a great fan of putting things as simply as possible. However, his ideas, and the psychological processes they point toward, are often complex, and that is certainly true in this case.

Of course, the "relation of a psychic content to the ego" *may* be simple. For instance, I am aware that I am typing a sentence right now. It is early January and it's cold outside. I think I'll get up and turn on the heat. The "relation" of those "psychic contents" to my ego are clear and immediate— "the criterion of its consciousness" unproblematic.

However, the farther a psychic content exists outside of the limited daylight sphere of the conscious mind, the more shrouded in subconscious darkness it grows and the more fear it potentially inspires in the conscious mind, which senses, in a mounting mystery, its own diminishing control. This is why looking at subconscious and unconscious material takes courage. It is precisely *this* that makes it a moral act.

In the negatively hermeneutic Freudian view, the subconscious is a problem from start to finish—a psychodynamic junkyard littered with the steaming scraps of organs still writhing for gratification of every form of feral appetite, mostly the sexual ones. It is also the place where we stuff into the trash bags of secrecy all those memories of things that others have done to us, or that we have done to others, which we could not keep in consciousness and continue to function in the world.

The purpose of psychotherapy, in Freud's negative hermeneutics, was to bring as many of the dark secrets of the subconscious as possible into awareness. As he famously proclaimed, "Where Id once was, there will ego be!" In the consulting room these secrets could be adroitly brought to the surface, rationally examined, and finally dealt with, not just compulsively played out. The aim of therapy was either to expunge or harness those subterranean energies so that the person would become more socially functional in love and work.

In line with his positive hermeneutics, Jung did not see the subconscious as simply the repository of the reprehensible. He felt it contained positive elements as well. To distinguish his view of this realm of psychic functioning from Freud's, Jung used the term *shadow.*

The shadow certainly includes repressed psychic contents that are felt to be malignant—but it goes beyond that. Jung saw the shadow as "the 'negative' side of the personality, the sum of all the unpleasant qualities we like to hide, together with the insufficiently developed functions and the contents of the personal unconscious" (1966c, p. 66, fn. 5).

With the phrase "the sum of all the unpleasant qualities we like to hide," we hear echoes of Freud. But when Jung goes on to add that the shadow also contains "insufficiently developed functions," we see light in the darkness. For functions, although undeveloped, may still be good, or at least potentially good—and "good" in more than the Freudian sense of being socially acceptable, good in the greater sense of being true to one's soul.

In reading Jung we must not miss this crucial point: *the shadow contains not only hurt and hurtful parts of us but also simply undeveloped parts that have the potential of making us much more than we presently are—parts that may even offer hope of living in relationship with something much greater than we can presently imagine.* Even in its inquiries into the darkest landscapes of psyche, Jung's is a hermeneutics of hope.

But the ego, in its fear of whatever does not immediately seem to support its survival and sovereignty, is likely not to distinguish between what is truly negative in the shadow and what is merely underdeveloped there. From its frightened fortress, the ego simply registers *anything* that lies outside its small, highly defended circle of awareness and control as a threat. Of course the irony is that by not looking at such things, the ego invites—and sometimes invents—the very demons that it dreads.

None of this is meant to deny that the shadow contains real evil. There are things that are *deemed* inappropriate because they *are* inappropriate—even dangerous to self and others. It is simply to say that with the phrase "insufficiently developed functions" Jung is indicating another part of the personal subconscious that is essentially positive.

As an example of this, imagine a teenage girl who writes reams of poetry every week and dreams of living a Bohemian lifestyle abroad after getting a degree in creative writing. She fantasizes about mingling with other artists in cafés all day and writing poetry all night in an inexpensive studio. Instead, she eventually yields to her mother's blandishments that she be "practical."

So she goes to law school, where she excels and is editor of the *Law Review*. She joins a prestigious firm after graduation, pads her bank account, and winds up at forty-two with an impressive sum of money . . . and nothing but mountains of boring paperwork on her desk to look forward to as she grudgingly slumps into her well-appointed office every dispirited morning, aghast at the next eight hours that stretch before her like the Sahara. She notices that she is drinking too much, often has migraines, has stopped going to the gym, is sleeping poorly, and is experiencing anxiety attacks at company gatherings. As is often the case at the outset of a midlife crisis, it is announcing its advent in *somatoform disorders.* It is getting physical.

One Sunday afternoon, going to a local Barnes and Noble bookstore to be alone instead of hanging out with friends (none of them share her love of poetry), she wanders into the fiction section, picks up a volume by Mary Oliver, her favorite poet as a girl, and begins to read. By that evening, she has written the first draft of her first poem in twenty years.

All next week, she comes home immediately after work instead of going to the bar. She tells her boss that she wants to cut back on her caseload. Within a month, she has written and submitted to some good poetry journals several pieces that she is quite pleased with. She is also back to the gym again on the weekends, starting to sleep decently, and making some new friends at a poetry circle she found online and attends every Wednesday night. The migraines have disappeared.

What she had consigned to the shadow of oblivion, herself as a poet, has emerged and she has invited it to stay in what is a promising start to successfully handling a midlife transition.

We are a spectrum of desires that are integral in our life. Some of them may have been exiled to the Siberia of the shadow because we learned early on that they are unacceptable to *our* socioeconomic class, *our* political party, *our* ethnic group, *our* religion, *our* family, and just *our* way of doing things. Some of these shadow elements not only can, but must now be brought to consciousness and incarnated in action in our adult life.

The Inferior Function

Also residing in the shadow are yet other "insufficiently developed functions." As is the case with our hidden talents, we have banished *these* functions as well to the land of shadows. However, unlike with our disowned talents, these exiled functions are fields or skills that we deny or dismiss in our lives because we do not feel good about them. In fact, they make us feel awkward and vulnerable. But by ignoring them and leaving them undeveloped, we ensure our continuing inadequacy in things that we could at least achieve *some* level of competency in, things that might enrich our lives in numerous ways.

Jung (1971) called the domain of a person's limited competencies his *inferior function*, and this is also part of the shadow. Examining one's shadow requires that a person see and work through his limitations as much as possible, trying to develop them as much as he can. For if he does not, his inferior function will strike back and subvert him in those areas where he *is* especially competent—his "superior function"—and also the function he is next best at, his "secondary function." In this, as in everything, balance, the reconciliation of opposites, is essential—a key notion in Jungian psychodynamics as we will see later in examining his idea of the "transcendent function."

Jung's idea of the inferior function has many educational implications and applications. Psychoanalytically oriented educational scholars have examined the subconscious forces involved in how and why a person does not learn, the psychological and cultural validity of a good many of them, and the considerable psychological damage that can be done to students when these forces are not honored and worked with by an educational system. [3]

THE SHADOW IN ALCHEMY, THE MATURATION OF THE EGO, AND THE PREFACE TO INDIVIDUATION

In the last phase of his lifework, Jung turned to the study of alchemy. In medieval and Renaissance alchemy, Jung discovered a system that confirmed his discoveries about the unconscious. Jung's critics, already suspicious of his privileging of spirituality, found further damning evidence of him being just a mystic, not at all a man of science, in his sudden fascination with something as eccentric as alchemy. In fact, Jung's alchemical studies would turn out to be his crowning achievement.

In his magisterial *Alchemical Studies* (1968b), *Psychology and Alchemy* (1968d), and *Mysterium Coniunctionis* (1970b), Jung announced that "the world of alchemical symbols definitely does not belong to the rubbish heap of the past, but stands in a very real and living relationship to our most recent discoveries concerning the psychology of the unconscious" (Jung, 1970b, p. xiii).

Because alchemy allowed Jung to bring his lifetime of psychological investigations to a culminating expression, we will continue to visit his psychospiritual interpretation of it from various perspectives throughout this book. Different aspects of alchemy proved to be excellent vehicles for Jung to convey various dimensions of his vision of psyche.

Jung almost singlehandedly revived and rehabilitated scholarly interest in the lost art of alchemy. What he found was that, unlike the quick fortune that the alchemical hacks were trying to trump up, what the great Christian alchemists such as Gerhard Dorn and Michael Maier were attempting to devoutly produce in their "retorts" (or test tubes) was not earthly but spiritual gold. Theirs was the *aurum nostrum, aurum non vulgi,* "our gold, not vulgar gold," as they called it, also dubbing it the *lapis philosophorum*, the "philosopher's stone." The spiritual alchemists, far from being get-rich-quick artists, were striving to manifest spiritual gold. It was a rarefied, perhaps even astral, substance, "translated matter," that they wrote about and labored to produce, and it was not for sale.

---

3. In educational theory, the realm of the student's individual experience in and of the classroom is called "the subjective curriculum" (Cohler, 1989). Salzberger-Wittenberg (1989) offers what is still the best general exposition of the subjective curriculum in psychoanalytic terms regarding what she calls "the emotional experience of teaching and learning." I have also explored this topic over the last two decades from a Jungian perspective in my work as an educational psychologist, with special reference to the shadow and the inferior function in a recent study (in press, 2016).

Jung found that their work, their *opus*, was symbolic of the psychic formations and processes that he had been writing about over the decades. This
was nowhere truer than regarding his idea of the shadow. The engagement
with the shadow was the precondition of psychological growth according to
Jung, just as it was symbolically the initiating stage of the alchemical process.

The spiritual alchemists purposefully gathered particularly grim sub-
stances that they then set about to transform into a heavenly substance. It had
to pass through a critical stage called *sublimatio*—sublimation—which
means "to make sublime." The parallel here with the process of sublimation
in psychoanalysis, where the muck of unacceptable libidinal passion is trans-
muted into something rare and fine, was already a clue to Jung that alchemy
was emblematic of deeply meaningful psychological processes.

The spiritual alchemist began in his laboratory with base matter that he
had found in the streets late at night, typically haunting some slum-scape in
the most (literally) "marginal" parts of town. What the alchemist collected
there would become the "primary matter," the *prima materia,* with which the
whole affair began. It comprised such things as excrement, crusts of blood on
rags, rotting trash, dead animals, and other debris. Through steps developed
over millennia by other similarly dedicated practitioners, the alchemical project was to change the base material of the first stage of this process—
working with the blackened substance, the *nigredo,* as they called it; the
confrontation with the *shadow,* as Jung called it—into spiritualized matter,
alchemical gold, symbolic of the redeemed psyche.

All of this, said Jung, indicated that alchemy was a symbol of the transformation of psyche from a debased, tortured state to a honed condition of
wholeness—lustrous consciousness. And just as the priest officiated over the
transubstantiation of pounded wheat and crushed grapes into the body and
blood of Christ on the sacrificial altar, so the medieval and Renaissance
Christian alchemist saw himself as effecting the transubstantiation of de-
graded matter into glorified matter within his roiling retort (Jung, 1968b,
1968d, 1970b).[4] Alchemy was not protochemistry. It was protopsychology.

The Christian alchemist felt it essential that the process begin in genuine
engagement with not only the darkness of the world but also his own. The
nightmarish stuff in his retort would become purer only to the degree that he
did, too. He would therefore monitor and write about his own changes along
with those of the morphing substance as both he and it proceeded, just as the
patient and psychotherapist would keep a close eye on their own transformations in the course of therapy.

Shadow work demands the ego's *withdrawal of its shadowy projections.*
This idea, briefly discussed in chapter 1, entails acknowledging the darkness

---

4. See also Jung (1969a) for transformation symbolism in the Mass.

in oneself so as not to *project* it onto others. The advance that analytical psychology represented over alchemy, Jung felt, lay in its recognition that the changes that were taking place in the alchemical laboratory were not finally in the material in the retort but in the substance of the soul—"in internal difference," as Emily Dickinson wrote, "where the meanings are."

A pressing theme running throughout *The Collected Works* is that the most significant ethical obligation laid upon a person is to look at his shadow as fearlessly and totally as possible. Doing so makes him more tolerant, less prone to point the finger of reproof not only at other individuals but at "other groups and other forms and levels of culture" (Neumann, 1973, p. 97)—a point that has begun to occupy post-Jungian multicultural research.[5]

Jung often drove home the point that there is no surer cure for a "holier-than-thou" attitude than looking long and hard at one's own shadow. Therein, one will find every evil that besets the world (1967, p. 183, fn 14). Of course, there is social injustice, and no one can plausibly lay claim to an ethical life if he is insensitive to and inactive about it. A constant theme in Jung's writings, however, is that we must first each face our *own* evil as individuals. We must descend to what Yeats called "the foul rag and bone shop of the heart" where, as all the great religions teach, the source of darkness exists first and foremost in the individual. Otherwise, all our social programs will finally amount to self-deceptive rhetoric, evasions of the corruption in our own hearts that breed social injustice in the first place.

Is this not the reason, asked Jung, why programs of social salvation imposed by a political elite—whether on the right or the left is beside the point—spawn more evil than they eradicate? Who among us is not the proverbial physician who must first heal himself before presuming that he has the ethical medicine to heal others? The fruit of doing one's shadow work is that one evolves into a more compassionate, less perfectionist person who, having looked at his faults and weaknesses, can gently laugh at himself and is less likely to derisively laugh at others.

Dealing with one's shadow is the first step on the long and winding road through the forest of transformation that leads to an integrated and empowered personality. This is one of the ego's primary life tasks, and it never ends. The encounter with the shadow is more than just an off-handed admission that one has some nasty habits. It is an ethical engagement *with* one's total being *of* one's total being. "The growing awareness of the inferior part of the personality," Jung declared, "should not be twisted into an intellectual activity, for it has far more the meaning of a suffering and a passion that implicate the whole man" (1969b, p. 208).

---

5. See especially Adams (1995), Alister & Hauke (1998); Gray (1996); Samuels (2001); and Singer, T. (2000).

WITHDRAWING PROJECTIONS

Withdrawing projections, or seeing our own role in having created emotion-ally and ethically injurious situations—it was this that would also release us from staying stuck in the role of the personal and political victim. Shadow work is thus, Jung insisted, a precondition of individual and political matura-tion, of becoming the *archetypal wise elder* (Jung, 1969b, p. 208).

For we cannot transcend the *puer* and *puella* archetype—we cannot get over being the archetypal "boy" or "girl," in other words—until we stop blaming others for all of our woes. However much we have indeed been sinned against, and sometimes horribly so, we must finally locate the source of our pain and the possibility of our freedom in ourselves. This is what it means to be a *subject* moving toward a future of liberty, not an *object* stuck in a history of abuse—a truth, Jung implies, that holds at the political level no less than the psychospiritual one.

The core of Jung's idea of projection is similar to the proverbial wisdom that we condemn most harshly in others what we refuse to see in ourselves. Of course, Jung is not claiming that *whenever* we assess something or some-one as ethically problematic in some respect we are simply projecting our shadow. Having witnessed the horrors of two world wars, Jung knew about evil and wrote a great deal on the subject. Evil is real. It cannot be theorized away.[6] And there are times when it must be exposed and named as such, which Jung never hesitated to do.

Jung's point was simply that until we face our own shadow we will never know if the evil we are "observing" is truly there or is just a projected problem in ourselves. Before we set out to save the world, we had better be sure we have put plenty of effort into reforming ourselves. This is why the shadow comprises "the true moral problem of the individual" (Frey-Rohn, 1974, p. 61) and why shadow work is "a suffering and a passion that impli-cate the whole man" (1969b, p. 208).This idea was so important to Jung that some reckon it the central theme of his later work (Frey-Rohn, 1974, p. 3).

We call up, confront, get to know, and learn to work with our shadow largely as it appears in our dreams. In classical Jungian dream analysis, the shadow is usually the same gender as the dreamer. The dream character might have a dark complexion and/or dark hair, a fact which sometimes

---

6.   One reason that Jung rejected traditional Christian dogma was its Augustinian insistence that evil is not real in itself (for God created everything, and it is unthinkable that he could create anything evil) but is, rather, the "absence of good"—a *privatio boni.* Especially in light of the concentration camps of World War II, Jung felt it was not only philosophically indefen-sible but morally grotesque to say that evil does not *really* exist in its own right but was simply an accidental absence of good. Various Jungians have criticized Jung for his caricatured por-trayal of Christian doctrine regarding evil. Very few theologians would take the "Augustinian" argument to the extreme that Jung did. In fact, Augustine himself probably did not (White, 1982).

seems to be true for patients of color as well as for white patients (Adams, 1995); the figure may be wearing dark clothes; sometimes he or she is literally standing in or peeking out of a shadow.

When "outcast" figures make an appearance in a dream, it is important to consider that they might be embodiments of the shadow, bearing vital information about what needs to be acknowledged and, in some instances, *used* by the ego for higher purposes. Decoding that information is where inner exploration begins in earnest. But it requires a commitment that indeed involves "a suffering and a passion that implicate the whole [person]." Perhaps alluding to Christ's proclamation that "many are called but few are chosen," Jung spoke of the psychospiritual aristocracy who alone were capable of this:

> [O]nly those individuals can attain to a higher degree of consciousness who are destined to it and called from the beginning, i.e., who have a capacity and urge for higher differentiation. . . . In this matter men differ extremely. . . . Nature is aristocratic. . . . So too with the possibility of psychic development: it is not reserved for specially gifted individuals. In other words, in order to undergo a far-reaching psychological development, neither outstanding intelligence nor any other talent is necessary, for in this development moral qualities can make up for intellectual shortcomings. . . . Each can take what he needs, in his own way and in his own language. (1966c, pp. 116f)

But what is perhaps more typical is that a person undertakes shadow work less because he is impelled by the "urge to higher differentiation" and more because the ego is in distress and menaced by emerging shadow energy that has never been adequately dealt with. The person is in pain. This pain may lead the person to a psychotherapist.

Hopefully, the psychotherapist is one who will go deeply with the individual. But Jung feared that therapy would, as the corporate state of the twentieth century gained more and more ground, become simply a matter of the superficial thought adjustment and behavioral management of the "client." The aim would not be the psychospiritual growth of the patient, Jung felt, but simply to get him back to work. For the companies that would be paying for the therapy, or the state that would be mandating it, would expect a good return on their money in the form of a more efficient worker and more obedient citizen (Jung, 1966a, pp. 104ff).[7]

At any rate, the best, and the timeliest, reason for engaging in deeper exploration of oneself is that the ego has developed enough strength within itself and within the world to now look beyond itself, to "go transpersonal," to search out something higher in life (Wilber, 2000). By midlife, said Jung, a person has generally established himself professionally as well as in a

---

7. For the corporatization of education, see also Cohen (2002); Cremin (1988); Mayes (2009a); Slife (1993); Spring (1976, 2000); Tyack (1974).

relationship with a mate. Often they have started a family together. And in general, the individual has received a sufficient number of blows from life's school of hard knocks to have gained some measure of judgment and stability. With such emotional and social ballast in his life, the individual would now be solid enough within himself and as a responsible member of society, felt Jung the conservative, to press beyond conventional limits without becoming a problem to himself or to society. This made the time ripe for individuation, in Jung's view.

However, there are prominent Jungians in its "developmental branch" who disagree with Jung here (Samuels, 1997). They see ample evidence of the person's need to be individuating at every point along the lifespan—from at least the early school years on, possibly even from birth—not only at some artificial demarcation point named "midlife" (Fordham, 1994; Wade, 1996). Of course, what the impulse to individuate will "look like" at any given developmental stage will vary because of the differing inner and outer circumstances and resources available to the individual (Fordham, 1994). I agree with this view and have thus argued that individuation should be a central purpose of schooling (Mayes, 2005a, 2007, 2009b).

Nevertheless, it is probably true, as Jung suggested, that it is at midlife and beyond that individuation becomes an especially pressing matter, He used a simple simile to make this point. Comparing our lifespan to the course of a day, Jung wrote:

> From sunrise to noon, which is to say from birth until about 35 to 45, the ego consolidates, establishes itself, increases its control, and attempts to master the reality-principle—all of this with more or less success, of course, depending upon the individual's talents and opportunities. But in most cases, the ego strives to become—and grow as—a "going concern."

The business metaphor is not gratuitous, for much of what the ego is doing in the first half of life is to understand and "work" the "rules of exchange" in order to "transact" all sorts of "business" with others in the world—the ego's goal being to win for itself as much fiscal and symbolic capital as possible, its mission to maximize its social positioning (Adler, 1930; Bourdieu, 1977). One is out to define and defend one's personal identity, settle into a career, choose a partner, perhaps have children, contribute to and benefit from the existing socioeconomic order, and, in general, plant one's flag in the ground of consensual reality.

Jung had no quarrel with this. Far from it. Conservative in many respects, Jung felt it essential to the survival of any culture that its youth be prepared to take these psychosocial jobs on and carry them out (1966c, p. 74). On this conventional terrain, the ego can proclaim: "This is the world of 'me and mine.' This is how I fit. This is what I offer. And this is what I want in return.

If my psychosocial vehicle breaks down, I will take it to the company's psychological 'healthcare provider' to get it fixed."

At some point, however, the rules of engagement needed to change, said Jung—from psychosocial guidelines to psychospiritual imperatives.

The Possible Poetry of Aging

Jung was the first to discuss in psychological terms the confusion and even despair that many people suffer in midlife and that many poets after their own fashion have written about. Jung undoubtedly felt that he was rendering in psychotherapeutic language what poetry already knew.[8] He would render that poetic knowledge in his own psychological lexicon, as I have called it. That Jung was, in his own way, at least as much a poet as a psychiatrist is an important point to bear in mind in reading him on virtually any topic (Rowland, 2005).

Thus, Dante's *Divine Comedy* begins with the poet lamenting that

> Midway in our life's journey, I went astray
> From the straight road and woke to find myself
> Alone in a dark wood. How shall I say
> What wood that was! I never saw so drear,
> So rank, so arduous a wilderness!
> Its very memory gives a shape to fear.

Finding itself at its zenith in midlife, the ego also begins to sense the possibility of descent under the pull of the first disquieting signs of aging. One is less physically resilient, aches and pains start to grate, and it is more difficult to bounce back from physical and emotional shocks. Cosmetic surgery and medications can retard the aging process somewhat but they cannot stop it.

In what we might call the "arrival syndrome," a person realizes that many of his major life decisions have now been made and he must live with the consequences—good, bad, or indifferent. The partner(s) one has chosen, the family that one has perhaps created, the networks of friends established, the experiences accrued (both gracious and gruesome), and the profession pursued—all of these existential elements and more make up the horizons, both fixed and blurry, of one's life in middle age (Chinen, 1989).

It is from this existential vantage point that the individual wonders—after all the whirr and buzz of the working day, alone in the den with his thoughts when everyone else is asleep: "Is what I have created of real value? Have I been true to myself in creating it? Can it sustain me emotionally and ethically through the rest of my life? If not, what changes need to be made—and what

---

8. See Edinger, *Ego and Archetype* (1973, p. 53, fn. 16) for his and Jung's view that the midlife crisis cannot be resolved without a spiritual awakening of some sort, whether or not it involves a formal "religious" commitment.

sacrifices will such changes require? Where are the new challenges that make life exciting—and, indeed, *are* there any new challenges that will make life even half as exciting as the first half of life? And above all, how can I cope with the fact that my death—once such a distant, unreal thing—is now within sight at the end of the tunnel, approaching with what seems to be increasing speed?"[9] It is unsurprising that suicide and divorce rates mount dramatically in midlife (Wrightsman, 1994).

Life now poses what T. S. Eliot called in "The Love Song of J. Alfred Prufrock" an "overwhelming question," which Prufrock, a middle-aged man looking back on the first half of his life, is asking himself, or rather is trying *not* to ask himself. The question has many forms: "Are you willing to go more deeply into yourself to attain some new vision that will create a fresh sense of purpose in the second half of your life? Or will you just stay where you now are, feeling cramped in by not only your failures but also your successes in life, which have etched a circle you cannot move out of unless you have the courage to seek the Unknown, the Eternal, that awaits you—the Unknown-Eternal within you?" Wrote Eliot in *Four Quartets*:

> Old men ought to be explorers
> Here or there does not matter
> We must be still and still moving
> Into another intensity
> For a further union, a deeper communion.

Not everyone faces this summative season of life with the lyricism and daring that Eliot advises. Some simply dull themselves to it by "keeping on keeping on" with a tiresome, sterile regularity from which they dare not deviate and which they refuse to scrutinize. Their houses are more mausoleums in memory of a now dispersed family than a place where an evolving human being resides. As Thoreau said, "Most men lead a life of quiet desperation and go to the grave with the song still in them." They are stuck in an ego they cannot renounce but also cannot revive. It is entropy.

Or they engage in age-incongruous practices in a vain attempt to regain their youth. But this often results in them looking rather silly. Who has not seen the balding seventy-two-year-old man sitting in his new cherry-red sports car waiting for the stoplight to change, decked out like a teenager in shorts and a *Rolling Stones* T-shirt, a baseball cap with its brim turned to the back atop his head, and maybe even gunning the engine a little as he eyes two twenty-something women in the car next to his who are mostly just embarrassed for him?

There are two responses to midlife and its sometimes frightful impasse, according to Jung. The first is to dauntlessly face our own shadows. But those who do so are probably the minority. As we have seen, Jung christened

---

9. See Herzog (1967) for a study of death as an archetype.

as a psychospiritual aristocracy those individuals who confront the creatures of the deep that populate their interior life in its shadows. Membership in this elite has nothing to do with level of income or education but with psychological and moral courage. Indeed, for Jung, psychological courage and moral courage often seem to be pretty much the same thing.

The other response is to shrink from facing our shadows. In that case sooner or later we will become a mere caricature, a parody of ourselves, a study in resignation. Dispirited, dull, and without resurrected purpose for the second half of life, we become like Macbeth, lamenting his lack of ethical courage. He now finds, in an "arrival syndrome" that for him has become an opulent nightmare, that

> To-morrow, and to-morrow, and to-morrow,
> Creeps in this petty pace from day to day,
> To the last syllable of recorded time;
> And all our yesterdays have lighted fools
> The way to dusty death. Out, out, brief candle!
> Life's but a walking shadow, a poor player,
> That struts and frets his hour upon the stage,
> And then is heard no more. It is a tale
> Told by an idiot, full of sound and fury,
> Signifying nothing.

It is not that the universe has failed Macbeth. It is Macbeth who has failed the universe. He refused to take up the midlife challenge of spiritualizing his life, focusing instead on his ego ambitions. For Macbeth, this led to the murder of a king. For others, it may lead to the murder of what is regal within.

How, then, shall we live authentically from midlife until death against the backdrop of eternity? Jung's approach to this question is the theme of the next chapter.

Chapter Four

Approaching the Archetypes and the Collective Unconscious

The Second Half of Life

Developmental theories throughout much of the twentieth century dealt with maturation until about fourteen to twenty years old. This is the age when it was thought the ego's basic parameters had been formed and its general potential reached in terms of (1) facility with deductive and inductive reasoning, (2) the analysis of ethical problems, and (3) the construction of sexual identity.[1] From this point on, the ego's task was seen as one of refining itself within the boundaries of its more or less set contours and limits.[2]

Jung felt that Freud's failure to consider substantial development past the early years was a colossal shortcoming of his theory (1961)—and a shortcoming of any developmental theory that limited itself only to this first phase of life.[3] Was the consolidation of the ego in the first two decades the litmus test, asked Jung, by which all psychic functioning was to be judged? Were we to conclude that psychosocial adaptation and sexual functionality represented the fullness of what a human being is—or might become?

---

1. Conger & Galambos (1997); Crain (2010); Dusek (1994); Kohlberg (1987); Gilligan (1982); Piaget & Inhelder (1969).
2. See Crain (2010) for both an excellent presentation of standard developmental models and a critique of them.
3. Crain (2010); Ferrer (2002); Wade (1996); and Wilber (2000) offer important transpersonal critiques of and alternatives to standard developmental models.

"THE MASS MAN" VERSUS "THE SELF": PSYCHOSOCIAL
IDENTITY AND ITS LIMITS

As we saw in chapter 3, Jung warned that a psychology that concerned itself only with the socially functional ego ran the risk of becoming a creature of the corporate state, Right or Left (1966a, pp. 104, 107)—a tool for engineering "the mass man" (1954a, p. 85).[4] The mass man being a special focus of Jung's profound concern and pointed critique throughout *The Collected Works*, let us spend a bit more time examining him.

The Mass Man

The mass man cannot or will not see himself in ways that go beyond his role as a social creature. He is ideologically uncritical, emotionally undifferentiated, and therefore politically manipulable (1966a, p. 48). And now, with the proliferation of new technologies that Jung could not have imagined, the mass man rapidly succumbs to the waves of electronic images and messages that bombard his senses and colonize his consciousness. Put a group of such undifferentiated people together, said Jung, and what you have is not a programmatic political utopia but just "one big fathead" (Jung, 1966a, p. 6).

A *complete* psychology, Jung felt, will naturally include but must also go beyond the world of sexual and social functionality. It must extend into the deepest and highest reaches of the individual's psyche where that psyche merges with (perhaps is even transformed into) *spirit in search of the Ultimate*—whatever ultimacy may be for a given individual (Jung, 1967, p. 184; Tillich, 1987).[5] After all, the word "psychology" derives from the Greek word *psyche*, or spirit. If psychotherapy ignores—or even worse, denies—the individual's spiritual core, it betrays its fundamental calling, loses its bearings, and degenerates into a mere instrument of social control, a technically sophisticated but existentially empty tool for manufacturing creatures of the state on an ideological assembly line. Wrote Jung prophetically of our times:

> Whatever the conditions to which the individual wishes to adapt himself, he
> should always do so consciously and of his free choice. But, in so far as

---

4. Freud shared Jung's conviction that "the mass man" was a danger to a free society. In the psychoanalytic literature over the last century which I reviewed (Mayes, 2009b), virtually every psychoanalytic theorist who wrote about the uses of psychoanalytic theory and practice in the classroom has made the point that a society of individuals who have not done their own inner work is prone to being terrorized or seduced into one form or another of demagoguery and state control. (See for example Castoriadis, 1994.)

5. The reader of Kierkegaard (1969) will note that the individual soul, casting off all social self-definitions, in pursuit of its own entirely unique engagement with the Divine is one of his great themes as well, making it a bit puzzling why Jung had nothing positive to say about Kierkegaard. See Dourley (1981, 1984, 1990) for sensitive analyses of the multifaceted nature of the relationship of Jung's work to Kierkegaard and Tillich.

political aims and the State are to claim precedence, psychotherapy would inevitably become the interest of a particular political system, and it is to *its* aims that people would have to be *educated* [emphasis added] at the same time seduced to their own highest destiny. (1966a, p. 104)

Just as Jung predicted, the cognitive-behavioral "training" and "adjust-ment" of the individual to conform to the ideology of a certain political system to service its needs is now being accomplished primarily through state-controlled educational and psychotherapeutic means. Through these two psychoeducational mechanisms—public education and company-funded psychotherapy—the individual is now molded to fill a slot and become a fiscally profitable unit (what is now called "human capital") in the interlock-ing corporate structures that constitute the present arrangements of socioeco-nomic power. Of course, this inevitably hinders and may finally obliterate the individual's search for the unique and eternal within himself. For the truths of the individual soul, Jung pointed out, are not determined by com-mittee vote after a cost-benefit analysis.

To see people as *primarily* social beings is thus wrong on two counts, according to Jung. First, it is untenable because it shifts the center of gravity from the individual to the group—a fatal and ultimately unreal move, Jung observed, since it is the individual who "carries" political, cultural, and ethi-cal reality (1969a, p. 179). "Does not all culture begin with the individual?" (1966c, p. 205), observed Jung at the sociological level, while at the ethical level insisting that "morality . . . rests entirely on the moral sense of the individual and the freedom necessary for this" (1966c, p. 153). For these reasons, Jung found state "programs of salvation" dangerous and ultimately unsustainable, not being rooted in the firm soil of *individual* experience and hard-won *personal* commitment. Hence, "special attention must be paid to this delicate plant 'individuality' if it is not to be completely smothered" (Jung, 1966c, p. 155).

But the smothering of this plant was precisely what Jung *did* see, and lament, as he surveyed the proliferation of political "-isms" that were claim-ing the individual's total being in the twentieth century—as Huxley and Orwell were illustrating in their dystopian novels *Brave New World* and *1984* at the same time that Jung was producing his major works. Only half-jokingly did Jung observe that the devil was alive and well. "Who would suspect [the devil] under those high-sounding names of his, such as public welfare, lifelong security, peace among nations, etc.? He hides under ideal-isms, under -isms in general, and of these the most pernicious is doctrinar-ism" (Jung, 1969b, p. 86).

Communism and fascism excelled in the awful art of turning individuals into "slaves of an anonymous state" (1954b, p. 695). Doubtless, Jung's de-spair at the idea of social functionality as some sort of psychoeducational "ideal" was heightened by his having lived during the reign of horror driven by those two behemoth corporate states of the twentieth century, fascist Germany and communist Russia. He divided his scorn equally between totalitarianism on the right and the left. The farther away we move from the individual as the measure of all things in theory, the more he will become a puppet of the state in fact.

The inexhaustibly rich *subjectivity* of the individual will be reduced and then banished, in the indifferent metrics of the mathematics of "human capital," into the drear *objectivity* of the all-important state. Look, said Jung, at all the grand social schemes that have invariably wound up creating infinitely more grief than good—if any good at all. How many of the world's evils have been committed in the name of a "utopia" that some charismatic egomaniac cajoled, hoodwinked, browbeat, or simply muscled people into accepting?

Second, a merely socially functional view not only takes the individual out of the center of things; it leaves *his* center unattended to, *his* central dilemma unsolved, for he is now "modern man in search of a soul" in a world that was rapidly losing its own (1957).

Although his feelings about the United States were more positive, he suspected that it too could well degenerate into just another variation on the theme of the monolithic state. This was because of capitalism's tendency toward monopolistic corporations that would finally no longer need to *collude* with the state for the simple reason that, having joined themselves into interlocking, covert sites of power, they had now *become* the state.[6]

These loci of superconcentrated governance would settle for nothing less than total conformity of its citizenry in the name of efficiency and profit, while wrapping themselves, of course, in the cover of a flag that had originally stood for individual liberty. This is a classic instance of manufacturing "false consciousness" in the people—that is, making them erroneously believe that they have one thing while something quite opposite had been cleverly imposed upon them—and in the very name of the thing they had lost (Freire, 1970).[7]

In sum, Jung's critique of the modern state and its mass man (one shared by Freud, who also recoiled from "the herd mentality")—was that the corporate state of whatever stripe outlaws, surveils, punishes, and finally erases whatever is distinct and creative in the individual in order to hammer him into an anonymous cog in a totalist machine. What Jung was registering was a world-historical movement that had been brewing since the rise of the industrial-imperialist nation-state around the middle of the nineteenth centu-

---

6. See Gray (1996) for archetypal aspects of capitalism.
7. For archetypal analyses of this issue, see: Gray (1996); Flowers (2000); Zoja (1998).

ry and was now gaining full steam in Jung's era (Hobsbawm, 1999; Schumpeter, 1975).

This problem is reaching a climax in education, as I have argued in other studies, confirming Jung's prediction that education would, like therapy, become one of the state's dual tools for producing "the mass man" (Mayes, 2007; 2009a,b). So did the greatest of all American educational historians, Lawrence Cremin (1988), warn that the primary threat to American democracy in the twenty-first century would be the cancerous growth of the military-industrial complex into the military-industrial-*educational* complex (Mayes, 2005a; 2007; 2009b; 2016, in press). Jung and Cremin were right, and these times are now upon us.

INTRODUCTION TO THE "SELF"

The cure for this dilemma, both in the privacy of the consulting room and on the stage of world history, lay in the individual venturing beyond the small circle of the socially constructed ego and the personal subconscious to explore the much wider sphere of the *psychospiritual* realm. It is in this region that *the Self* is discovered *in* and *as* relationship with the Eternal, the Transcendent. And this has political implications. For "here," said Jung, "each of us must ask: Have I any religious experience and immediate relation to God, and hence that certainty which will keep me, as an individual, from dissolving in the crowd?" (Jung, 1970a, p. 292). Jung's was a politics of the spirit (Mayes, 2005a).

We will examine Jung's vision of "the Self" more extensively as we go on, approaching it from many angles—as indeed one *must* do to sense its multiplex nature. To begin with, however, let us simply picture *the Self* as a higher level of identity than the ego.[8] For according to Jung, *we have two sites of identity.* These two centers of identity not only can but must interact in a process that actually leads to a *unity of personality*, not its splitting. One form of our identity, the ego, is *temporal*. The other, the Self, is *supra-temporal*. The *ego* is our psychosexual "me" in a very broad spectrum of social contexts, *in time*. The *Self* is our psychospiritual "I" in an endless range of eternal contexts, on a plane of being that *transcends time*.

The Self is not selfish, however (Jung, 1967, p. 173). Although it exists primarily as the transcendent source and goal of the individual's total being (and thus in that sense *is* the individual's total being), the Self is ideally in

---

8. Although Jung generally used lower-case *s* in describing the core of the psychospiritual system, Jungians generally refer to it with an upper-case *S* to distinguish it from the ordinary use of the lower-case "self," which in popular language is similar to the "ego" of depth psychology.

constant and vital communication with one's temporal "base of operations," the ego (Jung, 1967, p. 184; 1969a, p. 5).

In the communion of ego and Self, the Self manifests itself responsibly and compassionately through the ego *in timely, practical action*. The Self is not only mindful of the psychosocial roles and responsibilities that the ego must bear, but it enables the ego to carry those tasks out with a grace and goodness it could probably not attain on its own. However, the Self is in its native psychospiritual element and is most its-Self in unconditional freedom, in the realm of the timeless.

Jung believed that the world's religions, East and West, have pointed to the Self as the substance of their common message, and that each religion has, at its best and in its own way, carved out paths to the realization of the Self *in* and *as* the whole person (Jung, 1970b).

Buddhism speaks of how the fully "awake" human being discovers that he finally *is* the Buddha at his core, that his nature *is* Buddha-Nature. St. Paul proclaims, "Not I, but Christ lives within me." Jewish mysticism pictures one's true nature as being a spark of the Divine Flame of God, which, returning to the Flame and incorporating itself in it, also *becomes* that Heavenly Fire. Hinduism proclaims that one *is* eternal consciousness when all the illusions of ego fall away and one sees oneself as a unique manifestation of Eternal Mind at the same time as one *is* that Mind. It is a philosophically compelling and therapeutically practical version of such things that Jung wished to render in his psychospiritual lexicon with what may be its most important term, the "Self" (1970b).

The interaction of the ego with the Self is what the Jungian theorist Edward Edinger (1973) called the "ego-Self axis."[9] An essential psychospiritual structure *and* process, the ego-Self axis enables one to operate from a position that is both realistic (the ego) and spiritually fruitful (the Self). Without the Self, the ego is superficial and arrogant. But Self without ego is unrealistic and given to delusions of grandeur. Not grounded in a healthy ego, the Self is all too prone to try to act out some wildly unrealistic scenario in daily life. This can destroy ego-structure and result in psychosis (1969b, pp. 24f). (We will look at some examples of this phenomenon in the next chapter.)

Nevertheless, Jung makes it quite clear at various points in *The Collected Works* that, in this transaction of ego and Self in forming and forwarding the integrated personality, the Self is superior to the ego, for the eternal is superior to the temporal. Thus it is the Self that should be the primary "organizer" of psyche, and it is from the vantage point of the Self that one should essentially live—in concert with a responsible ego *in time*, yes; but always under

---

9. See the post-Jungian Hauke (2000) for an excellent postmodern interpretation of the ego-Self axis.

the greater, determinative pull of the transcendent . . . the *timeless* (Jung, 1970a, p. 278).

The Wise Elder—and the Message He Bears

Jung declared that the second half of life had its own signposts and stages. Now, having learned so much from so many of life's trials, traps, and temptations, the wise elders had emerged and could engage in an inner journey while at the same time seeking out ways to contribute to their culture. Indeed, these inner and outer projects enriched each other.[10] As severely tested and finally proven elders of the community, these wise ones were both empowered and obliged to hand down to that community their peerless wisdom. The sage elder shows up universally in the sacred stories of cultures of all times, stimulating his or her culture's evolution.

To quote Jung at length regarding an image of his introduced in the last chapter:

> Our life is like the course of the sun. In the morning it gains continually in strength until it reaches the zenith-heat of high noon. Then comes the *enantio-dromia* [or, reversal of the flow of energy—an important concept in Jung]: the steady forward movement no longer denotes an increase, but a decrease, in strength. Thus our task in handling a young person is different from the task of handling an older person. In the former case, it is enough to clear away all the obstacles that hinder expansion and ascent; in the latter, we must nurture everything that assists the descent. . . . [I]t is a great mistake to think that the meaning of life is exhausted with the period of youth and expansion, that, for example, a woman who has passed the menopause is "finished." The afternoon of life is just as full of meaning as the morning; only, its meaning and purpose are different. Man has two aims; the first is the natural aim, the begetting of children and the business of protecting the brood; to this belongs the acquisition of money and social position. When this aim has been reached a new phase begins: the cultural aim. (1966c, p. 74)

By the "cultural aim" Jung meant that as an aging individual approaches death and sees himself or herself ever more clearly against the backdrop of eternity, they can hand down spiritual wisdom—"meaning and purpose"—to their culture. Contrary to the charge that Jung was a solipsist who did not bother himself about society but only the inner life of the privileged individual (Carier, 1976), the fact is that he was intensely concerned with culture, spending a great deal of time studying and traveling through First Nations.

---

10. See also the Freudian Erik Erikson (1997) for a developmental model that adroitly addresses issues across the lifespan.

The Wise Elder in First Nation Cultures

What he learned there was integral to his distinctive vision of psyche. This made of his work not only the first "multicultural psychology" of the twentieth century. It also helped invest it with the simple but absolutely indispensable element of "meaning and purpose." Without it, psychology would become, Jung prophesied, meaning-*less*. A first-rate scholar and innately a mystic, Jung was also a practical clinician who took his patients' suffering, that "pageant of despair" that passed through his consulting room every day, seriously.[11] He labored to alleviate it. And without the spiritual dimension, there could be—Jung is quite insistent on this point throughout *The Collected Works*—no "cure."

Jung's approach to psyche drew from the foundational stories of various cultures and times to find what is universal in them and therefore *archetypal*—another term from his lexicon that will occupy us a great deal in what follows.

In an age of especially vicious Western European colonialism, Jung severely reminded his mostly Continental and American readers that "the white race is not a species of *homo sapiens* specially favored by God" (1966a, p. 82). He made the then politically unpopular observation that "the crimes [the white man] has committed against the colored [*sic*] races are legion" (1970a, p. 211). Jung also acidly noted that people or groups who exercise political power and enjoy cultural privilege typically rationalize their favorable positioning with the outrageous claim that *their* social order is exactly what God intends and that "He" has put them at the top of it because "He" has a special love for them.

This is not faith in God, said Jung. It is a theologically ridiculous glorification of oneself—such privileging of one's own culture being nothing more than an extension of one's own ego. To this unholy alliance of twisted psychodynamics and cultural politics, one then personally presumes to affix God's seal of approval. And what is even more grotesque in all of this is that it easily leads to a catastrophic, self-issued invitation for one culture to decimate another.

Jung thus emerges as one of the early twentieth century's more important precursors of postmodern multiculturalism, despite his occasional lapses due to the cultural lenses through which he inevitably saw things—as do we all. In reading *The Collected Works* as historical documents as well as psychological ones, we must avoid the historiographic error of "presentism." This is to see the past through present lenses and then judge the past through those lenses, blaming those who did not possess our specific lenses (which are not always better) for not seeing through them (Barzun, 2000; Duberman, 1972).

---

11. A phrase I learned in conversation with Professor Sy Kahn, formerly chair, Department of Drama, University of the Pacific, regarding the plays of Tennessee Williams, May 1995.

As Jung probed into what counted as real and abiding wisdom, preciously carried and generously conveyed to him by elders in First Nation cultures, he noted examples of *the difference between knowledge and wisdom.*

Knowledge, a second-order phenomenon—a "secondary process" in the psychodynamic terms presented in chapter 2—is a cognitive grasp on something in the realm of propositional discourse, with an ofen ample serving of the ego investment that such discourse may contain, as noted in chapter 1. But it is *wisdom* that the elder uniquely offers. Wisdom is the ethical penetration of an existential situation, and also being penetrated *by* it, typically involving terrific pain in the getting, that ethically transforms us at our core.[12] As we come ever closer to the end of our mortal run, felt Jung, such things tended to become clearer.

This is what Heidegger (1964) called "living towards death" and doing so in "good faith" as existentialism puts it. Heidegger did not wish to be morbid in speaking of living towards death. He simply meant that to live any other way—as if one would never die—is just false and is therefore by definition living in "bad faith." It generates desperate immortality projects that cannot bear the light of reality and therefore can never constitute wisdom. In fact, in its anxious flight from the greatest lesson of the reality principle, the ever-present possibility and eventual certainty of death, it is precisely the act of *not* living towards death that generates neurosis (May & Yalom, 1995).

Because various First Nation individuals whom Jung met were so embedded in their cultures' foundational narratives, which situated their personal lives and deaths in an eternal context, they had much to teach the so-called advanced cultures, which would do well to humbly attend to many First Nations' attunement to the nature of things. We would do well to honor the wise elder and the messages he or she holds in spotted, wrinkled, trembling hands, whether that wise one was speaking from a First Nation or our own—rather than exhaust ourselves, indeed neuroticize ourselves, in the futile pursuit of endless youth, as is becoming "the fate of America," according to Michael Gellert (2001), a Jungian cultural critic.

Our glorification of everything young and dismissal of the aged and their wisdom bodes ill for US culture, says Gellert, which now hides away its aged members in lonely rooms to expire in heart-wrenching isolation. When a culture disprizes and exiles the aged, it loses its mor(t)al bearings and drifts into a sea of emotional disorientation and ethical unreality. Ignoring the wise elder's vision in a frantic pursuit of wealth, status, and sensuality, a culture invariably crashes and explodes on the rocks of its own psychospiritual folly.

Gellert argues that America is so obsessed with youth—so possessed by the archetypes (universal and deeply resonant images of basic patterns of the

---

12. Heidegger (1964) makes a similar distinction between "knowing" (instrumental/ontic) and "understanding" (existential/ontological) in *Being and Time.*

human experience) of the *puer*, the eternal boy, and *puella*, the eternal girl, who refuse to grow up—that it has wantonly disregarded the archetypes of the wise old man and woman. The collective cultural bill is now coming due, says Gellert. It may, in fact, be overdue.

No sentimentalist, however, Jung simultaneously noted a tendency toward a lack of ego differentiation among members of First Nation cultures.[13] That is, he saw a lack of self-conscious awareness of and critical reflection on oneself as an independent being, apart from the culture into which one was born, as well as on that culture itself. Such a person is simply carried away in whatever direction the collective might wander, stampede, or be herded.

Further, the ego-undifferentiated person is easily overtaken by the primordial impulses of the collective unconscious. We will look at the collective unconscious presently. For now, it is enough to say that in its negative manifestations it contains waves of primal energy that may lead a person or group to potentially dangerous, even ugly, acts if ego-consciousness has not been sufficiently established (Jung, 1966c, pp. 116f, 148). Such things, Jung felt, along with most Europeans of his day, merited the name "primitive," and he occasionally employed that unfortunate adjective. We must reject Jung's use of it in talking about First Nation peoples. However, Jung's conviction that some cultural practices are unacceptable was considered, and rooted in his Kantian belief in a universal "moral intuition."

Indeed, said Jung, morality, apart from any specific code, is itself an archetype—an inborn human capacity and universal need, and a guide for action. It is

> a function of the human soul, as old as humanity itself. Morality is not imposed from outside; we have it in ourselves from the start—not the law, but our moral nature without which the collective life of human society would be impossible. That is why morality is found at all levels of society. It is the instinctive regulator of action. (Jung, 1966c, p. 27)

Jung held that an ethically relativistic culture, such as was more and more the case with the "advanced" ones of the twentieth century—one that lacked at least some sense of the sacred, some shared spiritual and ethical assumptions—must inevitably collapse, as all disorganized things necessarily do. Jung would certainly have resonated to Paul Tillich's (1956, p. 103) observation that "religion is the soul of culture and culture the form of religion," for it is also a salient theme throughout *The Collected Works*.[14]

---

13.   However, see Samuels (1997, p. 44), who does believe that Jung was caught up in the "Noble Savage" mystique.

14.   See Dourley (1981, 1990) for groundbreaking analyses of parallels between Jung and Tillich.

For ultimately, at the core of any culture's modes of concrete and symbolic exchange are its foundational narratives. From these hallowed stories inevitably stem the rules, roles, and rituals of that culture. Such universally compelling (and thus, again, archetypal) narratives, wrote Jung, make up "the body of lore concerning the things that lie beyond man's earthly existence, and of wise rules of conduct." Jung here points out the need to attend to those sacred narratives, for they contain crucial principles of ethical behavior that derive from a culture's originating experiences and the ongoing behavior of the human being in light of the Eternal (Jung, 1966b, p. 96).

As Jung saw the Westerner's faith in his foundational cultural narratives eroding, he was fearful of a general social collapse, which he felt that the two world wars foreshadowed. This is why if a culture was to evolve, not degenerate, its "old myth needs to be clothed anew in every renewed age if it is not to lose its therapeutic effect" (1969b, p. 81). Jung celebrated cultural variation, but he was no friend to cultural relativism—the notion that there are no ethical absolutes, only socially constructed *mores,* that do not stem from any transculturally shared ethical ground and do not apply any farther than the specific culture in which they arose (Vygotsky, 1986).

Naturally, Jung understood the wide variation, culturally and historically, in *how* these principles will be defined, enshrined, and enforced within a given culture. As we will see in the following section, Jung's work relies on the fact of cultural variation on universal themes. However, despite all the diversity in the rituals, roles, and rules that a culture's sacred narratives generate, they are similar in their effect across cultures in that they picture the individual and the culture as existing against the backdrop of eternity and, on that basis, provide him with certain principles that satisfy his moral impulse and answer to his moral intuition. The distinguished British sociologist Sir Anthony Giddens (1991) has enumerated these:

> Amid the diversity of human cultural behavior, there are some common features. When these are found in all, or virtually all, societies, they are called *cultural universals. . . .* There is no known culture without a grammatically complex language. All cultures have some recognizable form of family system in which there are values and norms associated with the care of children. The institution of marriage is a cultural universal as are religious rituals and property rights. All cultures also have some form of incest prohibition—the banning of sexual relations between close relatives—such as father and daughter, mother and son, or brother and sister. A variety of other cultural universals have been identified by anthropologists—including the existence of art, dancing, bodily adornment, games, gift-giving, joking, and rules of hygiene. (1991, p. 46)

In the last analysis, as the sociologist of religion Peter Berger (1967) has concluded, a culture's foundational narratives have an ontological and frankly religious quality in that they are the way that human beings, individually and collectively, confront the cosmos and understand themselves in it, as mortal beings, and possibly as something even more than that but all of whom must someday die:

> Every human society is, in the last resort, men banded together in the face of death. The power of religion depends, in the last resort, upon the credibility of the banners it puts in the hands of men as they stand before death, or more accurately, as they walk, inevitably, toward it. (1967, p. 52)

In dreams, myths, literature, art, and cinema, it is the archetypal universal figure of the wise elder who uniquely embodies and prophetically announces this indispensable spiritual wisdom (Jung, 1969a, 215f). Since the knowledge that wise elders offer is of life-and-death importance, these personages often appear when a hero or heroine—in everything from culturally foundational narratives and fairy tales to movies and sitcoms—has reached a particularly dangerous and desperate pass (1968c, pp. 217f).

The wise ones come bearing talismans and potions that aid the young hero or heroine in their search for safety and greater empowerment (Jung, 1969a, p. 221f; see also Campbell, 1949, for the "monomyth" in which the wise elder is pivotal).[15] Sometimes the wise elder even appears as God, the synthesizing archetype of all archetypes, according to Jung (1969a, p. 226)—the *imago Dei,* or "image of God" within all of us that represents the culminating vision of the Self.[16] Occasionally Divinity descends in the form of fire (Jung, 1969a, p. 224).[17]

The Adventure of the Second Half of Life

Because the second half of life presents to the aging person not only the gnawing immediacy of physical decline but also the growing possibility of transpersonal insight, this stage of life needs to be tended to in its own terms,

---

15. See my (2009a) work, *The Archetypal Hero's Journey in Teaching and Learning: A Study in Jungian Pedagogy,* for an application of the ideas of "living in good faith" and "living towards death" in educational policies and practices.

16. See Heisig (1979), for the first and still the best study of the Self as the *Imago Dei*; see also Colman (2000); Martin & Goss (1985); and Ulanov (1999), for excellent treatments of this topic.

17. In other studies in educational psychology I have argued that one of the great promises of multiculturalism in the public school classroom is to help students see the many ways that First Nation cultures often value the wisdom of the elders more than (post)industrial cultures do (Mayes, 2009b, 2016). Including this perspective in the classroom through truly inclusive multicultural education would do wonders to deepen our students who come from privileged classes—and address a serious American cultural problem: the excessive glorification of youth to the extent that serial tummy tucks, face-lifts, and other cosmetic surgeries are now common for those with the money to get them—with "extreme makeover" programs as vicarious gratification for those not rich enough to do so.

not those borrowed from a time of life that, for it, is now long gone (Erickson, 1997).[18] To heed the call to adventure in the second half of life leads to vision. It attends to the sage statement of Edgar in Shakespeare's *King Lear* speaking the great truth of life's second half: "The ripeness is all."

Jung advised both the therapist and the patient to be aware that the goal of therapy, at any stage of life, is not to produce vapidly "happy" people, for there is a great deal about life that is not happy and it is no use pretending otherwise—despite what television commercials, New Age religions, and "positive psychology" would have us believe. The goal of therapy is rather to help the individual learn to endure suffering and make it creative through the discovery of meaning in one's pain. "The principal aim of psychotherapy is not to transport the patient to an impossible state of happiness, but to help him acquire steadfastness and philosophic patience in the face of suffering" (1966a, p. 81).

What Jung did *not* want for the aging individual was some sort of warmed-up model of ego management to keep the "senior citizen" superficially "sunshiny" all day—and therefore out of everyone's way. He wanted a psychology of vision—one that stood by the aging person rising to his full psychospiritual stature, even as he dwindled in physical power. The journey was not over for the aging person, to leave him in a "care center," dull and despairing or disoriented and fearful, watching game shows and gossiping to reluctant visitors about the person in the next room. Rather, the elder ought to be a pioneer, delivering notices from the Eternal to his people, to both challenge and orient them, disturb and also comfort them, but always to remind them of their sacred past and to point them to a more significant future.

Practicing what he preached, it was in the travails of his own soul and those of his patients that Jung began to develop an approach to psyche that, although not limited to the second half of life, addressed its issues in ways that no "model of psyche" had done before or has done since. And it was in

---

18. See Chinen (1989), and also Scotton, Chinen, & Battista (1996) for mythological and transpersonal clinical expositions of the psychology of aging. See Cortwright (1997), Ferrer (2002), and Hardy (1987) for excellent general expositions of transpersonal theory.

his radical postulation of archetypes and the collective unconscious that this emerged.[19]

We pick up the story of Jung's first substantial formulation of his approach to psyche, which started brewing when he was a college student, continued when he was a medical student, and began to take on the recognizable form of his psychospiritual lexicon, when he was a young psychiatrist at the famous Burghölzli Clinic, the "mental hospital" attached to the University of Zürich.[20]

APPROACHING THE ARCHETYPES AND
THE COLLECTIVE UNCONSCIOUS

Jung writes of a man[21] whom he was treating at the Burghölzli, a schizophrenic and megalomaniac who thought he was Christ. Jung's account of this man is worth citing at length since it is the best known example of the clinical experiences that finally led Jung away from Freud, returning his focus from personal psychodynamics to *trans*personal ones.

Making his daily rounds one day, Jung reports,

> I came across [the patient], blinking through the window up at the sun, and moving his head from side to side in a curious manner. He took me by the arm and said he wanted to show me something. He said that I must look at the sun

---

19. See also Erik Erikson (1997) for a lifespan developmental model that theorizes the gradations and complexities of the second half of life. Ken Wilber (2000) also offers a developmental model that not only accounts for the second half of life but does so with more of an eye to spiritual matters than Erikson's does. Wilber's model is deeply embedded in Buddhist psychology. Although Jung had profound interest in and regard for Buddhism and Hinduism, writing several important commentaries on Indian and Asian religious classics and stressing how the Westerner could benefit from the study of Buddhism and Hinduism (1978), he noted that the Western mind and spirit had been forged in a very different metaphysical tradition from the Eastern one. Jung considered it a mistake, therefore, for the Westerner to lose himself in an Eastern school of spirituality (1970b). From a certain angle, Jung's entire body of writings can be seen as an attempt to point the Westerner to a spiritual path that is basically Western because it is (1) individualistic and (2) rooted in the symbols of Western texts, secular and sacred. For all that, Jungian psychological terms and tools have been put to beneficial use in the analysis of Eastern spirituality as well as in adapting it for Westerners (Coward, 1985; Mocanin, 1986; Odajnyk, 1993; Spiegelman & Mokusen, 1984; Spiegelman & Vasavada, 1987).

20. Jung's (1965) autobiography, *Memories, Dreams, Reflections*, recounts this, and other pivotal moments in Jung's life, in Impressionistic strokes and shadings that make the volume as much a poetic account of his life as a typically biographical one. It has become clear that this book was written not only by Jung but in conjunction with one of Jung's closest friends and associates, the analyst Aniela Jaffé, which means that we must approach it with a certain degree of caution. Nevertheless, one still discovers in *Memories, Dreams, Reflections* that Jung's access to the archetypal realm began early on in his life as a spiritually and intellectually precocious child, whose early visions and dreams have been too easily explained away by Jung's detractors as evidence of psychosis. In fact, they were setting the stage, marking out the course, and presaging the power of Jung's thought.

21. Later identified as one Emile Schiflin (Bair, 2003).

with eyes half shut, and then I could see the sun's phallus. If I moved my head from side to side the sun-phallus would move too, and that was the origin of the wind. I made this observation about 1906. In the course of the year 1910, when I was engrossed in mythological studies, a book of Dietrich's came into my hands. It was part of the so-called Paris magic papyrus and was thought to be a liturgy of the Mithraic cult. It consisted of a series of instructions, invocations and visions. One of these visions is described in the following words: "And likewise the so-called tube, the origin of the ministering wind. For you will see hanging down from the disc of the sun something that looks like a tube. And towards the regions westward it is as though there were an infinite east wind. But if the other wind should prevail towards the regions of the east, you will in like manner see the vision veering in that direction." (1969b, pp. 150f)

Jung felt that the similarity of the two visions was striking, to say the least. What was more, there was no existing psychological school of thought that could even begin to account for this arresting correspondence between a schizophrenic's hallucination and an ancient creation myth.

Of course, Jung considered the possibility that this young man had heard this myth somewhere before, filed it in his murky subconscious, and was now producing it for Jung. On the face of it, this seemed a plausible explanation: patients often subconsciously manufacture dreams that they know will please the therapist, or at least be consistent with the therapist's orientation. Jung soon dismissed this possibility, however, because the patient was a person of limited education and far from being a man of the world who might have run across this information in travels or readings.

Jung was sensitive to the Freudian elements in the dream (the phallic sun) as well as its Adlerian overtones (the patient was a megalomaniac and the dream is painted in epic strokes). Still, after reading the Mithraic myth again, the young psychiatrist could not shake the suspicion that Freudian and Adlerian interpretations of the vision, as useful as they might be up to a point, did not do justice to its archaic grandeur and mythically suggestive pull. And of course they left unexplained how the patient's hallucination could so closely, even eerily, parallel an ancient cultic image. Something more was going on here than normative psychiatry could handle in its preoccupation with genitalia and regalia. But what? [22]

Could it be, Jung wondered, that the patient's hallucination came from a layer of psyche that went much deeper—or higher or wider, or all of these

22. It was in *Symbols of Transformation* (1967) that Jung evidenced his more profound approach to dream imagery and psychosis than Freud's. It is at this time and largely because of this book that the strain between Jung and Freud became very serious, resulting finally in a rupture in their friendship around 1913—one that was never mended, mostly because of Freud's egomaniacal insistence upon the absolute and exclusive truth of his theory but not without fits of pique in Jung, too, who was given from time to time to a certain *hauteur* and peevishness himself (Bair, 2003).

things—than the merely personal subconscious that Freud had mapped? In its echoing of an ancient myth, could this patient's vision be pointing to a primal layer of the psyche that revealed itself most clearly in psychosis? And why, if this were so, would it be in psychosis that it was revealed?

The answer, Jung was coming to suspect, was that in the psychotic the ego structure has been blown away by the force of psychic typhoons emanating from a deeper region of psyche than was being imagined in modern Western psychology.[23] This did not mean, Jung hastened to add, that that level was necessarily pathological. It just meant that psychosis offered the most opportune conditions for observing it, owing to the fact that, by definition, ego functioning was levelled in psychosis.

Could this undiscovered region, this *terra incognita,* of the psyche lie not only farther down than any region previously considered but that it might be the very bedrock of psyche—particularly obvious with patients in whom there was little or no ego structure to occlude its existence and operations?

If so, then this bedrock of psyche would be inherent in all people and cultures. And that would explain why it would manifest itself in both ancient myths and a modern young man's hallucinations. Lying much deeper than the subconscious, which was primarily just repressed fragments of consciousness that were not inborn but the encrustations of personal experiences that were too painful to live with, it should be called "the unconscious" to stress its singular profundity. Natively existing in all human beings, it could also be called "collective." Thus was born Jung's idea of the *collective unconscious.*

A competent scholar of ancient languages and mythologies, Jung began to see a connection between his clinical experiences during his busy work day with its full case load and his solitary reading in the hush of his book-strewn doctor's quarters at night. The scholar-physician plowed through ancient myths, often in their original languages, uncovering parallels in the characters, themes, and narrative patterns of the psychic material which his patients shared with him during the day and the religious/literary texts he would read at night. These correspondences were all the more impressive to Jung since many of his patients were ordinary citizens, some of them relatively unlettered village folk, who had probably never heard of a pre-Greco-Roman myth in their lives, much less a Mithraic one.

But there, under the shattering force of psychosis—that wrecking ball that reduces the ego-structure to rubble—emerged all the contents of the deepest

---

23. Hinduism and Buddhism have not only been aware of these layers of consciousness for millennia but have a treasure chest of spiritual "technologies" for working with them, even transcending them, to arrive at "imageless" states of unconditioned being. For a Jungian approach to these spiritual practices, see especially Mocanin (1986) and Coward (1985). For psychoanalytic approaches to Eastern religion and mysticism and their therapeutic applications, see Epstein (1995), Grotstein (2000), and Kawai (1996).

strata of the psyche. They gushed forth from his patients in torrents of images, characters, and stories that corresponded to ancient myths. Working at
a much deeper level than the merely personal *sub*-conscious, these contents
were not retrievable like subconscious contents are. They were *un*-conscious
and *supra*-personal. In fact, they were *trans*-personal.

Imagine the young psychiatrist's astonishment at finding that the most
hidden ancient mythologies ran side by side with his patients' dreams and
hallucinations. To be sure, the cast of characters in the patients' sleeping and
waking visions were clothed in modern garb and spoke modern German,
Italian, and French, not ancient Sumerian; the conflicts the patients reported
were more current; the dream settings more familiar. But that was only at the
surface of the dream or hallucination. Going beneath the surface, Jung found
that in the cast of characters and their symbolic roles, the general patterns of
the plots, and the messages lodged in the dream's themes—the correspondences between the patients' psychic products and the ancient myths were
simply undeniable.

Not all of his patients' dreams were of this universal quality. Some were
decoded well enough with the standard Freudian and Adlerian methods of
analysis.[24] However, a sufficient surplus of them did exhibit this more "universal" nature for Jung to wax confident that he had come across something
of the first importance about "the structure and dynamics of the psyche"
(1969b). "This discovery," Jung announced,

> means another step forward in our understanding: the recognition, that is, of
> two layers in the unconscious. We have to distinguish between a personal
> unconscious and an *impersonal* or *transpersonal unconscious*. We speak of the
> latter also as the *collective unconscious,* because it is detached from anything
> personal and is common to all men, since its contents can be found every-
> where, which is naturally not the case with the personal contents. . . . The
> primordial images [of the collective unconscious], however, are the most an-
> cient and the most universal "thought-forms" of humanity. (1966c, p. 66)

Elsewhere, Jung explained:

> This deeper layer I call the *collective unconscious.* I have chosen the term
> "collective" because this part of the unconscious is not individual but univer-
> sal; in contrast to the personal psyche, it has contents and modes of behavior
> that are more or less the same everywhere and in all individuals. It is, in other
> words, identical in all men and thus constitutes a common psychic substrate of
> a suprapersonal nature which is present in every one of us. (1968c, pp. 3f)

---

24. Some neo-Jungians have speculated that even dreams, projections, and fantasies that
seem to be merely personal have an archetypal core (Kalsched, 1997; Knox, 1998; Machtiger,
1995a, 1995b). I believe this is correct, for it is simply to say that there is a deeper ethical and
spiritual significance in what we think, feel, and do than is apparent at a merely personal level
of the ego and the subconscious.

Jung thus distinguished between (1) the personal *conscious,* (2) the personal *subconscious,* and (3) the *transpersonal or suprapersonal unconscious*—the collective unconscious (1969b, p. 151f).

Freud used the term *libido* to denote sexual energy. But Jung used it to mean *life force* in general. Jung asserted that as libido matured it began to seek out things that are both higher and deeper than sex and power. What libido was in search of, Jung said, was a much more compelling goal— namely, *the collective unconscious and the archetypes that comprise it.*

> We have now found the object which the libido chooses when it is freed from personal, infantile forms of transference. It follows its own gradient down into the depths of the unconscious, and there activates what has lain slumbering from the beginning. It has discovered the hidden treasure upon which mankind ever and anon has drawn, and from which it has raised up its gods and demons, and all those potent and mighty thoughts without which man ceases to be man. (Jung, 1966c, pp. 66f)

His research and writing, his clinical practice, and above all, his own inner explorations pointed with sharpening insistence to the ever-flowing font, universal, within each individual, of our mythico-religious nature— what Jung characterized as our "spiritual instincts"—in all cultures at all times.

Despite the cultural and historical variations in the way that religion has been practiced, the uncritical obedience it too often demands, and the horrors that have been committed in its name, Jung believed that religion at its best has aimed at bringing the individual and the eternal, the specific and the universal, into communion (Jung, 1970b). But for Jung, it did not matter if we experienced this connection within a set of traditional beliefs and practices, or in a strictly personal way, or somewhere in between. All that mattered was that it happened. And for Jung, this was often a clinical matter as much as a philosophical one, for he said that he had never seen a "cure"[25] in therapy that did not involve some sort of spiritual awakening.

This was because psychospiritual health in the latter half of life consisted in bringing our *temporal ego* into creative alignment with our *timeless Self* in the "ego-Self axis" mentioned above (Edinger, 1973).

---

25. We must take Jung's use of the word "cure" with a grain of salt, however, in light of his statements that it was not "cures" that psychotherapy should aim at but rather to help the individual cultivate a certain stoic patience in the face of life's inevitable adversities while continuing to live passionately and creatively. See, for example, 1970a, pp. 169f; 1969b, pp. 72f.

ON THE "SPIRITUAL" IN *THE COLLECTED WORKS*

Since the question of Jung's spiritual commitments arises for scholars in both camps most frequently around the question of the nature and meaning of the archetypes and the collective unconscious, now is an appropriate time to look at this issue in more detail.

As mentioned in the introduction, Jungian scholarship is pretty evenly divided on the question of Jung's "spirituality." One camp holds that his intent was to help the individual find a life-giving connection with Spirit. The other camp argues that his intent was mostly existentialist—a variation on the theme of living an authentic existence in this life without reference to something transcendentally beyond or immanently within this life.

Obviously, this book is in the first camp. Readers interested in excellent presentations of opposing lines of thought from the other camp might begin with Brooke (1991) for his phenomenological reading of Jung's work as well as Hauke (2000) for his postmodern interpretation of the idea of the Self. In the following section, let us go more deeply into the first line of thought.

A major thread running throughout Jung's work is his hope that a transpersonal approach to psychology would give the modern individual access to the spiritual domain. He believed this would be instrumental in revitalizing the spiritual lives of those who felt bereft of the transcendent in what he perceived to be the collapse of formal religion in the twentieth century. As both a cultural critic and a practicing psychotherapist, Jung observed that the absence of transcendence in many people's lives was having disastrously disorienting consequences individually and societally (Jung, 1957). Jung, the quintessential man on a mission, was out to help "modern man in search of a soul" to find it (1957).

In a passage in *The Collected Works* that is somehow consistently missed or dismissed by those who argue that Jung did not believe in a divine source and goal of Being, Jung wrote the following:

> Here, just for once, and as an exception, I shall indulge in transcendental speculation and even in "poetry": God has indeed made an inconceivably divine and mysteriously contradictory image of himself, without the help of man, and implanted it in man's unconscious as an archetype, an . . . archetypal light: not in order that theologians of all times and places should be at one another's throats, but in order that the unpresumptuous man might glimpse an image, in the stillness of his soul, that is akin to him and is wrought of his own psychic substance. This image contains everything he will ever imagine concerning his gods or concerning the ground of his psyche. (1954b, p. 667)

Elsewhere he portrayed the archetypes as "guidance from God" (1938, p. 213).

One could not ask for more unequivocal statements of belief in a God of some sort or a more direct assertion that the individual may approach the Divine by means of the archetypes. Indeed, in true gnostic fashion, Jung insisted that God not only existed but dwarfed all of our conceptions and descriptions of God by manifesting to human awareness as "an inconceivably divine and mysteriously contradictory image of himself" (Hoeller, 1982; Segal, 1995). In the face of the transcendent, we are both reduced and raised to stunned speechlessness, a Zen silence; or, if speaking, uttering only St. John of the Cross's mystically erasing "Nada" about everything one might say of that God-Beyond-God. The ultimate surpasses all of our thoughts or imaginings, even the cleverest, and probably *especially* the cleverest. For "a man can know even less about God than an ant can know of the contents of the British Museum" (Jung, 1966c, 235, fn. 6).

However, to say that Jung's work cuts a spiritual orbit is not to say that orbit was not eccentric, that Jung did not sometimes contradict himself about what spirituality might mean, or that his views of spirituality did not evolve. Jung's critics are correct to point these things out. The reader who comes to Jung, whether for the first time or the thousandth time, must be prepared to ride the sometimes choppy sea of Jung's highly idiosyncratic approach to spirituality. That Jung's purposes were spiritual seems to be beyond doubt. What he meant by "spirituality," however, is shrouded, and maybe purposefully so, in *The Collected Works*. Let us, then, briefly review a few of the major schools of thought regarding Jung and spirituality.

Approaches to Jung's Approach to Spirit

Some scholars suggest that the complexity of the issue of Jung's view of spirituality reflects the fact that he was to some degree attempting to appease the governing materialist-scientific presuppositions of his day, and that his "dream" of creating a "natural science" out of psychospiritual issues was inherently problematic (Shamdasani, 2003).

Other Jungian scholars look to the tradition of spiritualism that ran in his family on his mother's side. They see his work as an attempt to both honor and keep in check his spiritualistic roots and proclivities in the "scientific vessel" of medical psychiatry. One need not look far for support for this explanation. His doctoral dissertation, *On the Psychology and Pathology of the So-Called Occult Phenomena,* was written in 1902 when Jung was twenty-seven years old and, despite his lifelong interest in and experience of the paranormal, the ambitious young psychiatrist was attempting to fall in line with Freud's natural-sciences model of psyche. To add yet another layer of *both* Freudian and familial complexity, it later emerged that the medium whom Jung studied for his dissertation was not only his cousin but may have been in love with him (Bair, 2003).

At any rate, this hypothesis about the complexity of Jung's writings on spirituality says that the psychiatrist was trying to find a way to reconcile the paranormal experiences and mediumistic gifts which he shared with his mother and her family, on one hand, and his urgent desire to be a creditable man of medicine, on the other hand (Charet, 1993).

Yet others attempt to explain Jung's wide-ranging approach to spirituality by pointing to his highly idiosyncratic character. They suggest that Jung saw himself as a "religious" person in his own way, but one that defies any simple characterization or analysis. By this interpretation, Jung's spiritual views evidenced different kinds of religiosity in different periods in his life, even in different works in the same periods, and sometimes even within a single work (Chapman, 1988).

Too, there is the fact that Jung, a polymath, was fascinated by many religious traditions and practices—ranging from Native American shaman-ism to yoga, from ancient Chinese alchemy to the Roman Catholic Mass—and that he picked and chose from them as he pleased in his work—and indeed in his life. Considering the colonialist European milieu in which Jung lived and worked, he must be admired for the insight and delicacy with which he analyzed and wrote about the texts, doctrines, and practices of various religions, East and West. [26,27,28]

It should not surprise us that this unapologetic individualist should have possessed a spirituality so entirely his own. As we have had occasion to note at various points, Jung is not petitioning his readers to imitate *his* manner of dwelling in ultimacy. Rather, he is encouraging each reader to do so in *his* own way.

Memories, Dreams, Reflections

In his autobiography, *Memories, Dreams, Reflections* (1965), we see that Jung's convictions were indeed *his own*—not matters of speculative theory building. They were founded, formed, and forwarded in personal experience.

---

26. Jungian psychology offers ways of identifying and suggestions for minimizing racism. These revolve around the idea that racism is often the result of the projection of the shadow onto subdominant groups, and that owning our own shadow makes it less likely that we will project it onto a marginalized group (Adams, 1995; Gray, 1996; Gross, 2000).

27. On the other hand, there is no lack of hostile statements about Jung from conservative religionists from varied religious traditions. Despite their own theological differences from each other—they unite in condemning Jung for what they believe to be his attempt to turn "true religion" (always, of course, their own) into just a psychological "experience."

28. On the other side of the East–West religious table, Jung has been widely celebrated by certain Jewish (i.e., Kluger, 1995), Christian (i.e., Sanford, 1993), and Islamic (Vaughan-Lee, 1998) theologians, clergypersons, and faithful as pumping critically needed psychospiritual lifeblood into dogmas, rites, and other practices that were becoming stale and flat.

This would be made even clearer over forty years later with the release of *The Red Book* (2009).

Memories, Dreams, Reflections has become a matter of some contention in Jungian scholarship recently because it is not clear how much his collaborator, Aniela Jaffé, may have embellished the account. It is still worth citing some passages at length about Jung's spiritually pivotal experiences, however, since these are clearly in Jung's voice and give the reader access to intensely personal accounts of some of the most impressive spiritual moments in his life.

As in *The Red Book*, these reports of particularly significant breakthroughs of the Eternal into Jung's life (which, in fact, had been happening to him since he was a boy) give us close glimpses into his *felt* spirituality. These experiences, which came in steady succession just before he turned seventy, are important to the reader of *The Collected Works*. He explains that much of what he wrote after them, including "a good many of my principal works," were born of these experiences (1965, p. 297).[29]

In 1944 Jung had an accident that eventually led to a heart attack. This instantiated a series of visions while he was in hospital. For the rest of his life Jung insisted that these visions were not the product of a fevered mind but were real. As he wrote elsewhere about spiritual convictions in general but in words that might just as well have been referring to his own encounters with the Divine during this time: "A religious truth is essentially an experience, it is not an opinion. Religion is an absolute experience. . . . It cannot be discussed. . . . When somebody has a religious experience, he just has such an experience, and nothing can take it away from him" (Jung, 1954b, p. 289).

In one of his visions, Jung reports that he seemed to be:

> high up in space. Far below I saw the globe of the earth, bathed in a gloriously blue light. I saw the deep blue sea and the continents. . . . I knew that I was on the point of departing the earth. . . . After contemplating it for a while, I turned around. I had been standing with my back to the Indian Ocean, as it were, and my face to the north. Then it seemed to me that I made a turn to the south. Something new entered my field of vision. A short distance away I saw in space a tremendous dark block of stone, like a meteorite. It was about the size of my house, or even bigger. It was floating in space, and I myself was floating in space. . . . My stone was one such gigantic dark block. An entrance led into a small antechamber. To the right of the entrance, a black Hindu sat silently in lotus posture upon a stone bench. He wore a white gown, and I knew that he expected me. Two steps led up to this antechamber, and inside, on the left, was

---

29. See Owens (2010) in addition to Shamdasani in his introduction to *The Red Book* for foundational essays regarding how we must now read Jung's entire body of work in light of what *The Red Book* now offers us. If *The Red Book* is, as I believe it to be, a great new key in reading Jung, Owens and Shamdasani have given us great new keys in reading *The Red Book*. The world of Jungian scholarship owes both of these important Jungian scholars an as-yet unacknowledged debt.

the gate to the temple. Innumerable tiny niches, each with a saucer-like concavity filled with coconut oil and small burning wicks, surrounded the door with a wreath of bright flames. I had the feeling that everything was being sloughed away. . . . There was no longer anything I wanted or desired. I existed in an objective form; I was what I had been and lived. There I would at last understand—this too was a certainty—what historical nexus I or my life fitted into. I would know what had been before me, why I had come into being, and where my life was flowing. (1965, pp. 289ff)

Jung's also experienced some bouts of depression as he realized that he was recovering. He resisted this in body and spirit, loath to return from the threshold of what he could only compare to the beatific "Garden of Pomegranates" from Kabbalistic portrayals of heaven. But now before him was the drab realization that he would have to take up daily life again in the workaday world.

Disappointed, I thought, "Now I must return to the 'box system' again." For it seemed to me as if behind the horizon of the cosmos a three-dimensional world had been artificially built up, in which each person sat by himself in a little box. And now I should have to convince myself all over again that this was important. I might formulate it as an affirmation of things as they are: an unconditional "yes" to that which is, without subjective protests—acceptance of the conditions of existence as I see them and understand them, acceptance of my own nature, as I happen to be. . . . [W]hen one follows the path of individuation . . . we forge an ego that does not break down when incomprehensible things happen; an ego that endures, that endures the truth, and that is capable of coping with the world and fate. (1965, pp. 295ff)

Here, and in other epochs in Jung's life, we see the link between oneself-in-the-world as an ego, on one hand, and the Timeless-Self in the pre of eternity, on the other. This is something that must ultimately be *attained* to and *known* as a matter of experience. Conceptualizing is not enough.

It is in this light that we may best read some of the passages in *The Collected Works* that might seem vague or appear to contradict other passages. Too often, Jung's critics forget that this has ever been the case with mystics when they try to put into words experiences that go beyond the power of ordinary language to convey—even beyond specialized language to convey, and often *especially* beyond such language.

Indeed, it is often only through paradox and indirection—poetic attempts to "hold" and then "hold forth" an experience that transcends our limited A-or-not-A ways of thinking and speaking—that the mystic can even begin to communicate something of the transcendent nature of what he has *experienced*. It is only in poetry that language can push beyond itself a trajectory towards the Timeless.

Much of what Jung's critics call unclear or inconsistent in his writings is best understood as an organic outgrowth of Jung's mysticism—and his ultimately poetic invitations to his readers not to just *consider* other levels of being from an analytical distance, but to seek them out for themselves—up close, under the pull of spiritual adventure, and *trans*-rationally (Owens, 2010; Rowland, 2005).

As a seasoned physician and psychotherapist, Jung was well aware of the physiological and psychological factors that might have been causing him simply to have hallucinated all of this. Yet in the remaining seventeen years of his life, he never wavered from his certainty that "it was not the product of imagination. The visions and experiences were utterly real; there was nothing subjective about them; they all had a quality of absolute objectivity" (1965, p. 295). As the editor of *The Red Book*, Sonu Shamdasani has made clear that Jung was similarly impressed by the "visions and experiences" that he recorded in it.

Jung the physician and Jung the scholar worked under the sponsorship of Jung the poet and Jung the mystic.

THE ARCHETYPES AND THE
COLLECTIVE UNCONSCIOUS, CONTINUED

The idea of the archetype is not an easy one, but it is central to any reading of Jung from whatever interpretive vantage point. Although the idea of the archetypes is, in Jung's own words, "controversial . . . and more than a little perplexing" (Jung, 1966c, p. 77, fn. 15), it is endlessly fascinating and brings with it a wide array of theoretical implications and practical applications that begin in the field of psychotherapy, of course, but extend from there to medicine to music, anthropology to theology, and physics to pedagogy. One cannot ask more of a single idea than what Jung gives us in his notion of the psychospiritual "archetype."

Jung wrote that the archetypes are "a functional disposition to produce the same, or very similar, ideas" (1967, p. 102), and, relatedly, that they underlie the human being's "inborn disposition to produce parallel thought-formations, or rather of identical psychic structures common to all men" (1967, p. 158).

From this, we gather that archetypes (1) are innate in all human beings, (2) are the origin of our thoughts and must therefore in some way come before those thoughts—thus being "supra-thinking thinking," as it were, (3) are the very thing that makes humans *human*, and (4) generate thoughts that, although obviously not the same in all people, *are* "parallel." Thus, all human thought evidences some sort of systematic, categorical (i.e., "structural") similarities at a deep level; and this is true even though the thoughts produced by this "deep structure" may look different at the "surface level" (Chomsky, 1968).[30]

Further, we learn that, taken as a whole, these archetypes make up "the stock of inherited possibilities of representation that are born anew in every individual" (Jung, 1967, p. 181). Thus there is a "stock" of archetypes, and where there is a stock of something, that stock is generally "contained" or "encircled" in something. This "container or encirclement"—which we are imagining here in terms that, although spatial, are still only metaphorical—is "the collective unconscious." And as we have seen, Jung equates the collective unconscious with the mystery of existence itself as it communicates to us through the archetypal structures that It has Itself generated and implanted in us that we might communicate *with* It (1969b, p. 68; 1954a, p. 667).

The Archetype "Mysterium Tremendum et Fascinans"

Jungians have pictured archetypes as "a kind of mold for the accumulation and discharge of psychic energy" (Odajnyk, 1976, p. 25).[31] As such, they are "irreducible and primary," "the structural nature of the psyche itself" (Palmer, 1995, pp. 8, 114). Samuels has said that archetypes "constellate experience in accordance with innate schemata and act as an imprimatur of subsequent experience" (1997, p. 27).[32]

Frey-Rohn (1974, p. 93) gives us a rather spartan definition of archetype as "preconscious categories which [channel] thought and action into [the] definite shapes [of archetypal images]." This sparse but useful definition reflects Jung's indebtedness to Kant (Pauson, 1988). In Kantian fashion, it makes it clear that the archetypes—which produce archetypal images in us that we *can* experience and work with using our "poetic faculty"—cannot themselves be directly known by us, *in and of themselves*, using only our mathetic faculty.

As we saw in the previous chapter, Kant declared that we can never know or see any "thing-in-itself" in its absolute and pristine nature and condition. We can know it only in a mediated way—through the "filters" that constitute mind. It is impossible to say how much, if any, of reality corresponds to our filtered images of it, for all we have to work with *is* our filtered images of reality. There is, by definition, no way to get behind those filters to see the filters that produce our knowing. Our "knowledge" of the Timeless "maxes

---

30. See Samuels (1997, p. 39) for similarities between Jung's idea of the archetype and Noam Chomsky's (1968) postulation of a grammatical and semantic "deep structure" of language.

31. A few Jungians have speculated that the archetypes might actually *be* patterns of energy at the deepest and most formative levels of the psyche (Spiegelman & Mansfeld, 1996; Stevens, 2000).

32. For more on schema theory in educational contexts, see Rummelhart (1980).

out" with the images that our filters both provide and enforce—archetypal images.

In a sense, therefore, all of our knowing is thirdhand, and there is no way around this exasperating situation. Why is our knowing necessarily third-hand?

At the first stage, there is the absolutely unknowable reality-in-itself. This is forever beyond us—this being the case at least given our limitations on this plane of being.

"Absolute reality" we can "register" only through the filter archetype, for it is our "organ" of knowing. This is the second stage. These filter archetypes produce our knowing, but we cannot "know" them either since all that we know is *through* them, and thus secondhand knowledge is also denied us.

But what we *can* know, at just one more step down the line, at this tertiary level, is what the filters produce. Indeed, that is *all* we know. These are the *archetypal images*, which both constitute the limitations and provide the fullness of our epistemological situation.

Frey-Rohn's spartan economy, although useful in clarifying the nature and primacy of the archetype, does not convey the poetic power and the sense of spiritual ultimacy that we *feel* when an archetypal image is so potent, so "in touch" with the archetype that generated it, and so organically shaped by it, that we are filled with the sense that this image is bringing us within close range of the archetype itself. We are then infused with waves of archetypal imagery and energy that emanate from the archetype and represent our closest means of "touching" and "being touched" by it.

When this occurs, then we feel that we are coming into some sort of credible contact with the aesthetic, ethical, and spiritual sources of our being, the archetypes, as they themselves exist *in* and *as* contact with the mystery that lies at the core of this whole process. We feel *in-spired* (literally, "breathed into") in this moment in and out of time. We stand in awe of the *mysterium tremendum et fascinans,* the *tremendous and fascinating mystery,* of encountering our own ultimacy as it presents itself to us in the form of an archetypal image—one that we intuit is so near the archetype itself—that the archetype seems for the space of that experience to become transparent, to stretch thin and become effaced in the intensity of the moment, so that we feel as if the mystery, in an act of grace, is revealing itself to us directly.

In short, the *mysterium tremendum et fascinans* is being *constellated* within us, through the mediation of the archetype, in archetypal terms and images that we poetically grasp and that fundamentally grasp us—and all of this taking place under the sponsorship of the mystery announcing itself as "the collective unconscious."

The phrase *mysterium tremendum et fascinans*, taken from Rudolf Otto's (1960) *The Idea of the Holy,* was important to Jung, who invoked it often to signify the individual's sense of having moved into (or better, having been gathered up into) the sacred precinct of the collective unconscious—an archetypally saturated psychospiritual zone that Jung characterized as the *temenos*. Through the mediation of the archetype, which stimulates this felt-proximity to the mystery, an archetypal image is produced in the zone of the *temenos*.

This archetypal image we *can* know, immediately and passionately. That is why we enshrine such images and may revisit them again and again in the grottos of memory, or we weave them into the more visible vestments of liturgy—but it is all done to retrieve that experience, relive that moment in and out of time, and thus reconstitute a basic sense of who we are as eternal beings in the filtered yet still effulgent light of the mystery.

In the "presence" of "the holy," which the archetypal image so authoritatively *re*-presents, or *symbolizes,* we wish to orient our life around its symbols, making them our own in our essential being, and acting in life under their inherent finality. This is living what Jung called "the symbolic life."

Consciously living the symbolic life, and this alone, invests our existence with *meaning*. Without those symbols and the revelation *within* us that they reveal *to* us, our lives become meaning-*less*. Then, nothing—no matter how appealing, empowering, or pleasurable in any other way—will finally prove capable of filling that void. Such things are distractions, and they may dull consciousness for a certain season like a drug. Indeed, sometimes they *are* drugs, which is why, according to a Jungian view of addiction, substance abuse is finally just an attempt to mask an inner emptiness and terror or to fill that emptiness with a counterfeit ecstasy.

At any rate, the soul, inevitably rebelling at being so ignored or gagged, will strike back at some point in the form of neurotic and psychotic symptoms. Unattended to, these symptoms will expand in the individual and assault the traitor-consciousness, sabotage it, and ultimately explode it in some form of humiliating collapse.

In brief, the core of psychopathology, said Jung, is spiritual—and so must the cure be too. For Jung, everything depends on the living symbol. Without it, we become desolate. We wither at our core, for its indispensable food *is* the living symbol. It is also our bridge to the Eternal. A symbol is not—as it is so often misunderstood as being—some sort of comfortable ornament that we hang on *an already-established visible reality*. Rather, a symbol is a sacramental crossing of our only portal into *the ever-elusive invisible Reality.*

The overarching problem of modern man, said Jung, is that he has been stripped of his symbols, culturally denuded, and emotionally exposed. He wanders "in search of a soul." He has been thrown into a world-historical moment that is a wasteland of de-symbolism, indeed of *anti*-symbolism. How to overcome that wasteland and find a way to psychospiritually flourish again, both personally and culturally, by becoming *re*-symbolized, is the overwhelming issue and first imperative for modern man. Jung wrestled with this and wound up venturing an answer in the notion of the archetypes and the collective unconscious, and in the psychospiritual lexicon that that notion generated.

Imagining the Archetypes and the Collective Unconscious

Not surprisingly, we best get a feel for what the archetypes and the collective unconscious are when we picture them in the same manner in which they present themselves to us—poetically. Thus the arts come much closer to the heart of the matter in *feeling* archetypal reality than merely discursive definitions can do in *scrutinizing* it. Here it is clear that Jung is not purely Kantian. Whereas Kant gave the mathetic domain equal weight to the poetic domain, Jung privileged the poetic (Mayes, 2009a).

Yet even in our symbol-starved state, we cannot help but live in symbols to some degree, whether we are conscious of this fact or not (and we usually are not). As we saw in chapters 1 and 2, primary processes inevitably precede secondary processes and weave in and out of them. There is a symbolic domain that our language is built upon so that we can hardly make even the simplest statement without at least some sort of indirect poetic reference, image, or appeal that is embedded in that statement—again, usually without being consciously aware of this fact. Thus the great philosopher of aesthetics Bendetto Croce (1953) reminds us that

> the relation between knowledge or *expression* and intellectual knowledge or *concept*, between art and science, poetry and prose, cannot be otherwise defined than by saying that it is one of *double degree*. The first degree is the [poetic] expression, the second the [discursive] concept: the first can stand without the second, but the second cannot stand without the first. There is poetry without prose, but not prose without poetry. Expression, indeed, is the first affirmation of human activity. Poetry is "the mother tongue of the human race"; the first men "were by nature sublime poets." (in Vivas & Krieger, 1953, p. 86)

Deploying poetic imagery to (as Croce put it) *express*, not just *conceptualize*, the *experience* of the archetypes and collective unconscious, we might picture an archetype as a living strand of spiritual energy among many such vibrant strands which, woven together, make up the mobile blanket of the collective unconscious, within whose sacred fabric we are finally wrapped.

We might also depict the collective unconscious as the womb from which all existence emerges—as in the ancient Chinese philosopher-poet Lao Tzu's *simulacrum*. Chinese Buddhist paintings often render the blurry outlines of the top of a mountain shrouded in mist and clouds, suggesting how the beauty of nature comes from a cloudy realm that is not so much formless as above form—the land of pure archetypes and the collective unconscious, with the landscape we presently see in the picture being an archetypal image of it all. An anonymous English Christian mystic of the fourteenth century, in another symbol, called this "void"—which is not empty as we know emptiness but simply transcends anything we might call either empty or full—"the Cloud of Unknowing." "The Cloud of Unknowing" matches up well with Jung's characterization of the collective unconscious as the Unknown (1969a, p. 68).

Let us also "image" the collective unconscious as a perpetually changing wind. This wind cannot be seen. It is very like what Jesus, that master poet of simple but galvanizing imagery, talks about in the Gospel according to St. John. There he describes the Spirit to Nicodemus: "The wind blows wherever it pleases. You hear its sound, but you cannot tell where it comes from or where it is going" (John 3:8). The wind is not so much spiritual as it *is* Spirit. Indeed, in Hebrew the word for "spirit" and "wind" is the same: *ruach.* The wind, in our metaphor, is thus the collective unconscious, the *mysterium tremendum et fascinans,* "the Unknown as it immediately affects us" (1969b, p. 68). We cannot see or measure it, identify its source, or predict its destination.

But all is not lost in our attempt to establish a connection with this wind and its stirrings. It does not just uselessly blow about and blow away. In this metaphor, the patterns it carves upon the sand are the *archetypal images*—the way an individual or group sees, feels, and thinks about the wind of the collective unconscious—and these sandy, wind-carved images we *do* see.

Archetypal Images

Whether an archetype—that mediating force between the collective unconscious and our ways of seeing, feeling, and understanding—itself morphs or whether each archetype is some sort of constant "bundle" of transcendent "energy," we cannot say. However, the archetypal images that "incarnate" the archetype *do* vary upon coming into contact with a specific person or group at a specific place and time in history. In other words, the energy of the archetype, epistemologically infrastructural to us, may or may not be constant. This is an ongoing topic of debate in Jungian theory (Robertson, 1995). However, the specific imagery through which that experience is made visible—the *archetypal image*—is by definition variable.

For example, the Egyptians had the dying, resurrected, and culturally redemptive god of Osiris; the Greeks had Dionysus; the Mayans had Quetzalcoatl; and the early Christians a carpenter-cum-preacher from the backwoods of Nazareth named Jesus. These different figures are culturally variable *archetypal images* that are expressing the same *archetype*—in this case, the archetype of the god slaughtered as a sacrifice, the god whose resurrection restores life for the people and their culture. These are all *archetypal images* of the *archetype of the savior.*

Take another common archetype that we've looked at a good deal already: the archetype of "the wise old man." This archetype has assumed many archetypal forms: in the archetypal image of Merlin, in later Shakespearian drama as Prospero in *The Tempest,* in popular culture as Obi-Wan Kenobi, in American history as Abraham Lincoln, and for many children around the world as Santa Claus. The archetype of the savior and archetype of the wise old man or woman are crucial to how we understand our place in the world *sub specie eternitatis*—as creatures of eternity.

Another instance of this is the archetype of the Great Mother. She is, in Lao Tzu's imagery above, the cosmic womb from which all things come and to which all things finally return. In Mahayana Buddhism she is Kwan Yin, "she who hears the cries of the world." In the Western tradition, she is Mary, the Mother of God, the Mother of Mercy. In Steinbeck's *The Grapes of Wrath,* she is the gracious Rose of Sharon Joad, who tenderly nurses a starving man.

Some of the most frequently appearing of these archetypal symbols are given below. Caution must be used, though, in not automatically assigning Self-meaning to any of these symbols since the uniqueness and sovereignty of each person's symbols must be respected—a point that James Hillman (1976), the father of "archetypal psychology," insists upon.

Archetypal psychology, one of the most important current schools of Jungian psychology, objects to the tendency in classical Jungian psychology to be too formulaic in its interpretation of symbols (Samuels, 1997). Hillman correctly warns that assigning a "standard" interpretation to a symbol may miss, erase, or even do violence against the idiosyncratic meaning and feel that the symbol has *for a specific individual.* This turns that person into an *object* of an interpretative system. It does not nurture him as an infinitely rich *subject*—one who is engaged in an intensely subjective pursuit of his own path.

However, the archetypal symbols listed below *do* have the virtue of suggesting some of the most persistent and consequential themes that define the human condition. This takes "the archetypes" out of the realm of a sort of "in-cognizable" abstraction as theoretical "entities" and helps us understand what they in essence *are*, or what, in any case, they must essentially mean to *us*. Identifying and categorizing archetypes is pragmatic, allowing us to give them what Shakespeare called a "local habitation and a name."

Some of the most important archetypes embodied as persons or animals include king, queen, trickster, lover, bride and groom, wise one/teacher, disciple, divine child, eternal child, shadow, magical helpful animal, an animal or ethnic minority sidekick, dragon/leviathan, nurturing mother, virgin, witch, harlot/temptress, Amazon, psychic medium, law-giving father, priest/

priestess, evil king, rogue, warrior, senex (the grumpy old man, not a wise one), devil, and savior.

Archetypal events include birth, baptism, initiation, education, vocation, courtship, matrimony, warfare, friendship, ritual sacrifice, descent to the underworld, death, resurrection, and final judgment.

Some of the most prominent archetypal landscapes and structures are the wilderness, city, home, place of instruction, temple, battlefield, heaven and hell.

Certain geometrical shapes are also archetypally salient: circles, squares (especially crosses), and triangles (especially in three-person godheads).

Certain numbers also seem to have particularly profound psychospiritual significance and are therefore archetypal: one signifies unity; two, duality; three, the reconciliation of tension in a new (i.e., third) perspective that unites but transcends the opposing polarities, like the apex of a triangle; four, the creation of a new foundation upon which the new perspective can become established; and five, as the essence of the whole process—the *quint-essence*. The prime numbers also seem to have particular psychospiritual significance. Indeed, Jung felt that numbers are only secondarily a means of counting; their primal function is psychospiritual in that they are "an archetype of order which has become conscious" (Jung, in von Franz, 1991, pp. 268f; also see Jung, 1968a, 1968c, 1968d, 1970b). Certainly, numbers come rich with symbolic significance when they occur in dreams.

I would like at this point to offer the following definition of archetypal images, the archetypes, and the collective unconscious by way of summing up what has been discussed thus far.[33]

The collective unconscious is the dynamic psychospiritual matrix from which all our other psychic functioning—conscious and subconscious—emerges. It is composed of archetypes, which can be pictured as constantly interacting, occasionally overlapping, and subtly morphing "patterns of energy." Through the archetypes, we interpret and shape our subjective and objective worlds in a distinctly human manner that has, in the most essential ways, remained fairly constant throughout history and across cultures. Because the archetypes are the irreducible *basis* of how we experience our inner and outer worlds, they can never be the direct *object* of that experience.

How an individual experiences and uses archetypal energy is variable, depending largely upon his native health, character, and personal experiences as well as upon the many cultural factors, past and present, that have shaped him—cultural factors that are themselves in large measure the products of collective archetypal processes. These personally and culturally variable "in-

---

33. This definition is taken from my 2007 study *Inside Education: Depth Psychology in Teaching and Learning,* and is reproduced by the kind permission of Atwood Publishing.

carnations" of archetypes in and to the human psyche in specific imagistic form are *archetypal symbols*.

Archetypal symbols manifest themselves in forms that suit the personal, cultural, and historical circumstances of the person who is both producing and experiencing these symbols. An individual or culture that loses touch with its archetypal symbols grows disoriented and falls psychologically, politically, culturally, and ethically ill since that person or culture has lost access to the source of meaning, in both individual and cultural life, in the *mysterium* of the life-giving collective unconscious, which lives within the individual just as the individual lives in it.

IS THE ARCHETYPE A SCIENTIFICALLY SOUND IDEA?

By definition, archetypal reality precedes any scientific way of knowing for the simple reason that archetypal reality is fundamental to any and all of the many valid ways of human knowing, of which current conventional science is just one.

As the physicist and historian of science Thomas Kuhn (1970) has argued, any "normative science" is ultimately a methodological elaboration of the scientist's already-existing assumptions about what the universe is.

In my own Jungian-oriented, pastoral-counseling work, I have often found that the inexhaustibly rich worldviews and practices of Native American medicine men and women are much more relevant to me than the models and terms of current psychotherapies. Other Jungians have found the same thing (Sandner, 1991; Stein, 1995; Walsh, 1990).

Here, let us recall a point made in chapter 2 in the discussion of Jung's philosophy of psychology. The collective unconscious and archetypes are in a sense a theoretical construct. Although the archetypes and the collective unconscious are a powerful model, they may or may not have ontological status as self-existing entities. Jung's critics along these lines have done us a service in making this point clear, as well as highlighting Jung's occasional ambivalence about whether his writings were essentially scientific or poetico-religious.[34]

On the other hand, Jung's intentions may have been more artistic than scientific in his writings as he approached the cognitively ungraspable fact of the collective unconscious from many points of view, much as Picasso rendered from multiple perspectives the subjects whom he painted in his Cubist period. In that case, the charge of "inconsistency" melts away and one is left admiring the unexpected, subtle artistry in *The Collected Works*.

---

34. For a particularly insightful treatment of this subject, see Rowland (2005), who examines Jung's writings as essentially poetic. See also Charet (1993); Glover (1956); Homans (1995); Segal (1995); Shamdasani (2003).

Furthermore, it is not necessarily true that archetypes are *not* ontologically actual in some way and to some degree, either. After all, Plato accorded the archetype the highest level of metaphysical status. But this seems to matter little in these decidedly un-Platonic times in academia. Let us therefore limit ourselves to saying of the archetypes and the collective unconscious that they are *fundamental* facts of human existence—what Jung called *esse in anima* (a thing in the soul)—though whether or not they are *transcendent* facts in an ontological or metaphysical sense—Kant's *esse in res* (a-thing-in-itself)—must always remain an open question (Jung, 1971, pp. 6, 44f, 51).

The Nobel Prize winning physicist Wolfgang Pauli, who had been in psychotherapy with Jung and became a close friend, wrote about the archetypal structures and images in Kepler's cosmological theories, suggesting how the physical sciences rest on archetypal ways of observing and organizing those observations (Pauli & Jung, 2001). In this sense, the shift from a Newtonian worldview to an Einsteinian and then post-Einsteinian one in modern physics may be as much the result of profound cultural metamorphoses at the archetypal level as the result of new evidence within the old paradigms.

Kuhn (1970) maintains that changes in what is considered normative science occur not primarily because new evidence suddenly pops up as a result of continuing experimentation along standard lines. In fact, such evidence generally serves to confirm scientists in old assumptions rather than spur them on to new ideas. Instead, it is a shift in the paradigms that organize experience itself (and what are these if not archetypes?) that causes scientists to ask new questions; look for evidence in previously unknown, even previously unthinkable ways; and now accept as evidence in the first place certain things that would not have been allowed, maybe not even seen, under the assumptions of the old paradigms.

In sum, it is not evidence that causes paradigm shifts, according to Kuhn. Evidence is ultimately a self-referring system of verification of what is already fundamentally assumed at the archetypal level about the nature of things. Rather, it is paradigm shifts[35]—cultural and historical changes in what counts as reality under a new paradigm, *archetypal transformations* at a culture's very base—that cause the search for new types of evidence.

A few scientists of note who do not feel overly constrained by reigning paradigms in normative science have begun to theorize in their respective fields in ways that are reminiscent of the archetype, sometimes even using that word or one like it. For instance, the noted physicist David Bohm has postulated an "implicate order" out of which empirical reality emerges as a

---

35. Kuhn coined the phrase "paradigm shift," which has found its way into popular usage.

second-level order of existence.[36] Discussing what could be called a quantum archetypal field, Bohm opines:

> In the enfolded [or implicate] order, space and time are no longer the dominant factors determining the relationships of dependence or independence of different elements. Rather, an entirely different sort of basic connection of elements is possible, from which our ordinary notions of space and time, along with those of separately existent material particles, are abstracted as forms derived from the deeper order. These ordinary notions in fact appear in what is called the "explicate" or "unfolded" order, which is a special and distinguished form contained within the general totality of all the implicate orders. (Bohm, 1986, p. 183)

Note how the implicate order resembles the collective unconscious teeming with trans-temporal, trans-spatial archetypes—those "different sort of basic connection." Bohm's hypothesizing requires us to imagine our local space/time field as a by-product of an order that is at once higher and deeper than anything we can conceive of. But Bohm goes even further, speculating that there may be a "general totality of *all* the implicate orders." In other words, there may be more than just the one implicate order that has produced the explicate order in which we live, and each of those implicate orders may result in corresponding explicate orders in alternate universes.

Bohm's suggestion that all of these implicate orders might be gathered into a totality of all the implicate orders is reminiscent of Plato's definition of God as the archetype of all archetypes. In turn, one cannot resist the temptation to go one step farther in noting the similarity of both Bohm's and Plato's ideas to Jung's definition of the Self as the archetype that contains and unifies all the other archetypes at play in the collective unconscious (Jung, 1968a, p. 223).[37]

At any rate, when we experience these archetypes, we must do so by means of the epistemological filters of space and time.[38] It is at this crucial

---

36. This is possibly an affirmation in quantum physics and cosmology of Heidegger's distinction between the ontological and the ontic (1964).

37. A possible relationship exists among (1) Bohmian cosmology, (2) Platonic metaphysics, and (3) Jungian theory. This is fertile territory for further theorizing and cross-disciplinary studies. Another interesting area for further study is the relationship between Hinduism and Jungian psychology, where the ground of being, the center of the Self, and God are so intertwined that it may be impossible to tell where one leaves off and the other begins. Indeed, they may all be the same "thing." There has been some work done by Jungian scholars on the similarities between Hinduism and Jungian psychology (de Gruchy, 1991; Main, 2004; Spiegelman & Vasavada, 1987).

38. Space and time may themselves be the two symbiotic primordial archetypes that enable archetypal images to arise in the human mind—indeed, that give birth to the human mind in the first place. But following this line of speculation would take us too far afield into realms of phenomenology and ontology and beyond the purposes of this book. See Kelly (1993), Nagy (1991), Pauson (1988), and Solomon (1994) for in-depth studies of philosophical issues in Jung's work.

juncture, where the timeless collective unconscious and its archetypes touch time and space that *archetypal images* arise—those embodied representations of the un-representable archetypes as they incarnate in a specific, imagistic, time/space form. Thus it is that one *archetype* will blossom forth as countless *archetypal images,* which vary because of the personal, geographical, cultural, and world-historical circumstances that have channeled the archetype into these specific forms.

In a similar key, the physicist David Peat asks: "Is it possible . . . that the archetypes and morphic fields have a universal aspect, being formative fields of information that have an active role within the processes of matter, thought, and behavior?" (1988, p. 166). The physicist Victor Mansfeld, in conjunction with the Jungian theorist Marvin Spiegelman, have also speculated along these lines in their research into the quantum dynamics of the phenomenon of synchronicity (Spiegelman & Mansfeld, 1996).

There have been corresponding developments in the field of biology over the last thirty years or so. The noted biochemist Rupert Sheldrake (1981) has suggested the existence of biological morphic fields, which strikingly resemble some of Jung's speculations about archetypes as fields of trans-temporal/ trans-spatial "energy." These fields may govern the emergence of a specie into visible, quantifiable shape and play an infrastructural role in the evolution of species. Sheldrake's theory unites biology, psychology, and ontology in ways that Jung (1970a) suggested would be necessary if archetypal psychology were to grow in a fashion that, although not bound by normative scientific models, need not be at war with them.[39]

Michael Conforti (1999), a biologist and Jungian analyst, points out that these outlying but important scientists are attempting to convince a scientific world which—even post-Einstein—seems to believe only what is physically observable or statistically probable, that things might be more complex than they seem to the merely physical eye and its extension in all sorts of instruments.

The idea of the collective unconscious and its archetypes may well provide a viable model for other-dimensional realms out of which observable forms and phenomena emerge and metamorphose. We do well to heed Kuhn's conclusion that scientific revolutions are radical, even poetic reimaginings of the universe, not ever-more laboriously detailed elaborations of a particular model whose privileged status blinds it to new possibilities.

---

39. Main (2004), Pauli & Jung (2001), Peat (1988), Shamdasani (2003), Stevens (1999, 2000), Wilber (2000).

THE SPECTRUM OF MATTER AND SPIRIT

Implicit throughout Jung's writings, and often enough explicit in them too, is the notion that human beings have souls, that they are essentially free, and that they are destined (if they will only take up the challenge) to grow psychospiritually in this life and perhaps beyond it. Little wonder that a materialistic age such as ours does not know what to make of a man and a psychology that will not blink in testifying to the uniqueness and sovereignty of the individual spirit in the context of the timeless, for

> a spiritual goal that points beyond the purely natural man and his worldly existence is an absolute necessity for the health of the soul; it is the Archimedean point from which alone it is possible to lift the world off its hinges and to transform the natural state into a cultural one. (Jung, 1954a, p. 86).

Lord Tennyson wrote that nature is "red in tooth and claw." Contrast this with the use of the archetypally pregnant color violet in many religions to represent spirituality and mysticism and we can understand how Jung employed the color spectrum as a metaphor of the range of instincts (Tennyson, "In Memoriam," 2013).

At the lowest pole, the infra-*red* zone of our animal instincts, lies the insatiable craving for sex and power. This is where Freudian and Adlerian psychology are at home. But at the other pole of our instinctual nature, the ultra-*violet* zone, are the archetypes, which are spiritual and transcendent (Jung, 1969b, pp. 211ff)—and this is where Jungian psychology shines. But the caution must immediately be issued that this does not mean that the spirituality of the archetypes is all sweetness and light—a misconception that besets New Age misinterpretations of Jung (Tacey, 2001).

THE LIGHT AND DARK SIDE OF THE ARCHETYPE

Every archetype has a light *and* a dark side—spiritual light is impossible without spiritual darkness in our dialectical universe. The archetypal figures of Christ and Satan in the Western foundational narrative are both necessary players in the cosmic drama, as the Christian gnostics well knew—a fact that intrigued Jung and that he examined in extraordinary detail in his work on alchemy and psychology (Jung, 1968a, pp. 32, 36, 70, 96, 109, 174ff).[40]

This might well be Jung's psychospiritual gloss of St. Paul's assertion that there is subtle "wickedness in high places" (at the ultraviolet pole), which is not to be confused with the bestiality of "flesh and blood" at the

---

40. Also see Jung's alchemical studies (1968b, 1968d, 1970b) for elaborate (and sometimes mind-bogglingly elaborate) expositions of this point in gnostic Christianity that informed the work of the medieval and Renaissance alchemists.

ultrared end (Ephesians 6:12). Still, the fleshy ultrared and mystic ultraviolet do not preclude each other. To the contrary, they require each other. The infinite gradations that exist between the primordial and the ethereal witness to how matter and psyche interact (Jung, 1969b, pp. 215, 232ff, 234; von Franz, 1992).

However, there *does* seems to be a hypothetical "point" on the spectrum when psyche breaks loose from the compulsions of its biological bonds and becomes "will" or "spirit":

> The psyche as such cannot be explained in terms of physiological chemistry, if only because, together with "life" itself, it is the only "natural factor" capable of converting statistical organizations which are subject to natural law into "higher" or "unnatural" [i.e., supranatural] states, in opposition to the rule of entropy that runs throughout the inorganic realm. How life produces complex organic systems from the inorganic we do not know, though we have direct experience of how the psyche does it. Life therefore has a specific law of its own which cannot be deduced from the known physical laws of nature. (Jung, 1969b, pp. 180f)

Although psyche is probably always involved with the natural realm to some degree, it must essentially transcend it if it is to evolve into an *opus contra naturam* (Jung, 1970b, p. 201; E. Jung & von Franz, 1986, p. 43). Jung often used this phrase, literally translated as "work against nature"— although a "work transcending nature" would probably be more accurate in catching Jung's meaning—to indicate psyche's higher goal: its teleology.

> The psyche is an emancipation of function from its instinctual form and so from the compulsiveness which, as a sole determinant of the function, causes it to harden into a mechanism. The psychic condition or quality begins where the function loses its outer and inner determinism and becomes capable of more extensive and freer application—that is, where *it begins to show itself accessible to a will motivated by other sources*. (1969b, pp. 181f; emphasis added)

What is this "will motivated by other sources"? Jung goes on to explain that it is an escape from the corral of biological determinism into the vast highlands of "freedom of choice" (1969b, p. 183). Here, the individual, in the unique exercise of his ethical vision, discovers his spiritual destiny. "Just as, at its lower reaches, the psyche loses itself in the organic-material substrate, so in its upper reaches it resolves itself into a spiritual form about which we know as little as we do about the functional basis of instinct" (1969b, p. 183).

In sum, Jung is claiming that at one end of the spectrum lies the mystery of matter itself. Here, psyche would devolve into entropic nonexistence in the primal mud were it not also the case that, at the other end of the spectrum, spirit enigmatically draws psyche on to ever higher realms of supratemporal, supraspatial evolution (Peat, 1988; von Franz, 1992).

Jung was fond of citing Goethe's lines at the end of *Faust* as poetic warrant for his own teleological optimism: "Formation, transformation, / Eternal Mind's eternal recreation." In suggesting that the human being is part of an eternal evolution that embraces the entire universe, and that may indeed *be* the universe, Jung stands in the company of philosophers from Hegel (1992) and Bergson (1987) to Chardin (1975) and Harsthorne (1984) who see the universe and everything in it in eternal evolution to ever-higher states of being.

Chapter Five

Anima/Animus, the Transcendent Function, the Ego-Self Axis, and the Self

ANIMA AND ANIMUS[1]

Using the typical metaphor of psyche as a landscape, let us picture ego-consciousness approaching the subconscious. As it does so, the figure of the *shadow* begins to make its appearance. The shadow lies closest to conscious awareness. It is a very proximate archetype. Holding everything we repressed because it was too agonizing to remember, it also contains all that we felt we needed to disown to form and maintain an ego that could function in its various social contexts, but some of that material is retrievable now that ego-consciousness is more mature.

Later, as this ego moves even farther on in its life journey, beyond the personal subconscious into more deeply forested regions (vast and enticing, both alluring and spooky), it arrives at the threshold of a kingdom called the Collective Unconscious. It had heard about this land in special stories throughout its life, had even visited it in dreams, felt its pull in art and ritual, but had never really credited it as being actual.

But now that it has arrived at its threshold, the wayfaring ego sees that this forest of the Collective Unconscious is very real indeed. And it is filled with many animals who roam within it. They are called archetypes—varicolored creatures who sometimes seem quite bright, sometimes quite dark. And puzzlingly, they never show themselves as who and what they really are but,

---

1. Passages of this discussion of the *anima* and *animus* are drawn from my book *Inside Education: Depth Psychology in Teaching and Learning* published by Atwood Press.

instead, are covered, each one uniquely, in a sort of force field of images that, for some reason, are all the wayfarer will ever see of them.

Those two other figures who, as it were, stand guard at the entrance of the kingdom with its many archetypes, are named *Anima* and *Animus*—the female and male forms of Latin for "soul." Upon closer scrutiny they appear to be beckoning the journeying consciousness to enter, not barring its way. They too have often appeared to consciousness, for instance in dreams, guided fantasy, artistic creation, religious ritual, and private experiences of the Timeless. Their presence signals at this stage that one is within hailing distance of "the sacred precinct," or *temenos*, of the collective unconscious.

The *anima*, a female, is the figure who in classical Jungian psychology symbolizes for the male the portal to the archetypal realm; the *animus*, a male figure, symbolizes it for the female.

"We know well enough," Jung wrote, "that the unconscious [of the male] appears personified: mostly it is the anima who in singular or plural form represents the collective unconscious" (Jung, 1970b, p. 106). Conversely, the *animus* personifies the collective unconscious for the female, Jung concluded (Jung, 1966c, pp. 209f). In romances and fairytales, the hero's pursuit of the maiden as well as the maiden's longing for the hero symbolize the desire of ego-consciousness to connect with the collective unconscious through union with the inner contrasexual other (von Franz, 1997).

Since the collective unconscious is the deepest of psychospiritual mysteries, Jung felt it natural that it should make its first major appearance in the form and under the pull of the contrasexual other. Jung held that the female will always be the primary "other" for most men, just as the male will be the primary "other" for most women. The oldest story in the world, after all, is the mutual attraction of the sexes—but also their puzzlement at each other. Accordingly, because the draw of the collective unconscious is so powerful and mystifying, it made sense to Jung that female figures would embody it for men and male figures would do the same for women.

The cultural politics of sexual identity over the last five decades have made Jung's claims regarding gender more than a little debatable. Some scholars now see in them evidence of sexist stereotyping. These are important points and we must attend to them. At the same time, we must remember that from the early twentieth-century cultural landscape on which *he* was standing and from which he necessarily operated, Jung was making a bold statement in declaring that each of us has a contrasexual element. Jung was the first modern psychologist to propound this notion, and it radically challenged the then-conventional views of gender, probably playing a part in causing us to rethink gender. As noted in the last chapter, we must avoid "presentism" in reading Jung.

Furthermore, examples of this idea also lie in Western culture's mythical core. Plato's story of the primordial person being a conjoined male and female in an archetypally perfect circular form is one. Another is the figure of the hermaphrodite who is prominent in various ancient stories. And then there is the melding of the King and Queen in alchemical lore into one regal bisexual figure who represents the alchemical gold.

Learning how to integrate one's contrasexual elements is important in the classical Jungian view. As Paracelsus, a Renaissance physician-alchemist whom Jung admired and identified with, wrote of the internal/eternal union of the male and female principles in religious alchemy: "When the heavenly marriage is accomplished, who will deny its superexcellent virtue?" (cited in Jung, 1968b, p. 163). Jung called this psychic synthesis of the male and female principles a *syzygy,* a term taken from astronomy, another area of interest to Jung because of its archetypal richness (1969a, p. 64). The *syzygy* refers to the conjunction of the sun and moon, classic symbols of the male and female principles, respectively.

Jung saw the *syzygy* evidenced in religious texts, doctrines, and practices everywhere throughout history: the incestuous royal marriage of the prince and princess, which was called the *hierosgamos* in ancient Egypt; the synthesis of the masculine principle of *yang* and the female principle of *yin* in Taoism; the spiritual seeker's quest for the Divine Beloved in Yoga and Sufism; and the mystical marriage of Christ and Holy Mother Church, *sponsus et sponsa*, the Heavenly Husband and Wife, in Catholic theology (1969a, 64).

Finding and embracing one's contrasexual nature is not easy. Like everything else in the process of becoming whole, it demands emotional maturity and ethical commitment. Again, one sees the need, as Jung appraised it, for this psychospiritual process to occur in its fullness after midlife—after one has firmed up a functional ego-identity. Indications and instances of individuation may occur earlier (Fordham, 1994), but one is usually too busy in the first half of life consolidating one's gender identity and performing various roles to focus on inner contrasexual exploration. So goes the classical Jungian view. This is not to say that such things cannot or should not happen before midlife. It is just that they generally happen more naturally, most deeply, and with the greatest finesse in the second half of life. *Not* to engage in this developmental task in the second half of life may exact a grave psychospiritual price.

The man in the second half of life who refuses to look at his feminine side and the woman who will not do the same with her masculine side will become controlled by it, Jung observed in his clinical practice, for nonconscious material will always strike back if ignored. This specific instance of it is called *anima possession* in a man and *animus possession* in a woman. It exemplifies an axiom of all depth psychologies that we are ultimately dominated by *any* unconscious elements that we do not integrate into consciousness. Inevitably, we will project this unmetabolized stuff onto others. Pro-

jecting it onto others, we invite the ethical catastrophe of erroneously evalu-
ating (and usually judging) others as a way of not facing our own inner
dynamics (Jung, 1970b, p. 168).

The best course of action is thus for the man to "court" and "wed" his
anima—that is, to explore and embrace his own archetypal depths, just as the
woman must do with her *animus*. This will require the male to cultivate and
express more delicate sensibilities and emotions than he has perhaps been
used to doing in the past; it will require the female to exercise more analytical precision and exert more force on people and events than has perhaps
been her habit.

Again, these are gender generalizations that Jung made in an age whose
sexual politics were different from ours, and they are understandably problematic to certain Jungians today (Lauter & Rupprecht, 1985). Nevertheless,
they continue to represent gender-rooted tendencies and tasks that are quite
common.[2] But whatever one's assessment of Jung's view of gender, it is the
general truth of the second half of life that it is unproductive, indeed counter-
productive, to ignore the call to psychospiritual adventure by refusing to go
deeply within oneself—that recently discovered forest, those shape-shifting
animals.

Neglecting to probe into one's inner contrasexuality, said Jung, men grow
anima possessed. They begin to look like a caricature of the archetypally
feminine principle—snappy, sentimental, given to gossip and erratic moods,
and irrational at crucial moments of decision. When *animus possessed*, wom-
en begin to look like caricatures of the archetypally male principle—opinion-
ated, stubborn, and caught in twisted webs of pseudologic.

In sum, Jung felt that the *anima* stands sentry at the gates of the male soul
just as the *animus* does for the female soul. He believed we gain entrance to
the mysteries of the collective unconscious—and thus to our psychospiritual
core—to the extent that we honor and incorporate the ancient archetypal
wisdom of the other sex into our total psychospiritual functioning.[3]

THE EGO-SELF AXIS

In previous chapters we looked at the ego as both the icon and instrument of
psychosocial functioning. We noted that the personal subconscious, or shadow, if neglected, will clamorously make itself known through a series of
ruptures to the ego, which, although generally still able to function, does so
in pain. These ruptures are the neuroses—fissures in the ego which are some-

---

2. Belenky et al. (1986), Chodorow (1978), de Castillejo (1973), Gilligan (1982), Stevens
(1999).

3. Dourley (1987) discusses celibacy, especially in the context of certain religious traditions,
as a powerful means of accomplishing the inner marriage of oneself and one's contrasexual
element.

times taken to therapy. There the client and depth psychotherapist will, hopefully, attempt to deal with them in such a way that the client deepens in character by looking at the shadow issues at the core of the problem, not simply "manage" them so that the client just returns to the same old treadmill that is being run by unseen cultural and political forces and using it as its pawn.

Of course, the ego can never be entirely free of shadow tensions. That is not a realistic option in this life. Nevertheless, it remains the case, according to Jung, that a major developmental goal of the first half of life is to try to come to grips with one's shadow, where what has not been folded into consciousness cries out for attention from its prison. Only if one has achieved some real measure of success in this can one begin to move to a higher level of identity.

As we also saw in the last chapter, that other locus of identity in the individual is the Self. In Buddhism, the Self is revealed in the enlightenment experience that one *is* the Buddha. One *is* absolute, unconditioned consciousness, beyond the dual illusions of life and death, to which timeless fact one has finally awakened after a long and terrible mortal sleep. It is also the Hindu proclamation: *Tat tvam asi,* "Thou *art* that," "you *are* Divinity"—this, the realization of *Shuddhadvaita*. It is the liberating comprehension, but much more *experience* than comprehension, that we are not *only* our particular identity but are simultaneously at one with the ontological center around which all revolves. *We realize our center as The Center.* Therefore, "if you meet the Buddha on the road, kill him," for no Buddha who is external to himself could ever really be his timeless Self (Kopp, 1972).

The kernel of the problem, according to Buddhism, is that, having forgotten this fact, our thoughts and emotions—and the ego is finally nothing other than these things—are ceaselessly oscillating in a futile sine-wave between frenetic peaks and horrifying troughs that are equally unreal. The task of this life is to cut all ties to the illusion-bound ego—its rollercoaster ride between clinging joy and terrified misery—and to take our rest in the compassionate impartiality of our Buddha-Nature. Some post-Freudians who invoke Buddhism's wisdom have made this the goal of their work as individuals and as psychotherapists, and the results have been healing for both them and their patients (Epstein, 1995; Grotstein, 2000; Kornfield, 1993).

The West has tended to see the realization of the Self in somewhat different terms.[4] In the Christian tradition, redemption has been the experience of
Christ taking up residence on the throne of our soul—where our personal
identity fuses with that of the Savior. According to Jung, the merger of the
ego and the Self in the formation of a strong ego-Self axis expresses in
psychospiritual terms what St. Paul was speaking of when he declared, "Not
I, but Christ lives within me" (Galatians 2:20)—a verse that appealed to Jung
greatly and which he saw as the Christian analogue of the discovery of the
Hindu notion of the Self as God-within.

Eastern and Western religions have called for the transcendence or cruci-
fixion of the ego until nothing is left but a timeless core. However, Jung was
a psychotherapist. Integral to his work was the practical task of helping
people carry on with their lives in the world. He had to concern himself with
helping the patient not erase ego but make it more vibrant, viable, and more
in touch with the person's organizing center.

For although a very special, sequestered monk might be able to live in a
state of perpetual unitive bliss in merger with the Eternal, other people could
not go throughout the course of a day with its necessary roles and responsibilities without being checked in to a psychiatric hospital. *The goal of
therapy must be the alignment of the dynamic ego with the timeless Self in
spiritualized action and grounded spirituality.* In this way, the individual
could lead a socially productive life that was transcendentally situated. Such
a person would constantly be experiencing and exploring his soul in depth in
a way that would not render him personally or socially problematic but, to
the contrary, would make him personally and socially even more generative.

For if the ego dominates, muscling and muzzling the Self so that it has no
real influence in the individual's total functioning, the result is a banal and
greedy personality, cocksure in its materialistic illusions. One becomes merely a boastful ego—an uninspiring person to be around, and the only thing that
is "archetypal" about him is that he is an "epic bore." There is no radio
contact between his imperial but still banal ego and his ignored, timeless
source, his Self.

We all have seen the type: the rich corporate executive who is always
going on and on about his financial and/or sexual prowess, commandeering
all conversations at social gatherings so that they revolve around him,
smooth in public but cruel at home. He measures his strides in life by the

---

4. However, in the writings of such Christians mystics as Hildegard of Bingen, Juliana of
Norwich, Meister Eckhardt, and St. John of the Cross, one finds experiences of God that seem
very much like Buddhist enlightenment in their obliteration of binary thinking and immersion
in a transcendently unitive view of all things. Ralph Waldo Emerson, the American transcen-
dentalist essayist and poet, gives us a glimpse of this unitive experience in the final couplet of
his poem "Each and All": "Beauty through my senses stole; / I yielded myself to the perfect
whole."

price of his latest luxury car, its license plates aggressively emblazoned with his initials. Even beyond middle age, he keeps trying to relive the glory days of his twenties and thirties He gets a face-lift and a new Mercedes convertible every year, maneuvers gullible young women with father issues into empty relationships with him, and, in general, perfectly plays the role of the aging fool in the drama of the second half of life—all the while believing he is the romantic lead. As we saw in the previous chapter, this person is clinging to the archetype of the boy, the *puer* (von Franz, 1981). He would do better to be putting on the modest robes of the archetypal *wise old man,* who finds new life in his venerable station, offering his wisdom to his people.

The American male is culturally prone to this archetypal pathology. Hemingway called him "the Great American Boy-Man." This is not surprising in a decaying society that prostrates itself before the idol of youth. Holding the aging in contempt and relegating them to rest homes, a culture forgets the moral wisdom contained in the sacred narratives of its past. Without these, a society is disoriented in "a runaway world," as the British sociologist Anthony Giddens puts it with sobering accuracy (2002).

The female counterpart of the *puer,* is, as we have seen, the *puella,* the archetypal girl. We notice her everywhere: the fifty-something mother who dresses in unflatteringly low-cut blouses and lacey jeans. She styles her hair like her daughter's, is giggly and flirtatious, and tags along with her daughter and her daughter's girlfriends for an afternoon of shopping at the mall, topped off by going with "the girls" to the latest romantic comedy at the Cineplex. Instead of having transitioned gracefully into the enchanting and potent role of the *aging wise woman,* she spends hours every day trying to make herself look like a debutante (de Castillejo, 1973; Harding, 1970; Woodman, 1990).

The opposite but equally destructive situation arises when a person's experience of the *Self* becomes overbearing in its "transcendence" and "purity." Its contempt for the ordinary world that we all must live in becomes so great that it more or less obliterates the ego along with the ego's healthily constraining functions. Religious fanaticism is a variation on this possession by the Self archetype, and it is a burden to the people who must interact with someone who exhibits it. They love him but they are now alienated by how he constantly bludgeons them with the sledgehammer of his newly discovered dogma.

As an example, take the person who no longer seems to exist as just an individual because he has become a self-appointed apostle of, say, a New Age religion. He showers the platitudes of his shallow piousness upon his friends like too many bags of artificial sweetener poured over the bitter taste of life's hard facts. He begins to call his friends to repentance because of their lack of purity in diet, exercise, and meditation.

This person no longer exists as an individual but has turned himself into a stereotype. He is also obsessed by an archetype—that of the prophet and seer, which he plays out with great fervor but little finesse, passion but little poise. The Zen tradition has a wry way of characterizing monks who are so enthralled with their own "enlightenment" that they clearly feel superior to others, despite their veneer of humility, which fools no one except themselves. They are said to "stink of Zen" (Suzuki, 1964).

The fanatic is recklessly trying to live above the existential safeguards built into healthy ego-functioning. The Greeks called this archetypal possession *hubris,* pride. Jungian psychology calls it *inflation,* an overidentification with an archetype (Jung, 1969b, p. 225).

With this, we begin to move into the outskirts of psychosis. Like the wolf in the fairy tale, archetypal energy in its darker aspect has blown the house of ego down. Psychiatric wards are filled with people who believe they are John the Baptist, Napoleon, Joan of Arc, the Virgin Mary, Buddha, or Christ. Their ego-functioning has been short-circuited by the superpotent energy of an archetype. Instead of drawing from that energy in health, the person has identified with it in psychosis.

The ego is arid if it does not partake of archetypal energy, but it is mad if it gets drunk on it.

Two Examples of Interactions of Ego and Self

I ask the reader's indulgence in giving what I hope will be two useful examples from my own life of how crucial it is for the ego and the Self to come into alignment. The first example comes from my days as a graduate student in literature at University of Oregon.

Because of certain traumatic realizations and system-wide changes that seemed to be coming all at once in the life of my dearest friend—a young man of enormous gifts, sensibilities, and charm—he simply broke down and came to believe that he was Christ, or at least some sort of divinely appointed prophet. When I tried to talk with him in more measured tones about all of this, he would look at me with great compassion because I simply could not see what had become so clear to him, and would soon become clear to the whole world.

For in the music of his favorite folk-rock artist, Joni Mitchell (and so many other things too), he began to decode personal messages from God that he needed to go to the United Nations to deliver a message that would change the world. In the patterns of the fields that he saw beneath him from his window seat on the plane that was speeding him to his momentous destiny in New York City, he discerned symbolic messages that confirmed him in his calling.

I heard the next day that he was in a psychiatric hospital, having been found late at night by the police—naked and shivering on the onramp to a freeway in the Big Apple. I sat in the café he and I went to almost every evening to smoke too many cigarettes, drink too much coffee, and spend hours happily discussing a painting by Chagall or Jackson Pollock (my friend was an art history major—and a brilliant one).

But on that evening, I sat there alone: I had just been told by a mutual friend that he, one of the most intellectually and personally captivating men I had ever known, was being filled with massive doses of antipsychotic drugs in some grim, neon-lit, state crazy bin. I recoiled, thinking of what had to be his stunned humiliation, fear, and rage. I imagined the sterile ward he was in—so horrifying to a man of his exquisite artistic perceptions. I didn't know what to do. I walked home in the midnight rain.

From a Jungian perspective, I see now that my friend had been possessed by the archetype of the savior—reduced to rubble by its obliterating force. Had he found a way to establish a more realistic relationship with the archetypal Christ—understanding that he could be enlivened by the energy of the savior archetype but that he was not the savior—he would have found a way to forge a creative ego-Self axis. It would have suited his poetic nature so well—such an inherently mystical, mythical man. Instead, when he "came to" and left the hospital, he grew more and more cynical about anything spiritual.

On the other hand is an example of a life-giving marriage between ego and Self. An old man whom I knew was dying in the hospital—which happened to be a Catholic one. I had been sitting by his bed with his granddaughter for hours. Now at 3 a.m. I needed to get up and walk around to stretch my legs for a few minutes. Meandering down a deserted hall in the basement level of the hospital, I saw that a letter was posted on the locked door of the chaplain's office. I walked to the door to read it. "Dear Father Montoya," it began, "thank you for all you do to help so many people in such terrible pain in this hospital. Your work is deeply appreciated! But please don't feel that you need to save everyone. That's my job. (Signed) Jesus."

This priest had such a realistic relationship with the core archetype in his life—the archetype of the savior as embodied in the archetypal image of Christ—that he could draw from the power of that archetype while understanding his own limits as a humble priest. And as is usually the case when we understand our limits, the result is a gentle sense of humor, usually at our own lighthearted expense, as in the "letter" to Father Montoya.

The Primacy of the Self in the Ego-Self Axis

It should be stressed here, as was mentioned briefly in the last chapter, that in the ego-Self axis, the Self is in a superior position relative to the ego, for the timeless is superior to the temporal. However, the Self must genuinely honor the healthy ego's demand that spirituality also be sustainable, creative, and not socially destructive—unless the society itself is sick, in which case the ego-Self axis must be marshalled to resist the reigning social order. Examples of this are the lives of Mahatma Gandhi and Dr. Martin Luther King Jr. In any event, whenever the psychospiritual balance between ego and Self is successfully struck, the ego is invested with ethical and spiritual energy that fills its daily operations with *numinosity* and meaning on a secular landscape.

We see this dynamic interaction of the temporal and eternal in the works of Renaissance artists who painted haloed saints living and moving on a very ordinary landscape where farm animals graze in an unremarkable village (Janson & Janson, 2006). When this equipoise is actualized in one's life, the spiritualized and responsible ego then serves the function of providing ballast to the Self so that the Self does not rise so high into the heavens that it is no longer relevant to the ego or to the culture in which it is embedded, and may even be a threat to them. Like Icarus, the Self that flies too high will sooner or later find that its wings of wax have melted in the unforgiving sun of ordinary life, and the individual must finally suffer a terrible fall.

That balance of ego and Self is the aim of Jungian psychology, its crowning gem: *individuation*. The reconciliation of opposites is a defining feature of individuation. It is accomplished through what Jung called the transcendent function.

DIALECTICAL TENSION AND THE TRANSCENDENT FUNCTION

"No Pain, No Gain"

One of the differences between Freud and Jung lies in how the two viewed and dealt with psychic tension and pain in the patient. Recall that Freud took a negative view of it, applying a "hermeneutics of suspicion," where the question is always: "What is fundamentally wrong here? And is it possible to root it out like a cancer or, failing that, find some way for a person to go on in life without *excessive* pain by managing the pathology and limiting its spread?"

Conversely, Jung, operating from a hermeneutics of hope, felt that nature was wise in her patterns, not crafty in her designs (Homans, 1989). She was not out trying to gore her creatures on the horns of impossible dilemmas. Where there is tension and pain, reasoned Jung, it is the organism's way of saying that there is a problem, but also that where there is a problem there is the possibility of growth. Psychic tension and pain are opportunities for psychospiritual advancement—but how this happens will necessarily be different in each individual.

This is not to say that Jung—who suffered greatly at various times in his life—in any way minimized psychospiritual agony. He would have resonated to T. S. Eliot's hard but true admission that "we only live, only suspire / Consumed by either fire or fire." But this made it all the more urgent, Jung felt, in his calling as a psychiatrist, that he tend as skillfully as possible to his patients' distress and dolor.

This could only be done by helping the patient look at his pain straight on, living through it to see what psychospiritual wisdom it was trying to convey, and then creatively attending to that message in practical action. If one did this, then the agony could lead to psychospiritual maturation. Recent Jungians have taken this insight about the generativity of pain to new heights, especially in Kathryn Madden's (2008) *Dark Light of the Soul* and Michael Gellert's (1994) *Modern Mysticism: Jung, Zen, and the Still Good Hand of God.*

Freud was ultimately a pessimist. Jung—although well-traveled through the darkness within himself, others, and the universe—must finally be reckoned an optimist.

The Transcendent Function and Evolution

In any psychic conflict, there exists the possibility of resolution by honoring both sides of it—and then transcending the tension to arrive at a third, more satisfactory, higher position. This creative process was what Jung called "the transcendent function."

Picture the base of a triangle defined by endpoints A and B. This represents the tension between two opposites. The apex of the triangle, C, is the higher resolution of the lower-level, A-B, dialectical tension. This resolution honors and perpetuates the truths in positions A and B, but it also makes a quantum leap to a new level of awareness that transcends anything A or B could have seen, given the assumptions of the plane on which they operated.

Jung was thus intrigued by the medieval Christian alchemists' formula known as the *Axiom of Maria:* "Out of the first comes the second, out of the second comes the third, and out of the third comes the fourth as the first."

This cryptic equation could only be understood by a spiritual calculus, Jung concluded in his massive, groundbreaking studies in the psychospiritual significance of alchemy (1968b,1968d, 1970b). The number one represents the original wholeness of the psyche, its primal self-sufficiency and repose, what the poet William Blake called "Innocence." Two represents the conflicts that life showers upon us in the acid rain of what Blake called "Experience." Three is the resolution of a psychospiritual tension in the apex-solution of the transcendent function, Blake's paradisiacal state of "Organized Innocence"—enlightenment *now* in the Eternal *Now.* Here was becoming a smaller, symbolic Christ or Buddha in and as *one's Self* (Diel, 1988).

Four was the elevated foundation for constructing a new approach to life, its grounding in Self-realization, and the witnessing to all of this in personal and social service to others.

The pivotal three was also the psychospiritual meaning of another enigmatic Latin axiom favored by Jung and a leitmotif in his work: *Tertium non datur*, "The third is not given." Like all animals, human beings live in a state of tension. But unlike other animals, human beings can seek meaning in that tension through an elevated vision—one that makes the tension not only endurable but creative. This is the transcendent function, the "third." But this "third" is not "given." What does it mean to be human if not to strive for ever-higher resolutions? And these are never just "given" but require the most extreme effort.

This is why Jung declared that individuation is an *opus contra naturum*—another emphasis in his writings. Individuation is a "work against nature," which, as noted in the previous chapter, would be better translated as "a work transcending nature" (Jung, 1970a, p. 201). These tensions are part and parcel of life for the simple reason that without them there is only stasis, something quite unacceptable to the teleologically optimistic Jung. Without tension, entropy would soon take over and shut the whole business down. Thus, we mustn't interpret this "against nature" to mean that nature is bad or that our fate is to be in a constant state of enmity with it. It means simply that *the human being is precisely that creature whose evolution is toward spirit, toward transcending nature.*

The French Jesuit priest and archaeologist Teilhard de Chardin (1975) proclaimed that the whole universe, including the Godhead, is involved in one grand cosmic evolution. The theologian Charles Hartshorne (1984), expanding upon the British mathematician and philosopher Alfred North Whitehead's (1929) view of the universe as an eternally evolving process, also saw God as coevolving with humanity. Known as "process theology," this has much in common with the idea of individuation.

It did not matter to Jung—personally, clinically, or theoretically—how one found the royal road leading to individuation. All that mattered is that one found a way to this inner sanctum—*to which* one does not so much *go* so much as *in which* one ultimately *is*. It is symbolized and sometimes even made real and experienced in the construction of mandalas (Jung, 1968b). In the mandalas that some patients would produce throughout the therapeutic process, Jung saw the patient drawing images of people, structures, and events in each of the circle's quadrants. Jung observed that these quadrants tended to increasingly "communicate with" and protect the numinous core of the mandala at the center as the therapy progressed. This was indicative of the consolidation of the Self and the creation of an ego-Self axis.

THE LIGHT AND DARK SIDE OF THE ARCHETYPE AND ARCHETYPAL PROJECTION

We live between the dialectical poles of light and dark. We carry on in shades of gray. Sir Thomas More says in Bolt's (1988) play *A Man for All Seasons:* "God made the angels to show Him splendor, as He made animals for innocence and plants for their simplicity. But Man He made to serve Him wittily, in the tangle of his mind."

This is the same Thomas More, by the way, who was later made a saint in the Catholic Church. It seems to be the greatest saints in every spiritual tradition who focus most on their darkness, the tangles of their minds, since pride in one's spiritual "accomplishments"—the Jungian idea of "inflation"—is always the last temptation of the saint: the final irony of vaunting oneself for being so humble.

Conversely, biographers who study the life of a notoriously evil person sometimes find that this presumed devil was not without some light, what remained of what had been all but snuffed out by some form of abuse in his youth (Miller, 1978). Of course, we do not condemn the saint for his small darkness any more than we excuse the monster because of his little light. We simply understand that no one is purely light, no one purely dark, and that we all have varying shades of gray in us. In these shifting gradations of gray we exist—striving for the light but also aware that the dark has a hold on us too.

A brief glance at a few essential archetypes confirms that every archetype has a dark side and a light one (Jung, 1969a, pp. 124, 135; Jung, 1969b, p. 183).

Over and against the archetype of Christ the Redeemer is the archetype of Satan the Destroyer. The archetype of Christ as "the way, the truth, and the life" is the cosmic opposite to the archetype of Satan, who is the father of all lies and the Prince of Death.

The wise old man like Obi-Wan Kenobi plays the role of the "good father" to Luke Skywalker. His Jungian lesson about becoming an integral personality is, in a play on words, the same as his name: "O, be one!" But where there is the good father, there must be the dark father, "Darth Vader"—his harsh, Germanic-sounding name echoing the name "Dark Father."

A wise old woman like Cinderella's fairy godmother stands in the starkest possible contrast to Dorothy's creepy nemesis, that murderous old woman, the Wicked Witch. That crone is the archetypal mother of misery—like Medea in the Greek drama, who slays her children. Naturally, a mother of death, like the Wicked Witch who plagues Dorothy, cannot survive the touch of the essence of life, which makes her shrivel up and die: water—which, in a perfect irony, is a maternal symbol, suggestive of amniotic fluid.

The very common archetype of the good magician, like Albus Dumbledore, must, according to the Jungian rule of psychic dialectics, constellate the

equally common archetype of the bad magician, Lord Voldemort—*de mort*
echoing the French "of death." As the Lord of Death, Voldemort is a variation on the archetype of the devil.

The point to be underscored here is that *just as we project personal
subconscious issues onto another person, we project archetypal energy from
the collective unconscious onto him as well.* This is especially true of those
who hold some kind of power and, therefore being instinctively "attractive"
to us *because* of that power, seem to summon our light and dark archetypal
projections. In Jungian psychology, a person whose role excites projections
is called "a hook" because we hang our projections upon him, whether or not
he has actually invited them.

In twentieth-century US politics, President John F. Kennedy was a hook
for the archetypal projection of the good king who brings peace and fertility
to the land (Frazer, 1935; Weston, 1957). We who were there then even
called the amiably handsome Kennedy's administration Camelot, after virtu-
ous King Arthur, thus unconsciously acknowledging the mythical filter
through which many of us saw JFK.

His assassination was particularly wrenching for Americans since it was
not just the death of a man, and not even the death of a president that
occurred on that black late-November day in Dallas in 1963. It was the
horrifying ritual slaughter of the archetypal good king (Weston, 1957) that
was being constellated in the American cultural unconscious—and viewed
on TV.

What is more, those of us who lived through this terrible thing somehow
sensed (although it would not have occurred to us to put it this way) that it
must follow the complete archetypal pattern in which a time of calamity
under a bad king must now take place before the archetypal time of restora-
tion could begin. And to confirm this suspicion, we were soon plagued by the
full fury of the Vietnam War.

The horror that flooded Americans upon Kennedy's assassination was,
primarily and primally, a spiritual one, at the archetypal level, at the apparent
triumph of evil. The redemptive narrative of Camelot had been disrupted in
the sickeningly dull pops of a few gunshots on a grassy knoll in Texas. It was
an archetypal necessity that world-historically dark days lay ahead of us. We
knew it at the level of "the cultural collective unconscious" (Adams, 1995).

Confirmations seemed to keep on coming, like boulders in a landslide.
Not much later appeared a man who was the perfect hook for the projection
of the archetypal king of darkness. His elevation to the now vacated throne
was probably an archetypal narrative necessity. He was Richard Milhous
Nixon.

Even his name had the sound of someone Dickens would have thought up
to suggest a particularly depressing and dangerous character—a house of
millstones, a millhouse, suffused with the gloom of negativity—something

an evil magician had put a "Nix-on." With his growly voice, shifty and falsely friendly eyes, perpetually dark stubble on his saggy jowls, and slight stoop as he walked, Nixon answered with uncanny accuracy to another dark king of the same name—Shakespeare's vile King Richard III, but now in his modern American used-car-salesman edition. As Kennedy's political nemesis, Nixon fit the archetypal bill of the evil king perfectly. In fact, Kennedy was no saint, as we now know, and Nixon was undoubtedly not without his virtues. But that is not the point. They were archetypal hooks.

Of course, much of the force that finally pushed Nixon from the Oval Office was strictly (one hesitates to say "purely") political. Political causation is what students read about in history books and no one doubts its reality. But there are, additionally, subtler powers at play in what Eliot called history's "many cunning and devious passages." Those world-historical energies may emanate from the archetypal realm—what St. Paul wrote about regarding "spiritual wickedness in high places" (Ephesians 6:12), alluding to a universal darkness that infuses not only our personal histories but our collective ones, too, in the archetypal dynamics of "cosmos and psyche" (Tarnas, 2011).

Nixon's collapse, then, was not only political but also archetypal—the result of the collective projection of anguished archetypal energy that had built up in the American psyche during the angry 1960s. Perhaps banishing Nixon was a collective attempt at a sort of exorcism. But this much seems certain: at a more profound level than the political, the JFK–Nixon showdown was emblematic of a fundamental archetypal dialectic, the opposition of light and dark. [5]

It is this tension between light and dark that generates the energy—again, understanding the word "energy" symbolically as an imagistic rendering of unimaginable, nonmeasurable archetypal power—that is the atomic core of our psychospiritual processes (Harding, 1970; Riegel, 1979). This dialectic is the essence of our existential situation as sojourners here through the Land of Gray. And it is the tug-and-pull between the light and dark side of every archetype within us that finally "authors" the tragicomedy of life. How we handle that tension is the governing question of the second half of life, said Jung.

And of this we may be sure. The person who claims to possess some sort of special righteousness is probably attempting to conceal from others and, worst of all, from himself his own inner darkness. This darkness is woven into us and can never be completely dispelled, no matter how strict the person's outward adherence to a moral code. Even that legalistic Pharisee

---

5. Professor Mark Grandstaff, a military historian and Jungian theorist at both the War College and the University of Maryland, has also spoken of the light and dark archetypes that presidents invoke and evoke (whether consciously or unconsciously) in addresses to Congress when they are urging the nation on to war (in conversation, March 2010).

and onetime champion of conventional "righteousness," St. Paul, makes this point in the seventh chapter of his Epistle to the Romans. Mercilessly bringing his own corrupt heart to task, he laments: "When I want to do right, only wrong is within my reach. . . . Wretched creature that I am." Examining the archetypes of Christ and Satan as the light and dark sides of the Self, Jung thus wrote:

> If we see the traditional figure of Christ as a parallel to the psychic manifesta-
> tion of the [S]elf, then the antichrist would correspond to the shadow of the
> [S]elf, namely, the dark half of the human totality, which ought not to be
> judged too optimistically. So far as we can judge from experience, light and
> shadow are so evenly distributed in man's nature that his psychic totality
> appears, to say the least of it, in a somewhat murky light. The psychological
> concept of the [S]elf . . . cannot omit the shadow that belongs to the light
> figure, for without it this figure lacks body and humanity. (1968a, p. 42)

We must deal with our personal, cultural, and archetypal darkness. We must admit to ourselves that to some degree we have generated our problems.

But in all this, we must above all avoid lapsing into despair and bitterness. Jung was an optimist. He knew that darkness plays its essential role in our lives. "For without [the darkness] this figure [of the Self, the integral human being] lacks body and humanity." However, even that is not the last word. Rather, it is that, by facing our own shadow, we can transmute its energy into ethically serviceable power, and we can do so all the more because we have learned throughout the first half of life how to be effective in the world.

Our light can grow stronger by skillful handling of our darkness. True, this is a paradox—but life's great truths usually *are* paradoxical. Jung had much to say about this.

PARADOX IN JUNGIAN PSYCHOLOGY

"The test of a first rate intelligence is the ability to hold two opposed ideas in the mind at the same time, and still retain the ability to function" (Fitzgerald, 1936). Jung would certainly have agreed with F. Scott Fitzgerald's maxim. For Jung, paradox is the key that opens the gate into the realm of the collective unconscious, the kingdom of the transrational. The word "transrational" should emphatically *not* be taken to imply that the collective unconscious is *ir*rational. Indeed, "rationality" is itself probably an archetype of the collective unconscious and the embodiment of Kant's mathetic domain.

As we saw in chapter 1, the word "transrational" comes from transpersonal theory, which entered academic discourse and therapeutic practice a half century ago and has grown since (Maslow, 1970).[6] Transrational refers to those living truths—deeply personal, psychospiritually stabilizing—that go far beyond the reach of mere rationality and propositional discourse, and that alone give us reasons for living: "the courage to be" (Tillich, 1952). The answers to the most important questions in our lives do not usually fall into logical dichotomies of "either/or." They come to us in the "good-news/bad-news" form of "both/and." To work with this fact requires the transcendent function.

William Butler Yeats, toward the end of his poetic career, captured it philosophically: "I call it death-in-life, and life-in-death." Paradox is the warp and woof of things. It cannot be learned in neat conceptual packages, systematically and risk-free. Rather, in a mix of dark and light, paralyzing pain and grateful growth, the individual must fully experience and somehow find a way to endure the reality of paradox in order for it to lead him to higher ground, where he can now move forward again—but in greater self-awareness and service to others.

Here we see again the difference between mere knowledge, which requires only conceptualization, and wisdom, which demands the whole person. Heidegger called it the difference between "knowledge" and "understanding" (Heidegger, 1964). Finally, it is not knowledge that Jung wished to convey, despite his vast erudition. It was understanding that counted.

The story is told of Akiva ben Joseph, a late first/early second century Jewish scholar and one of the founders of rabbinical Judaism. He exemplifies the archetype of the wise old man whose wrinkled brow has been carved with the plough of paradox.

In the last seconds of his life, Rabbi Akiva, a frail elder being flayed with hot pokers and then burned at the stake by the Roman state, which feared his influence, lifted his eyes to heaven . . . and declared, "Ah, at last I see! The love of God!" We intuit the truth of this despite the rational mind's outraged protest that such a cruel death inflicted on such a good man could *ever* reveal the love of God, could *ever* be anything but grotesque, could *ever* demonstrate anything but the absence of God. Yet as we meditate on it more and more, we also *feel* that Rabbi Akiva's one-line, dying sermon is not irrational. It is beautiful, not grotesque. Rabbi Akiva's dying words make supreme ethical sense, but that sense is grasped intuitively. It is transrational.

The death by torture of another Jew and also a rabbi, Jesus of Nazareth, is another such paradox. Here was a man without sin, impaled on a cross, the most torturous form of state execution by Rome, one reserved for the worst criminals—this Jesus, strategically assassinated by a colonialist empire for just going about doing good, proclaiming the eventual advent of God's king-

---

6. For excellent expositions of transpersonal theory, see Ferrer (2002), Wade (1996), Wilber (2000).

dom of love, which was even now being made manifest in his own lowly figure. Paradox upon paradox.

Another less bitter one comes from the East in Lao Tzu's declaration in the *Tao Te Ching* that "He who thinks he knows the great Tao does not know. But he who knows that he does not know, knows" (Yutang, 1948). In terms of formal logic, this statement fails the most basic tests. But as a transrational intuition about the greatness of the universe and its laws as compared to the puniness of the human being, it is peerless.

In the Zen tradition, too, paradox is central (Merton, 1967; Suzuki, 1964). A monk is given a *koan* to contemplate. "How can you keep the tiger that is crashing through the window this very second from breaking the window?" No rational answer *is* possible, which does not mean that there are no possible answers. There most certainly are, an infinite number of them, although what might count as a correct answer in one session with the head monk might not be correct in another session, for it all depends on the authenticity of the spiritual space from which the monk is answering at this very moment.

This the abbot *senses* with unerring accuracy. Teasing one out of rational thought, the *koan* requires of the student a better way of knowing and being: transrational intuition in the emerging reality of the present, which will provide a suitable answer, and a completely unpredictable one, if the student is attuned to—indeed, integral *with* and *in*—that emerging present. The monk answering, "But Master, isn't tomorrow laundry day?" might be precisely the right answer. Or the wrong one. It all depends.

Bucking the tide of our age's shallowly misplaced faith in reason and stubborn immersion in materialism, Jung was adamant about the primacy of the transrational. In what must be counted as one of his most daring challenges to the academic establishment of his time and ours, Jung declared, "Reason . . . is in point of fact nothing more than the sum total of all [of a person's] prejudices and myopic views" (1968c, p. 13). On the other hand, "wholeness is perforce paradoxical in its manifestations" (Jung, 1968a, p. 145; see also Zoja, 1998).

Another important paradox in Jungian psychology relates to Heraclitus's maxim that everything turns into its opposite given enough time. "The way up is the way down. The way forward is the way back," Heraclitus declared at the dawn of Western thought, calling this process *enantiodromia*. Jung borrowed this term to describe how our perspectives and commitments so often change into their opposites: "Old Heraclitus, who was indeed a very great sage, discovered the most marvelous of all psychological laws: the regulative function of opposites. He called it an *enantiodromia*, a running contrariwise" (Jung, 1966c, p. 72).

We do not have to look far to find examples of this. The enthusiasm of youth metamorphoses into the quietude of old age. Nor does it take an entire lifetime for great change to occur. It can happen quite dramatically.

David Horowitz, one of the most prominent radical leaders of the American Youth Movement in the 1960s—a young man who had been raised by his communist parents to advocate violent revolution to overthrow American capitalism and replace it with Soviet-style socialism—turned in a few years into one of the most vociferous ultraconservative speakers on the lecture circuits. The freewheeling atheist and artist in his twenties becomes a humble Benedictine monk in his thirties, as the poet-priest Thomas Merton (1947) chronicled in his spiritual autobiography, *The Seven Storey Mountain*. There is nothing constant except change. Psyche is no exception to this rule. Indeed, psyche *operates* by this rule. "Sooner or later," Jung wrote, "everything runs into its opposite" (1966c, p. 72).

THE NATURE AND PRIMACY OF THE SYMBOL IN JUNGIAN PSYCHOLOGY

As we have seen, we must deploy the transcendent function to intuitively get beyond the binary opposition in a problem on one plane of thinking and thereby ascend to a higher solution on a higher plane. We do this by means of symbols, which are what powers the transcendent function.

Our mathetic languages not only cannot raise us above binary oppositions; they guarantee them. Mathetic languages make binaries inevitable. Our mathetic languages are, indeed, the mechanism that *generates* our dualistic apprehension of things, and thus our contradictions, in the first place. For every linguistic item A, there is its opposite B. There is no right without left, up without down, yes without no.

Symbols alone are capable of breaking out of this linguistic-conceptual dilemma because only the symbol goes both deep and high enough to get beneath or above the plane of thinking on which an opposition resides and is presently working, and on which it is presently stuck. Why can a symbol do this? It is because "the symbol is the primitive exponent of the unconscious, but at the same time an idea that corresponds to the highest intuition of the conscious mind" (Jung, 1968b, p. 28).

When Jung wrote about the nature of a symbol, he would often point out that a symbol should never be confused with a *sign*. A *sign* is an arbitrary token that mechanically *stands for* something else in a one-to-one correspondence. Through a symbol, however, we *stand in* a complex reality—and not only in the best way possible but in the *only* way possible. A symbol can do this because, like fireworks, it simultaneously streams out into multiple directions and in diverse ways that boggle logical analysis and paralyze syllogisms but that move in the same rhythm as the free-flowing and multifaceted energy of the archetypal realm (Jung, 1966b, p. 77).

A sign, however—where one word means one thing and that is all—cannot do this. If a stop *sign* meant stop, go, turn around, get out of your car, dance in the streets, back up, have lunch, sit on the roof, and discuss cloud formations, it would make for interesting intersections—albeit dangerous ones. The stop sign, meaning more than one thing, would have failed as a *sign*. But meaning just one thing, it fulfills its function, which is necessarily a limited one. A sign is therefore unable to exist in the very different milieu of the limitlessness of the archetypal dimension.

Thinking symbolically is primary and creative. Thinking with signs is secondary and instrumental. Why is thinking symbolically creative while thinking in signs is not?

A sign can only exist within the strict confines of a certain way of seeing and being. Indeed, it is precisely the nature of a sign to obediently reflect and vigilantly guard a certain plane of thinking. The sign patrols this plane to make sure that nothing that does not conform to its rules may enter it or, if something foreign does appear, to expel or even destroy it. The sign fears what is new, but creativity must be ever in search of it, in the same way that one is always seeing something new in a symbol, which allows endless possibilities of interpretation on various planes of thought.

Furthermore, creativity involves the reconciliation of a tension between opposites by going to a higher plane to view the tension from a wholly new perspective and, from there, be able to resolve it in a novel way. A creative approach to a tension makes this move because the opposites exist on the same plane of thinking as each other, and they therefore share the same fundamental assumptions. Each pole of the opposition is simply a different interpretation and application of those assumptions. But it is precisely those limited assumptions that are limiting vision and therefore creating and confirming the problem!

Thus, Einstein famously observed, "The significant problems we face cannot be solved at the same level of thinking we were at when we created them." Moving to a higher plane of thinking to re-vision and re-interpret something from that higher perspective is the essence of the creative act and exactly the effect of a symbol on consciousness. To encourage someone to think creatively *is* to help him think symbolically.

The tension of opposites on one plane leading to a creative transcendence and resolution of those opposites on a higher plane is, again, Jung's transcendent function. Approaching an intellectual or psychospiritual dilemma as an occasion for a higher resolution of two equal but conflicting claims in a "third," higher answer, the transcendent function is the essence of the process of individuation in the classroom and in life in general, according to Jung (Miller, 2004). This third answer, as the synthesis of the two competing claims and then a transcendence of them on a higher plane, is a creative act in interpretive possibilities, which is the nature of symbolic thinking.

Like all creativity, this solution must be worked out and attained through considerable intellectual and often ethical effort that changes the individual in a new vision of not only the question under analysis but also a new vision of himself. Such difficult things are not just "given." Jung's *tertium non datur,* "the third is not given," thus suggests that the transcendent function, as the dynamic of individuation, requires hard work and personal *transformation.*

A symbol is a living one to the degree that it is an archetypal symbol, a manifestation of the ultimately unknowable archetype. As such, archetypal symbols are guesses about and glimpses into the core mysteries of life. Jung called the symbol "the best possible expression for a complex fact not yet clearly apprehended by consciousness" (Jung, 1969b, p. 75). He suggests something of the tremendous scope of the symbol, its depth and height—which does not deny ego-consciousness or its systems but, enfolding them, exceeds them, in a move that is not *irrational* but *transrational*—in observing that "the symbol is the primitive exponent of the unconscious, but at the same time an idea that corresponds to the highest intuition of the conscious mind" (Jung, 1968b, p. 28).

Symbols are thus not just the secondary, default position we take when the language of logic fails. Rather, symbols are existentially more powerful than logic and its rigidly defined, rigorously defended signs because only through symbols can we catch a vision of the complex contours of the archetypal realm, and only by symbols can we begin to express what we experienced in doing so—or grasp what someone else did. This is undoubtedly why, as we have noted throughout, Jung clearly favored the poetic over the mathetic domain.

To give body to these ideas about the nature of a symbol and suggest its difference from a sign, let us briefly look at the first line of a well-known poem. Allen Ginsberg's *Howl,* which ushered in the Beat movement in the mid-twentieth century, begins with the cry: "I saw the best minds of my generation destroyed by madness." Clearly, he is not referring to a group of people who scored high on intelligence tests ("the best minds of my generation") but, diagnosed as clinically ill ("madness"), were then put in an incinerator ("destroyed"). Such a literalistic, sign-based reading of that shocking opening line that changed the face of American poetry in the 1950s would obviously be way off track.

Ginsberg was referring to sensitive spirits of all sorts who were driven into various kinds of despair *and* protest by the aridity of the American cultural landscape in the United States of the 1950s. The "best" minds that he refers to were likely seen as useless misfits by "normal" society. We thus immediately register the tension between what is conventionally considered "good" and what Ginsberg considered "good." Ginsberg's view of the good involved radical politics, Eastern mysticism, gay sexuality, drug use, and other practices that "respectable" society then spurned.

His ironic use of "best" therefore invests the line with all sorts of meanings that bump up against and jar each other in various, sometimes vexing, but always thought-provoking, even thought-defying, ways. His symbols do not convince by logic but by paradox. Indeed, paradox is the living medium in which symbols swim.

Thus, Ginsberg's symbols in this first line of *Howl* are, at one and the same time, defeated and audacious, pathetic yet bold, ill and sane, damning and salvific. Like the archetypes of "the revolutionary" and "the poet" that they embody, in other words, Ginsberg's symbols contain both light and dark, play off the tension between them, and (by the end of the poem) have risen to a mystical vision of a restored, millennial America that is beyond what could have been imagined at the beginning of the poem. Such is the potency of the transcendent function.

Ginsberg's use of "destroyed" carries other meanings, too. For, to be "destroyed" by the culture in which he lived at the time *really* means, in Ginsberg's eyes, to have allowed oneself to be coopted into that culture's sterile marketplaces and mindsets. The conformity which society calls good, Ginsberg calls evil and *truly* destructive. Those who *seem* to have been "destroyed by madness" are, ironically, finally the only sane ones left standing. Despite these outcasts' suffering, they will not allow themselves to be just cogs in the machine of a soulless culture, like so many others had done. *Those* were the people who were truly "destroyed" by the "madness" of buying into an insane society. And finally, it is the culture that is destroyed because it has destroyed itself.

What is sanity? What madness? Ginsberg uses paradox to turn the ideas of sanity and madness on their heads. He is able, in one short line, to problematize every conventional notion of good and bad because he uses the word as a symbol, not as a sign, and thereby dwells, and invites us to dwell, on the archetypal plane, where his, and *our,* pain is redemptive because it eventuates in vision.

The general point to note for our purposes is this: the delicately constructive but also shattering potential of a symbol can accommodate many meanings, even contradictory ones, at the same time. This open-ended capacity of a symbol to hold any number of ideas of every sort within itself simultaneously in order to take us to a higher way of seeing something makes it the true language of the transcendent function.

The foremost problem of "modern man in search of a soul" was in Jung's day as in ours that we have few or no *really* meaningful, *really* living symbols—not just outdated tokens of something that used to be meaningful and living in a previous historical epoch but fails the test in ours—to organize and energize our spiritually adrift lives (Jung, 1954b).[7]

"Now, we have no symbolic life," lamented Jung in an address to a group of British psychiatrists,

> and we are all badly in need of the symbolic life. Only the symbolic life can express the soul—the daily need of the soul, mind you! And because people have no such thing, they can never step out of this mill—this awful, grinding, banal life in which they are "nothing but." . . . There is no symbolic existence in which I am something else, in which I am fulfilling my role, my role as one of the actors in the divine drama of life. . . . That gives the only meaning to human life. That gives peace, when people feel that they are living the symbolic life, that they are actors in the divine drama. . . . [E]verything else is banal and you can dismiss it. (1954a, pp. 274–275)

A CUBIST APPROACH TO THE GNOSTIC SELF

The idea of "ego" is not difficult to grasp. It does not stretch any conceptual limits to do so. Indeed, in a sense, our ego *is* our conceptual limits, and our conceptual limits *are* our ego. "Ego" and "concept" depend upon each other. They create and confirm each other, and then crown each other to legitimate their sovereignty on a tiny desert island in the middle of a teeming, endless ocean of which ego and concept know very little.

Besides, we are accustomed to the word *ego* at this point after over a century of Freudian psychology. But the transrational idea of the Self from lesser-known Jungian psychology is a great deal more difficult to take in. The existentialist educational philosopher Maxine Greene's (1974) idea of the "Cubist Curriculum" is helpful in approaching the *Mysterium tremendum et fascinans* of the Self.

Greene argued for a "Cubist" approach to anything that we wish to study and appreciate deeply. Just as Picasso in his Cubist phase has us regard, say, his *Woman Looking in a Mirror* from multiple angles at once, Greene advised that anything we wish to explore intensively and extensively should be viewed from multiple points of view. In this manner we enjoy a multifaceted participation in whatever is being apprehended.

Thus, let us continue approaching the pivotal, complex idea of the Self in *The Collected Works* in more detail and from yet another point of view. In this way, we enhance the richness of not only our "understanding *of*" but, even more significantly, our "dwelling *in*" this difficult yet tremendously generative notion.

---

7. Jung's view of the crucial psychospiritual importance of the symbol provides a principled basis for critiquing the present marginalization of art in public education in the United States as I (2007) argue in *Inside Education: Depth Psychology in Teaching and Learning.*

"For you are all one": The Gnostic Self [8]

Jung describes the Self as a *complexio oppositorum,* Latin for a "combination of opposites," existing in a lively balance. This was a crucial idea in medieval and Renaissance gnostic Christian alchemy.[9] For in gnosticism, "God" dwarfs our dichotomies. Indeed, God is the one who generates all dichotomies, has them within Its Being, but also transcends them in a unity which shatters mere conceptualization and can only be known in paradox and through our *own* experience (Jonas, 1958; Pagels, 1992). This God beyond any idea or image we might have of God—the God-beyond-"God"—goes above, below, around, within, without (or any other possible *metaphorical* use of a spatial preposition) all of our merely split-in-two ideas of things into good/bad, light/dark, male/female.

As did the gnostics, Jung often psychospiritually interpreted sacred writings. The interpretation of scripture is known as "exegesis." Jung performed exegeses on holy texts from a wide range of traditions. He felt this kind of thing to be an important exercise since the challenge facing the member of a modern Western culture was that, although he might no longer believe his culture's sacred narratives as literally true, he still needed spiritual sustenance—which Jung felt such texts remained uniquely capable of offering. An individual's *personal* reading of his culture's sacred narratives, not as literally true but symbolic of his own individuation processes, would still be relevant, compelling, and potentially quite growthful to him as a "modern man in search of a soul."

In this section, therefore, I propose to read one of St. Paul's most famous proclamations, Galatians 3:28, in order to interpret it archetypally. I do so in order to provide yet another perspective on Jung's idea of the Self, and thus respond to Greene's call for a Cubist view of complex matters, and also to offer an example of the kind of personal appropriation of a sacred text that Jung advocated for.

Paul declares in this oft-cited scripture: "There is neither Jew nor Gentile, neither slave nor free, nor is there male and female, for you are all one in Christ Jesus." This has often been taken as a call to promote a "democracy of believers" within an institutional church, where rights and responsibilities are divided equally, and previous political distinctions are obliterated, or rendered unimportant. But from a psychospiritual view, its meaning far exceeds this.

We begin by noting that the title "Christ Jesus" consists of two parts. They are (1) a specific historical person, "Jesus," an incarnation (as, in a sense, we are all specific incarnations) of (2) the Eternal Mind (the Cosmic

---

8. Elaine Pagels's (1992) gnostic readings of the Pauline letters have influenced me deeply, which I gratefully acknowledge here.

9. See also Edinger (1985), Hoeller (1982).

"Christ"). Hence, the composite title "Christ Jesus" can be interpreted as the axis between Jesus as an ego ("I"), although a supremely exemplary one, and a fully realized Self ("Christ" within). By this reading, then, "Christ Jesus" symbolizes the ego-Self axis, and is a *complexio oppositorum,* a combination of the mortal and the Timeless: individuation.

As a *complexio oppositorum,* "Christ Jesus" emerges as an archetypal symbol of that "archetype of wholeness," the *imago Dei,* toward which every person must strive if he is to become an integral human being (Jung, 1968b, p. 223).[10] And, in what is perhaps most important to the individual who is reading this scripture archetypally, "Christ Jesus" is potentially the reader himself, or what that reader may become, as he strives *to contain and unify opposites within himself.*

The mathetic reader, on the other hand, who can *only* see and talk about things as dichotomies—Jew *or* Gentile, slave *or* free, male *or* female— recoils at this Cosmic Christ, who obliterates all of the dualities that the mathetic man relies upon in his categorical world, his "box system," in which he feels safe—unlike Jung in his hospital visions, who felt fatally cramped in by the box world (Jung, 1965, p. 292). The mathetic man would shrink in terror at the *complexio oppositorum* of the Self, condemn it as ludicrous, sheer chaos blurring into a panicked "Nothingness." Not male *or* female? Not something *or* its opposite? Not "A" *or* "not A"? But that is logically impossible. It is absurd.

"Yes," Paul seems to be proclaiming here, it *is* to *nothing* that all of our dichotomies are reduced when we see them in the context of the Eternal. Male/female, Jew/Gentile, slave/free—such things are conditional, biased, transient, and dissolve in the presence of the Unitive Center. The mathetic mind is undone. And as if to make matters even more exasperating to the logical mind, Paul says that in this center "you are all one."

For "you are all one" refers, in its gnostic sense, not especially (and maybe not even) to a political fact—a "democracy of believers." The mathetic, rule-based mind would have no problem if Paul's proclamation were as easy as that. But it isn't. For political truths, however praiseworthy, fall short of the deeper truths that lie in the soul's core. "You are all, each and every one of you, *one.*" The gnostic Paul (Pagels, 1992) is underlining the *individual's* psychospiritual wholeness, the unique "oneness" of *each* person, as he finds the attainment of his life task through facing and embracing all of his own contradictions—as he becomes *integral.*

At this point, the individual may then employ this *felt knowledge* (for that is what *gnosis* is) of existential unity as a springboard from which he can leap into an *experience* of his own center—an experience, not a cognition, of it.

---

10. Cf. Diel's (1988) interesting but limited analysis of Jesus in the Gospel according to St. John as essentially just a picture of an individual staying true to his deepest beliefs.

And in fact, in uniting all contradictions within himself, he is already *in* that center. It resolves and dissolves all the warring binaries that have heretofore made up and tormented his poor, isolated ego, buffeted it from pole to pole in exhausting tension upon tension, seemingly never ending. And in this act of *centering his own center in the Universal Center,* he becomes both fully himself as an individual and also completely calibrated in God—the God-within. In that moment, for as long as that moment may last in time, he is *individuated,* and therefore timeless—timeless in time.

"One" also refers to the completion of all things in the universe, the totality of their realized purposes. And this abundance arises precisely out of what appears to the mathetic mind to be mere "Nothingness." For the reader who stays stuck in ego-mind and mere rationality, these paradoxes are too much. He can only flee in terror or strike out in wrath. But for the ego-mind that has risen above all dualities, then Nothingness—which is the ego-mind reaching and confessing its mortal limitations, and now resting in that recognition—will paradoxically but certainly become fullness, spiritual abundance in the understanding that one, having given up oneself and thus finding oneself, *is* at one with the Timeless One. The gnostics called this abundance the *pleroma,* Greek for "that which fills" (Hoeller, 1982; Segal, 1995). Out of Nothingness, abundance streams.

Gnosticism, which centered around the idea of knowing the *pleroma* through a personal experience of it, was gaining a certain currency in Jung's day with the discovery of ancient gnostic documents—especially those of important second-century gnostic Christians such as Marcion and Valentinus, who came very close to becoming the leaders of Christianity in its earliest stages (Chadwick, 1990). There is no doubt that Jung was influenced by gnosticism in his formulation of the idea of the Self (Hoeller, 1982).

This is the mystical experience (Underhill, 1961). And it is one which Jung had after his heart attack in 1944. He had had these experiences of an ultimate Unity in all contrarieties throughout his adult life, some of which he personally recorded and artistically rendered in *The Red Book* (2009).

In 1916 Jung privately published a manuscript of one series of such experiences of the *pleroma.* He titled it *Septem Sermones ad Mortuous (Seven Sermons to the Dead).* He made its author Basilides of Alexandria, a gnostic teacher of the first decades of the second century, when gnostic Christianity was influential. This manuscript he passed around to only a few people, since only they, he felt, would appreciate its mystical nature and not ridicule him for it, dismissing it, and him, as mad. Jung, a pioneer in Western psychology, already had enough trouble dealing with the psychiatric establishment to give it further ammunition to use against him.

In his writings, Jung (1969b, p. 189) also portrays the Self as the gnostic's Eternal Man—the *Anthropos*—in whom all dichotomies are reconciled, the archetypal Christ awaiting discovery within each person, and therefore (again) St. Paul's "Not I [ego] but Christ [the Self] within."[11] In Jung's idea of the Self we also see evidence of his fascination with the alchemists, for whom, as Jung demonstrated in his culminating research, the creation of the spiritual gold of the philosopher's stone symbolized the God-within: the Self (1968b).

Jung also conceived of the Self as the archetype that includes and unites all archetypes— embracing but also transcending their duality. Thus, Jung also characterized the Self as "the archetype of wholeness" (1969b, p. 223).[12] Here we note Jung's indebtedness to Plato—the *locus classicus* of the idea of the archetype. As Plato defined God metaphysically, Jung defined the Self psychospiritually as the archetype of all archetypes. This, Jung asserted, is why the experience of the Self has the feel of ultimacy, a religious epiphany. For as "the highest dominant," an archetype "always has a religious or philosophical character" (Jung, 1966b, p. 80).

Much more could be said about the gnostic exegesis of Galatians 3:28. Hopefully, this brief exercise in archetypal exegesis has given the reader another perspective on the Self and an example of responding to Jung's call to read scripture psychospiritually.

PERSONALITY TYPES [13, 14]

The shadow, projection, the archetypes, the collective unconscious, the transcendent function, individuation, and the ego-Self axis—these terms from Jung's psychospiritual lexicon are the most important ones in Jung's approach to psyche. However, what is much more widely known about Jungian psychology is his theory of personality types. What have become popular ways of talking about personality types began with Jung's seminal work *Psychological Types* in 1921.

---

11.   In the shape of the cross, many Catholic exegetes throughout history, and not only gnostic ones, discerned Christ, the Man on the Cross, as the Eternal Man, the Second Adam, who reconciles all temporal opposites and tensions, as symbolized by the vertical and horizontal beams of the cross (Brown, 1979). The four sections created by this geometry also reflected the archetypal significance of the number 4 to the medieval and Renaissance Christian alchemists. See the discussion above of the *Axiom of Maria:* "Out of the third comes the fourth as the first."

12.   See Smith (1990) for an excellent exposition of Jung's idea of the Self as the archetype of wholeness.

13.   Although Jungian typology is usually presented in the context of Jung's ego psychology, it must be borne in mind that there are fundamental archetypal dynamics that infuse one's personality type. However, since the superior function is one's primary way of dealing with the world, and furthermore since one's inferior function usually is primarily a shadow issue, it seems sensible to discuss personality as primarily an ego function, particularly since it is usually approached in this way.

14.   This discussion of personality types and synchronicity is taken from my book *Inside Education: Depth Psychology in Teaching and Learning* (2007).

In his studies of ancient literature as well as ancient science and medicine, Jung noted the importance of four-pointed symmetrical forms—*quaternities*. Many great thinkers throughout history have seen quaternities as the infra-structure of everything from the human body to the cosmos. To Jung it was clear that the quaternity and the number 4 were chock-full of archetypal import. He pointed out that quaternities often consisted of two paired oppo-sites within a whole: a cross within a circle, a "unification of a double dyad" (1969b).

Jung's interest in the phenomenon was equally scholarly and clinical. Many of his patients reported dreams that had quaternities—both imagistical-ly in the form of four-chambered mandalas, thematically in the form of characters who "squared off" as paired opposites, and simply of the appear-ance of the number 4 in a dream. Observing that his patients seemed to divide into four basic personality types, which he called the thinking, feeling, sen-sate, and intuitive types, Jung further categorized these types into two sets of paired opposites: thinking/feeling and sensate/intuitive. Wishing to avoid simplistic interpretations of his theory—which have turned out to be all too common in quick personality quizzes that simplistically color-code and mis-use Jung's complex assessment of personality—Jung was quick to add that everyone had elements of all four of these ways of interacting with the world within himself.

Furthermore, he insisted that no personality type was intrinsically better than the other three. Each was simply a different way of engaging with the world, and each had its own strengths and weaknesses. Although no one should be schematically reduced to just *one* psychological function, most people tend to use one particular function more than the others. For example, athletes tend to be sensate types, therapists intuitive, poets feeling, and scien-tists thinking. Jung called this the individual's *superior function*—the oppo-site of the person's *inferior function,* which is typically banished to the shadow. Knowing what a patient's superior function is can be therapeutically useful. It has also been used in educational research to identify teaching, learning, and leadership styles. Cultural anthropologists sometimes use Jun-gian typology to identify a group's primary way of being, seeing, and acting in the world.

The Four Functions: Thinking and Feeling, Sensation and Intuition

"Thinking is the psychological function which, following its own laws, brings the contents of ideation into conceptual connection with each other" (Jung, 1971, pp. 481–482). The thinking type is analytical. He utilizes para-digms and systems to negotiate his world. Feeling, which is at the opposite pole from thinking, is entirely a *subjective* process between the *ego* and a given content, a process, moreover, that imparts to the content a definite *value* in the sense of acceptance or rejection ("like" or "dislike"). The process can also appear isolated, as it were, in the form of a *mood* (1971, pp. 434ff). Feeling types see the world in terms of emotional preferences that stem from deeply held values.

The other paired opposites are the sensate and intuitive types. The sensate negotiates his world in terms of how it presents itself to him in immediate *perceptions and sensations*. The sensate type relies upon "the psychological function that mediates the perception of a physical stimulus. It is, therefore, identical with perception. . . . Sensation is related not only to external stimuli but to inner ones, i.e., to changes in the internal organic processes" (1971, p. 461). Intuition, by contrast, "is the function that mediates perceptions in an *unconscious* way. . . . In intuition a content presents itself whole and complete, without our being able to explain or discover how this content came into existence" (1971, pp. 453–454). The intuitive person always seems to sense how or why a situation came into being and what direction it will probably take.

Jung called a person's basic type his *superior function*. The opposite pole is the person's *inferior function*. Thus, thinking types tend to have the most problems with having, sorting out, and managing their feelings, whereas feeling types struggle most with thinking analytically about their emotions and judgments. Sensate types, whose inferior function is intuition, struggle with grasping the deeper causes and broader possibilities of a given concrete fact or situation, whereas intuitive types often inhabit a world of imagination and thus are not adequately tuned in to their immediate physical realities. Additionally, each person has an *auxiliary function*—or the thing at which he is "second best." Thus, a sensate type might also be inclined to have strong emotions about immediate situations, which would make feeling his auxiliary function.

The Two Attitudes: Introversion and Extraversion

To complete his typological system, Jung added one final dimension—that of the *attitudes*. There are two fundamental attitudes: *introversion* and *extraversion*—popular terms which originated with Jung. The four functions times the two attitudes yields eight basic personality types.

Introversion is "an inward turning of *libido*, in the sense of a negative relation to the object. Interest does not move toward the object but withdraws from it into the subject. Everyone whose attitude is introverted thinks, feels, and acts in a way that clearly demonstrates that the subject is the prime motivating factor and that the object is of secondary importance" (1971, 52f).

Conversely, *extraversion* is "an outward turning of *libido*. I use this concept to denote a manifest relation of subject to object, a positive movement of subjective interest toward the object [an 'object' in this case being not only a thing but also a situation, event, or person]. Everyone in the extraverted state thinks, feels, and acts in relation to the object, and moreover in a direct and clearly observable fashion, so that no doubt can remain about his positive dependence on the object. In a sense, therefore, extraversion is a transfer of interest from subject to object" (1971, 81f).

Just as each of the four major types must be thought of only as a tendency, introversion and extraversion must be seen as ways of relating to the external world that are "habitual" but by no means exclusive.

The popular Myers-Briggs Type Indicator was devised on Jungian principles. Gardner's (1983) theory of multiple intelligences also contains elements of Jungian typology. Indeed, many currently popular devices for categorizing personality can be traced back to Jung's seminal work in typology. Jungian typology has been quite influential in educational research and practice, especially in identifying and improving teachers' and students' styles of relating to each other and the curriculum. It has also found a place in cultural anthropology as a way of discussing the basic way(s) in which a culture processes reality and the social structures that stem from that preferred mode of being, seeing, and doing.

ARCHETYPAL TRANSFERENCE
AND COUNTERTRANSFERENCE

Archetypal Transference

The reader will recall from our previous discussion of Freudian and post-Freudian theory the idea of *the transference*. It is "the experiencing of feelings, drives, attitudes, fantasies, and defenses toward a person in the present which are inappropriate to that person and are a repetition, a displacement of reactions originating in regard to significant persons of early childhood" (Greenson, 1990, p. 151). Jung added greatly to the idea of the transference. We looked above at archetypal projections made at the cultural level. Let us now turn to archetypal projections and counterprojections in psychotherapeutic settings.

Jung observed that in addition to making purely personal projections onto the analyst, the patient might also be making *archetypal* projections onto him. Not only might transferences not be merely *sexual*, they might not even be merely *personal* (Jung, 1954a, pp. 184–185; 1966a, p. 153).[15] Indeed,

---

15. See also Conforti (1999, pp. 62, 66–67, 73); Edinger (1973, p. 59); Papadopoulos (1991); San Roque (2000, pp. 117–118); and Van der Heydt (1976).

some Jungians hold that at the nucleus of every personal complex[16] (and the transference is a *complex* that a client is projecting onto the analyst) is a *transpersonal, archetypal core.*[17] Its power radiates from the depths of the collective unconscious and permeates the individual's specific identity and issues. This interaction of the personal and archetypal in the transference can occur in any emotionally charged venue, but it happens with special intensity in psychotherapy.

Archetypal Transference in the Consulting Room

Consider the rather common example of the male client who craves unconditional moral, psychological, and sometimes even physical nurturance from a female psychotherapist. She may well suspect that the client is projecting onto her his personal Oedipal needs, which his mother was never able to satisfy, not having been a good-enough mother who offered a holding environment of safe transitional spaces and transitional objects—in Winnicott's (1992) terms. Nor did she provide the opportunity for Kohut's (1978) mirroring or idealizing transferences. The patient is now attempting to find all of this in the psychotherapist.[18]

Psychoanalytically based theories have many valuable things to say about this kind of problem. What they do not allow for is the possibility that the patient is imagining in and needing from the therapist the universal attraction exerted by the archetypal Great Mother back into the cosmic womb (Neumann, 1954).[19] Only a transpersonal analysis can bring this information to the level of ego awareness and provide ways of using it to clarify and liberate consciousness.

---

16. Although "having a complex" about something has come to mean something entirely negative in popular parlance, this was not how Jung saw complexes. As he wrote, having a complex "only means that something discordant, unassimilated, and antagonistic exists, perhaps as an obstacle, but also as an incentive to greater effort, and so, perhaps, to new possibilities of achievement. In this sense, then, complexes are nodal points of psychological life which we would not wish to do without; indeed, they should not be missing, for otherwise psychic life should come to a standstill" (1971, p. 529). See Ellenberger (1970) for the historical precedents of the idea of a "complex" in pre-Jungian psychiatry.

17. See Knox (1998); Mattoon (1985); Shamdasani (2003, p. 186); Stevens (2000).

18. See Barford (2002); Basch (1989); Cozzarrelli & Silin (1989); Ekstein & Motto (1969); Field, Cohler, & Wool (1989); Mayes (2002a, 2003); and Salzberger-Wittenberg (1989) for extensive treatments of the idea of transference in pedagogical theory regarding the relationship between teacher and student in the classroom.

19. However, Freud's *nirvana principle* and *death instinct*, which resemble the all-consuming aspect of the archetypal Great Mother, address this issue in some measure and in rather archetypal terms—additional evidence of the unnecessary breach between psychoanalysis and analytical psychology, as in Glover's (1956) often unfair characterizations of Jungian psychology, which serve to unnecessarily maintain a breach between it and Freudian psychology. The fact is that (post)Freudian and (post)Jungian thought can inform each other in both theoretical and practical ways (Redfearn, 1981; Samuels, 1997; Washburn, 1995).

Archetypal Countertransference

The therapist's countertransferences—or his projections back onto his client—also have personal and archetypal components.

As just one example, it is easy to see how a male therapist, the object of "God-the-Father" projections onto him, might let it go to his head. He might get inflated and possessed by the archetype. However, it is also true that, to some degree, the therapist may healthily embody the archetype of the healer, the wise old man or the wise old woman.

Now, it is not only legitimate for a psychotherapist to draw on the power of these archetypes, but it can be vitalizing to do so as long as he does not allow himself to become possessed by the archetype. *Not* infusing one's work with archetypal energy can lead to boredom with and alienation from not only one's work but also from others and thus finally from oneself. What de Castillejo has written about general practitioners in medicine, for instance, applies to many different people in various walks of life.

> [General practitioners] have been vociferous about their unjust remuneration and inferior status in the medical hierarchy, but I have never heard them mention what is much more likely to be the fundamental nature of their unhappiness: that the *archetype of a healer* which has sustained and nourished them throughout the centuries has fallen from their shoulders leaving them as little cogs in the great machine of modern medical practice. It is not a greater share of the world's wealth they lack, but "mana." (de Castillejo, 1973, p. 22; emphasis in original)

Transference, Countertransference, and Temenos

Because of their extreme psychological importance, the archetypes generate strong emotions in us when they emerge in the form of archetypal images, and "it is this emotionality of archetypal images that endows them with dynamic effect" (Jung, as cited in Adams, 1995, p. 102). As we have seen, Jung used the word *numinous* (from the Greek word for "spirit") to describe the spiritual intensity of encountering the archetypal realm as a *mysterium tremendum et fascinans.*

When archetypal energy is fully at play in the transferential dynamics in a consulting room, the atmosphere can become electric, supercharging the therapeutic setting and turning it into a *temenos* or "sacred precinct." Consulting rooms are not the only place where this happens. Wherever people are passionately engaged with each other in a potentially transformative experience—the battlefield, the classroom, the bedroom, the meditation hall, a football field, or even the dinner table—that location can morph into a *temenos* in a transfixing flash.

Some neo-Jungians even make the intriguing claim that the idea of the *temenos* is more than merely symbolic but may involve the actual generation of psychophysical forces that form a transpersonal, quantum field in which subtle energies of the analyst and patient come into contact (Spiegelman & Mansfeld, 1996). This may to some extent explain the paranormal events that often occur in shamanic practices (Eliade, 1974; Walsh, 1990). This quantum field is fertile ground for paranormal phenomena, especially for *synchronicity* (1969b, pp. 417–531).[20]

Most people have experienced synchronicity at some time in their lives. For instance, you dream of a person whom you have not seen in thirty years, think about only once in a blue moon, have never dreamed of before, and haven't corresponded with in the last twenty-five years. But the next morning after your dream, you open your e-mail and there is a message from her that she looked you up, is passing by your city on a business trip, and wonders if you'd like to get together for lunch to talk about old times. Or you and a friend are talking about a poem by your favorite poet over lunch and you become closer than ever in that moment. Later that afternoon wandering around in the library you pick up a book that has fallen off the shelf. It is opened to that very poem. We have all had these experiences. Jung was the first to try to make sense out of them from an archetypal, transpersonal perspective.

Whenever individuals are engaged in profound *I-Thou* relationship and dialogue, archetypal dynamics are set into motion, all of them pregnant with meaning, some of them manifesting as synchronicities, in the sacred zone of the *temenos*.[21]

A synchronicity is naturally important to the person experiencing it in a specific situation. Such a "rupture of time" (Main, 2004) is even more important, however, in the larger and ongoing possibility that its very existence opens up our view—namely, the infusion of the presence of the Timeless in our daily lives. Here, the realm of the archetype and the realm of the ego come together—generating meaning in the context of relationship. Synchronicity is not only an element of Jung's vision of psyche. It is a symbol of it.

---

20.   For superb treatments of the many aspects of the phenomenon of synchronicity, see Asiz (1990); Charet (1993); Main (2004); Marshak (1998); Peat (1988); and von Franz (1992).

21.   In addition to the above referenced examinations of Jung's idea of synchronicity, the reader might wish to consult Jung's essay "Synchronicity: An Acausal Connecting Principle." However, it is considerably less clear than the work of those who have written about Jung's conception of synchronicity, and contains obscure statistical analyses of questionable value. I have written about synchronicity in educational settings (Mayes, 2003, 2005a, 2007, 2009a).

Chapter Six

Psyche as Spirit

In this book I have discussed what are generally considered to be the major themes in *The Collected Works of C. G. Jung*. My hope is that the reader will now feel more confident in approaching Jung's writings and those of the several generations of Jungians who have followed him. I have tried in writing this book to be mindful of Jung's caution against the "concretization" of the language we use to talk about psyche.

The reader will recall that by "concretization" Jung said he was referring to the error of thinking that his "abstractions, concepts, views, figures," as he put it, could ever capture the mystery of psyche. They are, he said, "specific illusions" (Jung, 1973, p. 57). But this does not make them irrelevant. His massive labor in providing us his "abstractions, concepts, views, figures" to approach that mystery is sufficient evidence that he believed they were important. For they are, after all, *specific* illusions. Concentrated and directed, they point the reader to the outskirts of psyche so that the reader might then undertake his own engagement with it.

To seek out this engagement is wisdom. To neglect it will sooner or later cause a person to fall, often tragically—as ancient Greek drama illustrates. Or, as Jung put it, "The psychological rule says that when an inner situation is not made conscious, it happens outside, as fate" (1968a, p. 71). To the extent that Jung's, or anyone's, language about psyche brings us closer to the mystery of psyche, it performs a significant duty. But it is the finger pointing at the moon, not the moon. There is no substitute for experience. This is especially true of a mystery. That experience will necessarily be different for each person, Jung insisted.

Indeed, Jung suggests throughout *The Collected Works* that psyche is not only a mystery: it may be *the* mystery. Thus, although he was, in my view, the greatest psychologist of the twentieth century, Jung concluded: "I haven't the faintest idea what 'psyche' is *in itself*' (1973, p. 57). We must be as cautious in theorizing about psyche as we must be courageous in exploring it.

What Jung therefore left us with is what I called in chapter 1 a "psycho-spiritual lexicon." Its terms, ideas, constructs, and images emerged from his own studies and musings, travails and travels, clinical work and mystical unions. These are what he offered to us from *his* journey to aid us in *our* journeys, a journey we must carry on as individuals individuating. For Jung, a crucial part of his journey was the seven years he spent in close association with Freud. We have seen how Jung, Freud's "heir apparent," ultimately broke ranks with him over the role of sexuality in the psychic economy. At considerable personal and professional expense, Jung rejected the idea, which Freud had pleaded with him to elevate to the level of a "dogma," that the psyche operated exclusively in the service of sexuality. But Jung was no friend of dogmas. Ideas must work in the service of the individual, not the other way around.

Besides, to reduce all psychodynamics to the sex drive was demeaning, Jung believed. It was a diminution of the human being. Ricoeur's (1991) characterization of Freud's approach to psychological interpretation as the "hermeneutics of suspicion"—where everything is deconstructed to reveal its dark intent—and Jung's approach to psychological interpretation as the "hermeneutics of faith"—where things are evaluated in terms of their higher potential—captures one of the fundamental differences between the two men and their views of psyche. Jung felt that Freud was accurate enough in his explorations into man as *homo sexualis.* Jung publicly honored Freud for his work throughout his life—a favor Freud never saw fit to return, by the way. But Jung finally would not budge from the idea that sexuality was only one of the planets that orbited the psychic center. Psyche's sun, he declared, was a holy hunger to find the Eternal at one's core—and from that nuclear fire to forge a link between it and the ego. In this way, our being-in-the-world would be infused with meaning at the same time as our spirituality would remain rooted. This was the great life task. It was *individuation,* the eternal taking up residence within the individual.

This idea had been stirring in Jung from at least his college days, well before he met Freud, even before Jung the Zofingia Club undergraduate, famous for his dissenting lectures about taking spiritualism and philosophy seriously in psychology, became a medical student. They continued, albeit hidden (not least of all from himself, perhaps) during his years with Freud, and then resurged and picked up speed after that, stabilizing for a long period, and finally coming to a complex crescendo in his crowning works on alchemy.

In alchemy Jung discerned, through the mists of at least five intervening centuries, the full body of individuation in the triumphant hermaphroditic figure of the conjoined King and Queen. In the archetypally male and female principles united, Jung saw emblemized the reconciliation of *all* opposites in the integral psyche. This was the real alchemical gold, the currency of eternity, minted in and for the world—but finally for more delicate transactions of the individual soul with Something or Someone beyond this world yet immanent in it.

Still, Jung was a very practical Swiss. Although scholarly, he was not an academic lost in theorizing. He was a physician. He carried a heavy caseload most of his professional life. A man who loved being a clinician and took his responsibilities seriously, Jung had to concern himself with the patient as he found him. He must help him go on in the world—as a more spiritualized human being if the therapy were to be successful, but also one who was now more personally, professionally, and culturally generative. Accordingly, Jung added much to the repertoire of ego psychology.

His first contribution was to clarify the term *ego* itself and its relationship to the *persona*—one of the several important terms that Jung added to ego-psychology. Jung portrayed the ego as "a complex of ideas which constitutes the center of my field of consciousness [that] appears to possess a high degree of continuity and identity" (1971, p. 425). The persona is what the great nineteenth-century American psychologist William James (whom Jung deeply admired) calls the "me"—what others see when they look at *me*. But my understanding of the full range of myself as a conscious being in this particular moment in personal and historical time is my "I"—who *I* believe I *essentially* am as a limited but free agent in the world. The persona should only be a functional part of that "complex of ideas" that comprise the total "I."

Jung thus cast light on two facts. First was the fact that the ego is not a static entity. It is, rather, a "complex" of dynamically varying centers of attention that crystallize in the conditions of a present situation as a means of navigating it. He also highlighted the problem of what the psychoanalyst D. W. Winnicott (1992), possibly drawing on Jung (whom *he* admired), would later call "the false self." This is when an individual becomes so preoccupied with how he appears to others that it comes to dominate him. In Jungian terms, such a person has become *persona-possessed*. The persona-possessed individual has so confused his masks for the face beneath them that he no longer *has* a face—or has forgotten what it is. Such a person has forfeited his individuality to become just a social category—and caricature—and is then the perfect puppet of the state.

This is something Jung greatly feared would become—indeed, was *already* becoming—the lot of "modern man," who, vacated of those living symbols that alone give life, was now "in search of a soul" (Jung, 1965). But then again, Jung's career was carried on in every case in the service of the symbol, his mission to help symbol-bereft modern man find new ones—often, paradoxically, by restoring old ones in psychospiritual interpretations that would make those ancient symbol systems credible and creative once more. This would move the individual and culture forward. It was our only hope in the wake of two worldwide conflagrations, and with a third one, Jung feared, just around the corner—and this one with the potential to set the world aflame in a final fire. Against the charge by his hissing critics that Jung cared only about the individual and bypassed political problems, an entire volume of the *Collected Works* and many essays in the others provide a calm rejoinder (1970b).

Jung refined Freud's definition of the subconscious as merely the place where we stuff all our dirty laundry—whether we were the ones who soiled it or someone else who did. These things we banish to unawareness for the simple reason that they are too hard to be aware of. Therapy was the means, according to Freud, of surfacing such things so that we could examine and manage them, purposefully recognize and gradually rehabilitate them, in therapy. Otherwise they would continue to haunt and harry us.

Jung agreed with all of this in part. But he said that what Freud had called the subconscious and relegated to the status of a basement overflowing with trash was more than just that. Yes, that basement had plenty of trash in it. But it also had diamonds among the debris—proclivities, gifts, and hopes that we had banished to unawareness not because they were bad but because it was too hard for us to acknowledge them and still survive as a child or youth in an environment that condemned them. Now, as adults, there might well be ways to draw upon them in the furtherance of our psychospiritual unfolding.

In Jungian therapy the goal is not simply to bring to awareness difficult things so as to contain their effects; it is also to reclaim something beautiful in the shadow in order to resuscitate and empower it. The difference between Freud's hermeneutics of suspicion and Jung's of hope is nowhere clearer than in how they understood and worked with personal material that had been exiled to forgetfulness.

Jung also rather paradoxically advanced our understanding of ego dynamics by demonstrating their limitations. An inherent problem in psychotherapy that is concerned only with addressing the ego and its vicissitudes is that it tends not to see (or not to credit very much) the ego's desire to transcend itself, to move into the realm of the *trans*-personal. In other words, strictly ego-psychology is inherently limited because it is not *ecstatic*—taking that word in its etymological sense as *ex-stasis,* a going beyond oneself and the existential situation in which one is presently embedded—lifting oneself off the launch pad of temporality toward the timeless and universal, ascending from the personal to the transpersonal. Jung was one of the first modern Western psychologists—and remains the most impactful—to identify this transcendental need and offer a possible star chart for the trek to the transpersonal. It is for this reason that conventional psychology dismisses Jung as just a fuzzy mystic.

A mystic he was. Fuzzy he was not. He was as meticulous as he was fearless in carrying on his own journey toward the Eternal in himself, and in helping his patients do the same thing in the manner and matters that suited them best. And all of this he accomplished with a sense of the poetic that is still unequalled in the annals of Western psychology.

No starry-eyed romantic, Jung warned that this movement toward the Divine could never be valid or fruitful—would not really *count*—if it were merely an attempt to flee from dealing with ego issues that simply had to be resolved. The ego must be sound if its eventual ascent toward connection with the Eternal were to be viable. Living among the stars is lovely, but it requires a sturdy spaceship constructed on earth to get to them. New Age paperbacks gulped down in bookstore coffee shops along with vanilla frappes, he would abhor. The ego-structure must be practical and strong or else a person's "spirituality" would at best prove to be a lie and at worst would result in madness.

Jung was also the first modern Western psychologist to call attention to the fact that the second half of life is valuable in its own right—in many ways even more important than the first half of life. For the second half of our life we should aim at something more than the ultimately time-bound landscape of our will, work, romantic love, and family. Having carved out our social world with all the tools the ego can marshal, we find that that world is now "set" in most of its essential respects by middle age—defined and delimited by the choices we have made, and their often sad consequences.

For no matter how hard we try to deny it, one day we will come up against the hard fact that our ego-engendered world—however grand or small, ornate or simple—is one that must someday fall regardless of how hard we try to extend its length of days. We all live under the cloying sign of our eventual death as we run the short circuit of our transiting horoscopes. As T. S. Eliot wrote, "That which is only living can only die."

This recognition—along, perhaps, with a hope for a life beyond this life—will ideally stimulate us to pursue the transcendent life, the symbolic one, especially because evidence of our mortality begins to appear around midlife with a growing grimness. Our body shows increasing signs of wear and tear in its limited shelf life. Even worse, our heart is scarred with the jagged marks that commemorate how often it broke and how terribly, and—most terribly—how often it broke others'. Time begins to move more and more quickly as we see the terminal station at the end of the earthly train ride, approaching with mounting speed.

We must sooner or later look around at our world—the one we have created, the one that has created us, and its contracting horizons—and ask, "Is this all there is?" Jung's body of work urgently calls our attention to this critical developmental juncture. It has come to be known as the "midlife crisis"—another of Jung's ideas that he receives insufficient credit for. The midlife crisis can be either a calamity or a blessing, depending upon how skillfully we respond to it.

The root of the word "crisis" is Greek *krisein,* which does not necessarily connote something negative but simply means to arrive at a decision point, a turning point. Will we use this "crisis" as the occasion to choose the higher road to individuation—one where the imperiled ego will find new life in a transfiguring encounter with the Eternal? Will we dedicate ourselves to forging an ego-Self axis that both emanates from and finds its fruition in and as our Center? Or will we ignore the call to transcendence and merely follow the same externally imposed, linear state highway littered with outdated insurance policies, rusted golf trophies, divorce decrees, and empty whiskey bottles? This is the path to an inglorious death on the dull plains of an unregenerated ego. Equally inglorious is the path of cosmetic surgery, drugs, and sexual adventurism to try to recapture a youth that no longer applies, and (truth be told) is long gone in any case.

The choice could not be more dramatic or consequential. On one hand lies death by boredom or folly. On the other hand is a life satisfactorily led, and, in some individuals, the hope of a life beyond this life through the emergence of the Self and the growth of the ego in communion with it.

The better path—the road to individuation—is not without its own brands of pain. It is still life on planet Earth after all, where part of the job description of being human entails suffering. The first of the Buddha's Four Noble Truths is that "Life is suffering"—also the message of Christ from the cross.

Pain is integral to life despite all the promises (sometimes blaring, sometimes seductive) from both the Right and Left that we will be happy if we just follow their programs for political salvation. Pain is indispensable, even "good," when seen against the backdrop of eternity, and this is so despite the seductive claim of cognitive behaviorism that we can be glad and "functional" (i.e., machines running endless laps on the corporate racetrack) simply by changing negative thought and behavior patterns.

As Jung said, the purpose of psychotherapy is not to escape pain. A painless life is impossible, with or without therapy. Rather, the goal of psychotherapy is to find meaning in pain. This meaning *does* provide its own kind of comfort, but it is not the kind of comfort that the world can either understand or offer. "Peace I leave with you," Jesus said in the Farewell Discourse to his disciples at the end of St. John's Gospel—however, "not as the world gives peace, give I it unto you" (John 14:27). Rather, the peace and also the power, the certainty and also the creativity that may come in the second half of life lie in the humble knowledge that we are doing our best to move toward our spiritual center, where the Divine must reside in an individual—if it is to reside anywhere at all.

The Collected Works of C. G. Jung does not seek to impose upon its readers a paradigm of psyche. It shares with its readers how Jung pursued the

Divine within *himself,* helped others locate and live it within *themselves,* and stands as an open invitation to each of us to do the same. The major terms in Jung's lexicon that were presented in this book are each a possible aspect of the individual's search for the Self, a different vector of approach to the same mystery.

For instance, there is the stranger within us, the *anima* and *animus,* the interior "Other," whom we have always known yet never known. It is the voice within us always whispering: *Come hither. That which you have done and been is not all that you can do or be. There is more than the triumphs and tragedies of this world. You have triumphed. You have failed. Let those things now be. What you seek is in you. It is me. It is you. Tat tvam asi. Come hither.*

Anima and *animus* are enigmatically compelling because that is precisely what a mystery is. Both before and beyond our sexual identity, the *anima* and *animus* are ambassadors of the Self, Something or Someone who calls us, but whom we must also call out, court, and wed within in order to consummate the process in the inner intercourse of male and female, which is everyone's task.

Past the first, forbidding strangeness of that "other" realm over which the *anima* and *animus* have stood guard, just beyond that threshold, we find our natural habitat as a soul. But, although it is the soul's *natural* habitat, it is also a habitat that is an *opus contra naturam,* a work against nature—or better, beyond nature. Contrary to the nagging needs of the noisy ego, and to a different rhythm than the ordinary ticking of the clockwork rational mind, we find the zone of the *opus contra naturam* by *trans*-rationally reconciling opposites.

This is the potency and poetry of the transcendent function. It moves us to a higher plane. There, the language of the land is poetry. The people, things, and events we encounter are symbolic, sometimes synchronistic. And the shaping force in the wind of the collective unconscious that sweeps that landscape is the archetypes. "God has indeed, made an inconceivably divine and mysteriously contradictory image of himself, without the help of man, and implanted it in man's unconscious as an archetype, an archetypal light" (Jung, 1973, p. 57).

In that light, on that land, we, now in the *temenos,* exist under the numinous pull of the *mysterium tremendum et fascinans.* There, we discover that we have been invested with a dual nature. We are living in two intersecting dimensions of being at once: that of ego and Self, the normal and its paranormal ruptures; the daily round and the Eternal Circle; a wise involvement in the world and an even wiser transcendence of it.

These are the passages toward individuation. Passages toward it, not a final arrival at it. Individuation is a recursive process. We spiral up, we spiral down; we tend closer and closer to the Self's many habitations, never fully attaining them, but in ever nearer approximations of them.

Working with and witnessing to all of this in terms that are poetic *and* scientific—and, finally, more poetic than scientific—*The Collected Works of C. G. Jung* is not only *concerned* with symbols, but, taken all in all, is *itself* a symbol: the symbol of Jung's own pilgrimage to ultimacy. The "abstractions, concepts, views, figures" he offers—items of a partial language, entries in a potential lexicon—each invites the reader's personal interpretation in engaging the archetypal issue that must occupy us all: how best to live in the world under the sponsorship of the Divine.

References

Adams, M. (1995). *The multicultural imagination: "Race," color, and the unconscious*. London: Routledge.

Adler, A. (1930). *The education of children*. South Bend, IN: George Allen and Unwin, Ltd.

Ahlstrom, S. (1972). *A religious history of the American people*. New Haven: Yale University Press.

Aichhorn, A. (1935/1965). *Wayward youth: A psychoanalytic study of delinquent children, illustrated by actual case histories*. New York: Viking Press.

Aichhorn, A. (1990). The transference. In A. Esman (Ed.), *Essential papers on transference* (pp. 94–109). New York: New York University Press.

Alister, I., & Hauke, C. (Eds.). (1998). *Contemporary Jungian analysis: Post-Jungian perspectives from the Society of Analytic Psychology*. London: Routledge.

Almon, J. (1999). From cognitive learning to creative thinking. In J. Kane (Ed.), *Education, information, and transformation: Essays on learning and thinking* (pp. 249–269). Upper Saddle River, NJ: Prentice-Hall.

Ammerman, N., & Roof, W. (Eds.). (1995). *Work, family, and religion in contemporary society*. New York: Routledge.

Anthony, E. (1989). The psychoanalytic approach to learning theory (with more than a passing reference to Piaget). In K. Field, B. Cohler, & G. Wool (Eds.), *Learning and education: Psychoanalytic perspectives* (pp. 99–126). Madison, CT: International Universities Press, Inc.

Appel, S. (1996). *Positioning subjects: Psychoanalysis and critical educational studies*. New York: Bergin and Garvey.

Assagioli, R. (1965). *Psychosynthesis: A manual of principles and techniques*. New York: Penguin Group.

Assagioli, R. (1973). *The act of will*. New York: The Viking Press.

Asiz, R. (1990). *C. G. Jung's psychology of religion and synchronicity*. Albany: State University of New York Press.

Astor, J. (1998). Fordham's development of Jung in the context of infancy and childhood. In I. Alister & C. Hauke (Eds.), *Contemporary Jungian analysis: Post-Jungian perspectives from the Society of Analytical Psychology* (pp. 17–26). London: Routledge.

Augustine, St. (2000). *Confessions*. New York: Penguin Books.

Bair, D. (2003). *Jung: A biography*. Boston: Little, Brown.

Balota, D. (2004). *Cognitive psychology: Key readings in cognition*. New York: Psychology Press.

Barford, D. (Ed.). (2002). *The ship of thought: Essays on psychoanalysis and learning*. London: Karnac Books.

Barnaby, K., & D'Acierno, P. (Eds.). (1990). *C. G. Jung and the humanities: Toward a hermeneutics of culture.* Princeton, NJ: Princeton University Press.

Barrett, W. (1967). The flow of time. In R. Gale (Ed.), *The philosophy of time* (pp. 354–376). Garden City, NY: Anchor Books.

Barzun, J. (2000). *From dawn to decadence: 500 years of Western cultural life.* New York: HarperCollins.

Basch, M. (1989). The teacher, the transference, and development. In K. Field, B. Cohler, & G. Wool (Eds.), *Learning and education: Psychoanalytic perspectives* (pp. 771–788). Madison, CT: International Universities Press, Inc.

Bateson, G. (1972). *Steps to an ecology of mind.* New York: Ballantine Books.

Beck, J. (1995). *Cognitive therapy: Basics and beyond.* New York: Guilford Press.

Becker, C. (1966). *The heavenly city of the eighteenth-century philosophers.* New Haven: Yale University Press.

Beebe, J. (1986). Toward a Jungian analysis of character. In A. Casement (Ed.), *Post-Jungians today: Key papers in contemporary analytical psychology* (pp. 53–66). Routledge: London.

Belenky, M., Clinchy, B., Goldberger, N., & Tarule, J. (1986). *Women's way of knowing.* New York: Basic Books.

Belmonte, T. (1990). The trickster and the sacred clown: Revealing the logic of the unspeakable. In K. Barnaby & P. D'Acierno (Eds.), *C. G. Jung and the humanities: Toward a hermeneutics of culture* (pp. 45–66). Princeton, NJ: Princeton University Press.

Berger, P. (1967). *The sacred canopy: Elements of a sociological theory of religion.* New York: Doubleday and Company.

Berger, P. (1995). From the crisis of religion to the crisis of secularity. In S. Bruce (Ed.), *The sociology of religion* (pp. 636–646). Aldershot, UK: The International Library of Critical Writings in Sociology: An Elgar Reference Collection.

Berger, P., & Luckman, T. (1995). Sociology of religion and sociology of knowledge. In S. Bruce (Ed.), *The sociology of religion* (pp. 174–184). Aldershot, UK: The International Library of Critical Writings in Sociology.

Bergson, H. (1987). *Creative evolution.* Lanham, MD: University Press of America.

Bernstein, B. (1996). *Pedagogy, symbolic control, and identity: Theory, research, critique.* London: Taylor and Francis.

Best, S., & Kellner, D. (1991). *Postmodern theory.* New York: The Guilford Press.

Bishop, P. (2007). *Analytical psychology and German Classical aesthetics: Goethe, Schiller, and Jung.* London: Routledge.

Blackwell Mayes, P. (2005). The use of sandtray therapy techniques in examining the sense of calling among pre-service public school administrators. A dissertation: Department of Psychology, Southern California University for Professional Studies, Santa Ana, California.

Block, A. (1997). *I'm only bleeding: Education as the practice of social violence against children.* New York: Peter Lang.

Blumer, H. (1969). *Symbolic interactionism.* Englewood Cliffs, NJ: Prentice-Hall.

Bly, R. (1990). *Iron John: A book about men.* Reading, MA: Addison-Wesley.

Bockus, F. (1990). The archetypal self: Theological values in Jung's psychology. In R. Moore & D. Meckel (Eds.), *Jung and Christianity in dialogue: Faith, feminism, and hermeneutics.* New York: Paulist Press.

Bocock, R., & Thompson, K. (Eds.). (1985). *Religion and ideology.* Manchester: Manchester University Press.

Bodkin, M. (1974). *Archetypal patterns in poetry: Psychological studies of imagination.* Oxford: Oxford University Press.

Bohm, D. (1986). Time, the implicate order, and pre-space. In D. Griffin (Ed.), *Physics and the ultimate significance of time* (pp. 177–208). Albany: State University of New York Press.

Bolt, R. (1988). *A man for all seasons: A drama in two acts.* New York: Samuel French.

Bourdieu, P. (1977). Cultural reproduction. In J. Karabel & A. Halsey (Eds.), *Power and ideology in education* (pp. 487–507). New York: Oxford University Press.

Bowles, S., & Gintis, H. (1976). *Schooling in capitalist America.* New York: Basic Books.

Bradway, K. (2001). Symbol dictionary: Symbolic meanings of sandplay images. *Journal of Sandplay Therapy, 10*(1), 9–110.

Bradway, K. (2002). Response to Clifford Mayes & Pamela Blackwell Mayes paper. *Journal of Sandplay Therapy*, *11*(2), 125–129.

Britzman, D. (2003). *After-Education: Anna Freud, Melanie Klein, and psychoanalytic histories of learning.* Albany: State University of New York Press.

Brooke, Roger. (1991). *Jung and phenomenology.* London: Routledge.

Brown, G., Phillips M., & Shapiro, S. (1976). *Getting it all together: Confluent education.* Bloomington, IN: Phi Delta Kappa Educational Foundation.

Brown, R. (1979). *The community of the Beloved Disciple.* New York: Paulist Press.

Bruce, S. (Ed.). (1995). *The sociology of religion* (vol. 1). Brookfield, VT: Edward Elgar Publishing Company.

Bruner, J. (1996). *The culture of education.* Cambridge, MA: Harvard University Press.

Buber, M. (1965). *I and thou.* New York: Vintage.

Bultmann, R. (1971). *The Gospel of John: A commentary.* Louisville, KY: Westminster John Knox Press.

Burke, K. (1989). *On symbols and society.* J. Gusfield (Ed.). Chicago: University of Chicago Press.

Butcher, C. A. (2009). *The cloud of unknowing with the book of privy counsel.* Boston: Shambhala.

Campbell, J. (1949). *The hero with a thousand faces.* Princeton, NJ: Princeton University Press.

Camus, A. (2002). *The myth of Sisyphus: And other essays.* New York: Random House.

Carier, C. (1976). The ethics of a therapeutic man: C. G. Jung. *The Psychoanalytic Review*, *63*(1): 115–146.

Carotenuto, A. (1994). *The call of the Daimon.* Wilmette, IL: Chiron Publications.

Casement, A. (Ed.). (1986). *Post-Jungians today: Key papers in contemporary analytical psychology.* London: Routledge.

Castoriadis, C. (1994). Psychoanalysis and politics. In S. Shamdasani & M. Münchow (Eds.), *Speculations after Freud: Psychoanalysis, philosophy, and culture* (pp. 1–12). London: Routledge.

Chadwick, O. (1990). *A history of Christianity.* Oxford: Oxford University Press.

Chapman, J. H. (1988). *Jung's three theories of religious experience.* Lewiston, NY: Edwin Mellen Press.

Chardin, T. de. (1975). *The phenomenon of man.* New York: Perennial Library.

Charet, F. X. (1993). *Spiritualism and the foundations of C. G. Jung's philosophy.* Albany: State University of New York Press.

Chevalier, J. (1994). *A dictionary of symbols.* Oxford: Blackwell.

Chinen, A. (1989). *In the ever after: Fairy tales and the second half of life.* Wilmette, IL: Chiron Publications.

Christopher, E., & McFarland Solomon, H. (Eds.). (2000). *Jungian thought in the modern world.* London: Free Association Books.

Chodorow, N. (1978). *The reproduction of mothering: Psychoanalysis and the sociology of gender.* Berkeley: University of California Press.

Clift, W. (1993). *Jung and Christianity: The challenge of reconciliation.* New York: Crossroad.

Chomsky, N. (1968). *Aspects of the theory of syntax.* Cambridge, MA: MIT Press.

Cohen, S. (2002). Learning: A Jungian perspective. In D. Barford (Ed.), *The ship of thought: Essays on psychoanalysis and learning* (pp. 64–83). London: Karnac Books.

Cohler, B. (1989). Psychoanalysis and education: Motive, meaning, and self. In K. Field, B. Cohler, & G. Wool (Eds.), *Learning and education: Psychoanalytic perspectives* (pp. 11–84). Madison, CT: International Universities Press, Inc.

Coles, R. (1986). *The moral life of children.* Boston: Atlantic Monthly Press.

Coles, R. (1990). *The spiritual life of children.* Boston: Houghton Mifflin.

Colman, W. (2000). Models of the self. In E. Christopher & H. McFarland Solomon (Eds.), *Jungian thought in the modern world* (pp. 3–19). London: Free Association Books.

Comer, R. (1998). *Abnormal psychology* (3rd ed.). New York: W.H. Freeman and Co.

Conforti, M. (1999). *Field, form, and fate: Patterns in mind, nature, and psyche.* Woodstock, CT: Spring Publications.

Conger, J., & Galambos, J. (1997). *Adolescence and youth: Psychological development in a changing world.* New York: Longman.

Cooper, A. (1990). Changes in psychoanalytic ideas: Transference interpretation. In A. Esman (Ed.), *Essential papers on transference* (pp. 94–109). New York: New York University Press.

Coppleston, F. (1961). *Medieval philosophy.* New York: Harper and Row.

Corsini, R., & Wedding, D. (Eds.). (1995). *Current psychotherapies* (5th ed.). Itasca, IL: F.E. Peacock Publishers

Cortright, B. (1997). *Psychotherapy and spirit: Theory and practice in transpersonal psychotherapy.* Albany: State University of New York Press.

Coward, H. (1985). *Jung and Eastern thought.* Albany: State University of New York Press.

Cozzarrelli, L., & Silin, M. (1989). The effects of narcissistic transferences on the teaching-learning process. In K. Field, B. Cohler, & G. Wool (Eds.), *Learning and education: Psychoanalytic perspectives* (pp. 809–824). Madison, CT: International Universities Press, Inc.

Crain, W. (2010). *Theories of development: Concepts and* applications (6th ed.). New York: Pearson.

Cremin, L. (1988). *American education: The metropolitan experience.* New York: Harper and Row.

Croce, B. (1953). The primacy of the symbol. In E. Vivas & M. Krieger (Eds.), *Theories of aesthetics* (pp. 234–256). New York: Reinhart.

Dante. (1954). *The inferno.* (J. Ciardi, Trans.). New York: Signet Classics.

Dass, R. (1984). *The only dance there is.* New York: Anchor Books.

De Castillejo, I. (1973). *Knowing woman: A feminine psychology.* New York: Harper and Row.

De Gruchy, J. (1991). Jung and religion: A theological assessment. In R. Papadopoulos & G. Saayman (Eds.), *Jung in modern perspective: The master and his legacy* (pp. 193–203). Dorset, UK: Prism Press.

Devine, D. (1995). Prejudice and out-group perception. In A. Tesser (Ed.), *Advanced social psychology* (pp. 467–524). New York: McGraw-Hill.

Diel, P. (1988). *Symbolism in the Gospel of John.* (N. Marans, Trans.). San Francisco: Harper and Row.

Dourley, J. (1981). *C. G. Jung and Paul Tillich: Psyche as sacrament.* Toronto: Inner City Books.

Dourley, J. (1984). *The illness that we are: A Jungian critique of Christianity.* Toronto: Inner City Books.

Dourley, J. (1987). *Love, celibacy and inner marriage.* Toronto: Inner City Books.

Dourley, J. (1990). Jung, Tillich, and aspects of Western Christian development. In R. Moore & D. Meckel (Eds.), *Jung and Christianity in dialogue: Faith, feminism, and hermeneutics* (pp. 63–103). New York: Paulist Press.

Drew, E. (1949). *T. S. Eliot: The design of his poetry.* New York: Scribner's and Sons.

Duberman, M. (1972). *Black Mountain: An exploration in community.* Evanston, IL: Northwest University Press.

Dusek, J. (1994). *Adolescent development and behavior.* New York: Macmillan.

Dweck, C. (1999). *Self-theories: Their role in motivation, personality, and development.* Philadelphia, PA: Psychology Press.

Eagle, M. (1993). *Recent developments in psychoanalysis: A critical evaluation.* Cambridge, MA: Harvard University Press.

Edinger, E. (1973). *Ego and archetype: Individuation and the religious function of the psyche.* Baltimore: Penguin Press.

Edinger, E. (1985). *Anatomy of the psyche: Alchemical symbolism in psychotherapy.* La Salle, IL: Open Court.

Edinger, E. (1992). *Transformation of the God-image: An elucidation of Jung's "Answer to Job."* Toronto: Inner City Books.

Eisner, E., & Vallance, E. (1985). *The educational imagination: On the design and evaluation of school programs.* New York: Macmillan.

Ekstein, R., & Motto, R. (Eds.). (1969). *From learning for love to love of learning: Essays on psychoanalysis and education.* New York: Brunner/Mazel Publishers.

Eliot, T. (1971). *T. S. Eliot: The complete poems and plays: 1909–1950.* New York: Harcourt, Brace and World, Inc.

Eliade, M. (1974). *Shamanism: Archaic techniques of ecstasy.* Princeton, NJ: Princeton University Press.

Ellenberger, H. (1970). *The discovery of the unconscious: The history and evolution of dynamic psychiatry.* New York: Basic Books.

Emerson, R. W. (1958). *The collected works of Ralph Waldo Emerson.* New York: Modern Library.

Engler, J. (1986). Therapeutic aims in psychotherapy and meditation. In K. Wilber, J. Engler, & D. Brown (Eds.), *Transformations of consciousness: Conventional and contemplative perspectives on development* (pp. 17–52). Boston: Shambhala.

Epstein, M. (1995). *Thoughts without a thinker.* New York: Basic Books.

Erikson, E. (1963). *Childhood and society.* New York: W.W. Norton.

Erikson, E. (1997). *The life cycle completed.* New York: W.W. Norton.

Fairbairn, W. R. D. (1992). *Psychoanalytic studies of the personality.* London: Routledge.

Fay, B. (1987). *Critical social science: Liberation and its limits.* Ithaca, NY: Cornell University Press.

Fay, B. (2000). *Contemporary philosophy of social science: A multicultural approach.* Oxford: Blackwell Publishers Ltd.

Feinstein, D., & Krippner, S. (1988). *Personal mythology: Using rituals, dreams, and imagination to discover your inner story.* Los Angeles: Jeremy P. Tarcher, Inc.

Ferrer, J. (2002). *Revisioning transpersonal theory: A participatory vision of human spirituality.* Albany, NY: State University of New York Press.

Ferrucci, P. (1982). *What we may be: Techniques for psychological and spiritual growth through psychosynthesis.* Los Angeles: Jeremy P. Tarcher, Inc.

Field, B., Cohler, K., & Wool, G. (Eds.). (1989). *Learning and education: Psychoanalytic Perspectives.* Madison, CT: International Universities Press, Inc.

Fierz, H. (1991). *Jungian psychiatry.* Einsielden, Switzerland: Daimon Verlag.

Fitzgerald, F. Scott. (1936, February). The crack up. *Esquire Magazine.*

Flowers, B. (2000). Practicing politics in the economic myth. In. T. Singer (Ed.), *The vision thing: Myth, politics, and psyche in the world* (pp. 207–212). London: Routledge.

Forbes, S. (2003). *Holistic education: An analysis of its nature and ideas.* Brandon, VT: Foundation for Educational Renewal Press.

Fordham, M. (1978). *Jungian psychology: A study in analytical psychology.* New York: John Wiley and Sons.

Fordham. M. (1985). *Explorations into the self.* London: Analytic Press.

Fordham, M. (1994). *Children as individuals.* London: Free Association Books.

Foucault, M. (1961). *Madness and civilization.* New York: Vintage Books.

Foucault, M. (1972). *The archaeology of knowledge.* New York: Pantheon Books.

Foucault, M. (1979). *Discipline and punish.* New York: Vintage Books.

Fowler, J. (1981). *Stages of faith: The psychology of human development and the quest for meaning.* San Francisco: Harper and Row.

Frankl, V. (1967). *Man's search for meaning.* New York: Washington Square Press.

Frazer, J. (1935). *The golden bough.* New York: The Macmillan Company.

Freire, P. (1970). *The pedagogy of the oppressed.* New York: Seabury Press.

Freud, S. (1957). On narcissism: An introduction. In J. Rickman (Ed.), *A general selection from the works of Sigmund Freud* (pp. 104–123). Garden City, NY: Doubleday Anchor Books.

Freud, S. (1990). The dynamics of transference. In A. Esman (Ed.), *Essential papers on transference* (pp. 28–36). New York: New York University Press.

Frey-Rohn, L. (1974). *From Freud to Jung: A comparative study of the psychology of the unconscious.* New York: G. P. Putnam's Sons.

Frye, N. (1957). *Anatomy of criticism: Four essays.* New York: Atheneum.

Gadamer, H. (1980). *Dialogue and dialectic: Eight hermeneutical studies on Plato.* New Haven: Yale University Press.

Gardner, H. (1983). *Frames of mind.* New York: Basic Books.

Gauvain, M. (2001). *The social context of cognitive development* (vol. 4). New York: The Guilford Press

Gellert, M. (1994). *Modern mysticism: Jung, Zen, and the good still hand of God.* York Beach, Maine: Nicolas-Hays.

Gellert, M. (2001). *The fate of America: An inquiry into national character.* Washington, DC: Brassey's, Inc.

Giddens, A. (1990). *The consequences of modernity.* Stanford: Stanford University Press.

Giddens, A. (1991). *Modernity and self-identity: Self and society in the late modern age.* Stanford: Stanford University Press.

Giddens, A. (2002). *Runaway world: How globalization is reshaping our lives.* London: Profile.

Gilligan, C. (1982). *In a different voice: Psychological theory and women's development.* Cambridge, MA: Harvard University Press.

Ginsberg, A. (2001). *Howl and other poems.* San Francisco: City Lights Books.

Giroux, H., & Mirsiades, C. (2001). *The corporate university: Culture and pedagogy in the new millennium.* Lanham, MD: Rowman & Littlefield.

Gitlin, T. (1995*). The twilight of common dreams: Why America is wracked by culture wars.* New York: Holt.

Glover, E. (1956). *Freud or Jung?* New York: Basic Books.

Goethe, J. W. v. (1994). *Faust: Parts one and two.* New York: Continuum.

Goffman, E. (1997). *The Goffman reader.* C. Lemert & A. Branaman (Eds.). London: Blackwell.

Goldbrunner, J. (1964). *Individuation: A study of the depth psychology of Carl Gustav Jung.* Notre Dame, IN: University of Notre Dame Press.

Grant, C. (Ed.). (1995). *Educating for diversity: An anthology of multicultural voices* (pp. 143–147). Lanham, MD: Rowman & Littlefield.

Gray, R. (1996). *Archetypal explorations: An integrative approach to human behavior.* London: Routledge.

Greeley, A. (1974). *Unsecular man: The persistence of religion.* New York: Delta Books.

Greene, M. (1974). Cognition, consciousness, and curriculum. In W. Pinar (Ed.), *Heightened consciousness, cultural revolution, and curriculum theory* (pp. 69–83). Berkeley: McCutchan Publishing.

Greenson, R. (1990). The working alliance and the transference neurosis. In A. Esman (Ed.), *Essential papers on transference* (pp. 150–171). New York: New York University Press.

Greenspan, M. (2004). *Healing through the dark emotions:* The *wisdom of grief, fear, and despair.* Boston: Shambhala.

Grof, S. (1988). *The adventure of self-discovery: Dimensions of consciousness and new perspectives in psychotherapy.* Albany: State University of New York Press.

Gross, S. (2000). Racism in the shadow of Jung: The myth of white supremacy. In E. Christopher & H. McFarland Solomon (Eds.), *Jungian thought in the modern world* (pp. 71–86). London: Free Association Books.

Grotstein, J. (2000). *Who is the dreamer who dreams the dream? A study of psychic presences.* Hillsdale, NJ: Analytic Press.

Gutek, G. (2000). *American education: 1945–2000.* Prospect Heights, IL: Waveland Press.

Hall, A. (2002). Psychoanalytic research on learning: An appraisal and some suggestions. In D. Barford (Ed.), *The ship of thought: Essays on psychoanalysis and learning* (pp. 17–40). New York: Karnac Books.

Hall, J. (1985). Differences between Jung and Hillman. In L. Martin & J. Goss (Eds.), *Essays on the study of Jung and religion* (pp.144–164). Lanham, MD: University Press of America.

Halliday, M. (1978). *Language as social semiotic.* London: Edward Arnold.

Handy, W., & Westbrook, M. (Eds.). (1974). *Twentieth century criticism: The major statements.* New York: Macmillan.

Harding, E. (1963). *Psychic energy: Its source and its transformation.* New York: Putnam Publishing.

Harding, E. (1970). *The way of all women.* New York: Putnam.

Hardy, J. (1987). *A psychology with a soul: Psychosynthesis in evolutionary context.* New York: Routledge & Kegan Paul.

Hartshorne, C. (1984). *Omnipotence and other theological mistakes.* Albany: State University of New York Press.

Hauke, C. (2000). *Jung and the postmodern: The interpretation of realities.* London: Routledge.

Heath, S. (1983). *Ways with words: Language, life, and work in communities and classrooms.* Cambridge: Cambridge University Press.

Hegel, G. W. F. (1992). *Hegel's phenomenology of spirit: Selections.* University Park: Pennsylvania State University Press.

Heidegger, M. (1964). *Being and time.* Albany: State University of New York Press.

Heisig, J. (1979). *Imago Dei: A study of C.G. Jung's psychology of religion.* Lewisburg, PA: Bucknell University Press.

Henderson, J. (1984). Reflections on the history and practice of Jungian analysis. In M. Stein (Ed.), *Jungian analysis* (pp. 3–26). Boston and London: Shambhala.

Henderson, J. (1991). The Jungian interpretation of history and its educational implications. In R. Papadopoulos & G. Saayman (Eds.), *Jung in modern perspective: The master and his legacy* (pp. 245–255). Garden City, NY: Avery Publishing Group.

Henderson, J. (2000). The inner vision and social organization. In T. Singer (Ed.), *The vision thing: Myth, politics, and psyche in the world.* London: Routledge.

Herzog, E. (1967). *Psyche and death.* New York: The C. G. Jung Foundation for Analytical Studies.

Hick, J. (1989). *An interpretation of religion: Human responses to the transcendent.* New Haven: Yale University Press.

Hillman, J. (1976). *Re-visioning psychology.* New York: Harper and Row.

Hobsbawm, E. (1999). *Industry and empire.* London: The New Press.

Hoeller, S. (1982). *The Gnostic Jung and The Seven Sermons to the Dead.* Wheaton, IL: Theosophical Publishing House.

Homans, P. (1985). C. G. Jung: Christian or post-Christian psychologist? In L. Martin & J. Goss (Eds.), *Essays on the study of Jung and religion* (pp. 26–44). Lanham, MD: University Press of America.

Homans, P. (1989). *The ability to mourn: Disillusionment and the social origins of psychoanalysis.* Chicago: University of Chicago Press.

Homans, P. (1990). Jung: Christian or Post-Christian psychologist? In R. Moore & D. Meckel (Eds.), *Jung and Christianity in dialogue: Faith, feminism, and hermeneutics* (pp. 21–37). New York: Paulist Press.

Homans, P. (1995). *Jung in context: Modernity and the making of a psychology.* Chicago: University of Chicago Press.

Houston, J. (1996). *A mythic life: Learning to live our greater story.* San Francisco: Harper Collins Publishers.

Huebner, D. (1999). *The lure of the transcendent: Collected essays by Dwayne E. Huebner.* London: Lawrence Erlbaum Associates.

Huxley, A. (1950). *Brave new world.* New York: Harper and Brothers.

Huxley, J. (1945). *The perennial philosophy.* New York: Harper.

Hyde, L. (1998). *Trickster makes this world: Mischief, myth, and art.* New York: Farrar, Straus, and Giroux.

Jacobi, J. (1974). *Complex/archetype/symbol in the psychology of C. G. Jung.* Princeton, NJ: Princeton University Press.

Jacoby, M. (1984). *The analytic encounter: Transference and human relationship.* Toronto: Inner City Books.

Jadot, L. (1991). From the symbol in psychoanalysis to the anthropology of the imaginary. R. Papadopoulos & G. Saayman (Eds.), *Jung in modern perspective: The master and his legacy* (pp. 109–118). Dorset, UK: Prism Press.

Jaffé, A. (1975). *The myth of meaning: Jung and the expansion of consciousness.* (R. F. C. Hull, Trans.). New York: Penguin Books.

Jaffé, A. (1989). *Was C. G. Jung a mystic? And other essays.* Einseideln, Switzerland: Daimon Verlag.

Jansen, G., & Peshkin, A. (1992). Subjectivity in qualitative research. In M. LeCompte, W. Millroy, & J. Preissle (Eds.), *The handbook of qualitative research in education* (pp. 681–725). London: Academic Press.

Janson, A., & Janson, H. W. (2006). *Janson's history of art* (7th ed.). New York: Prentice Hall Art.

Jansz, J., & Drunen, P. van. (2004). *A social history of psychology.* Oxford: Blackwell Publishing Ltd.

Johnstone, R. (1997). *Religion in society: A sociology of religion* (5th ed.). Upper Saddle River: NJ: Prentice-Hall.

Jonas, H. (1958). *The Gnostic God: The message of the alien God and the beginnings of Christianity.* Boston: Beacon Press.

Jones, M., Jones, B., & Hargrove, T. (2003). *The unintended consequences of high-stakes testing.* Lanham, MD: Rowman & Littlefield.

Jung, C. G. (1938). *Psychology and religion.* New Haven: Yale University Press.

Jung, C. G. (1954a). *The development of personality* (vol. 17) (R. F. C. Hull, Trans.). Bollingen Series XX. Princeton, NJ: Princeton University Press.

Jung, C. G. (1954b). *The symbolic life* (vol. 18) (R. F. C. Hull, Trans.). Bollingen Series XX. Princeton, NJ: Princeton University Press.

Jung, C. G. (1957). *Modern man in search of a soul.* New York: Harcourt, Brace and World.

Jung, C. G. (1961). *Freud and psychoanalysis* (vol. 4) (R. F. C. Hull, Trans.). Bollingen Series XX. Princeton, NJ: Princeton University Press.

Jung, C. G. (1965). *Memories, dreams, reflections.* New York: Vintage.

Jung, C. G. (1966a). *The practice of psychotherapy: General problems of psychotherapy* (vol. 16) (R. F. C. Hull, Trans.). Bollingen Series XX. Princeton, NJ: Princeton University Press.

Jung, C. G. (1966b). *The spirit in man, art and literature* (vol. 15) (R. F. C. Hull, Trans.). Bollingen Series XX. Princeton, NJ: Princeton University Press.

Jung, C. G. (1966c). *Two essays on analytical psychology* (vol. 7) (R. F. C. Hull, Trans.). Bollingen Series XX. Princeton, NJ: Princeton University Press.

Jung, C. G. (1967). *Symbols of transformation* (vol. 5) (R. F. C. Hull, Trans.). Bollingen Series XX. Princeton, NJ: Princeton University Press.

Jung, C. G. (1968a). *Aion: Researches into the phenomenology of the self* (vol. 9.2) (R. F. C. Hull, Trans.). Bollingen Series XX. Princeton, NJ: University Press.

Jung, C. G. (1968b). *Alchemical studies* (vol. 13) (R. F. C. Hull, Trans.). Bollingen Series XX. Princeton, NJ: Princeton University Press.

Jung, C. G. (1968c). *The archetypes and the collective unconscious* (vol. 9.1) (R. F. C. Hull, Trans.). Bollingen Series XX. Princeton, NJ: Princeton University Press.

Jung, C. G. (1968d). *Psychology and alchemy* (vol. 12) (R. F. C. Hull, Trans.). Bollingen Series XX. Princeton, NJ: Princeton University Press.

Jung, C. G. (1969a). *Psychology and religion: West and East* (vol. 11) (R. F. C. Hull, Trans.). Bollingen Series XX. Princeton, NJ: Princeton University Press.

Jung, C. G. (1969b). *The structure and dynamics of the psyche* (vol. 8) (R. F. C. Hull, Trans.). Bollingen Series XX. Princeton, NJ: Princeton University Press.

Jung, C. G. (1970a). *Civilization in transition* (vol. 10) (R. F. C. Hull, Trans.). Bollingen Series XX. Princeton, NJ: Princeton University Press.

Jung, C. G. (1970b). *Mysterium coniunctionis: An inquiry into the separation and synthesis of psychic opposites in alchemy* (vol. 14) (R. F. C. Hull, Trans.). Bollingen Series XX. Princeton, NJ: Princeton University Press.

Jung, C. G. (1971). *Psychological types* (vol. 6) (R. F. C. Hull, Trans.). Bollingen Series XX. Princeton, NJ: Princeton University Press.

Jung, C. G. (1972). *Mandala symbolism.* Princeton, NJ: Princeton University Press.

Jung, C. G. (1973). *Letters* (vol. 1). (R. F. C. Hull, Trans.). Princeton, NJ: Princeton University Press.

Jung, C. G. (1978). *Psychology and the East* (R. F. C. Hull, Trans.). Princeton, NJ: Princeton University Press.

Jung, C. G. (1979). *Flying saucers: A modern myth of things seen in the sky.* Bollingen Series XX. Princeton, NJ: Princeton University Press.

Jung, C. G. (1984). *Psychology and Western religion.* Bollingen Series XX. Princeton, NJ: Princeton University Press.

Jung, C. G. (2009). *The red book: Liber novus* (edited and introduced by Sonu Shamdasani). New York: W.W. Norton.

Jung, E., & von Franz, M-L. (1986a). *Four archetypes: Mother, rebirth, trickster, spirit* (pp. 83–133). London: Routledge and Kegan Paul.

Jung, E., & von Franz, M-L. (1986b). *The Grail legend.* London: Coventure.

Kalff, D. (1980). *Sandplay: A psychotherapeutic approach to the psyche.* Boston: Sigo Press.

Kalsched, D. (1997). *The inner world of trauma: Archetypal defenses of the personal spirit.* London: Routledge.

Kane, J. (Ed.). (1999). *Education, information and transformation: Essays on learning and thinking.* Columbus, OH: Merrill/Prentice Hall.

Kant, I. (1781/1997). *The critique of pure reason.* Chicago: Hackett Publishing.

Kast, V. (1998). Can you change your fate? The clinical use of a specific fairy tale as a turning point in analysis. In A. Casement (Ed.), *Post-Jungians today: Key papers in contemporary analytical psychology* (pp.119–134). London: Routledge.

Kawai, H. (1996). *Buddhism and the art of psychotherapy.* College Station: Texas A&M University Press.

Kelley, A., & Moloney, F. (2003). *Experiencing God in the Gospel of John.* New York: Paulist Press.

Kelly, S. (1993). *Individuation and the absolute: Hegel, Jung and the path towards wholeness.* Mahwah, NJ: Paulist Press.

Kelsey, M. (1984). Jung as philosopher and theologian. In R. Papadopoulos & G. Saayman (Eds.). *Jung in modern perspective: The master and his legacy* (pp. 182–192). Lindfield, Australia: Unity Press.

Kerényi, K. (1966). *Hermes: Guide of souls.* Dallas, TX: Spring Publications.

Kierkegaard, S. (1969). *A Kierkegaard anthology.* R. Bretall (Ed.). Princeton, NJ: Princeton University Press.

Kimbles, S. (2000). The cultural complex and the myth of invisibility. In T. Singer (Ed.), *The vision thing: Myth, politics and psyche in the world* (pp. 157–169). London: Routledge.

Kirsch, J. (1995). Transference. In M. Stein. (Ed.), *Jungian analysis* (pp.170–209). Chicago: Open Court Publishing Co.

Kirschner, S. (1996). *The religious and romantic origins of psychoanalysis: Individuation and integration in post-Freudian theory.* New York: Cambridge University Press.

Kittelson, M. L. (Ed.). (1998). *The soul of popular culture: Looking at contemporary heroes, myths, and monsters.* Chicago: Open Court.

Klein, M. (1932/1975). *The psychoanalysis of children.* New York: Delacorte Press.

Kliebard, H. (1986). *The struggle for the American curriculum: 1893–1958.* New York: Routledge.

Kluger, R. (1995). *Psyche in scripture: The idea of the Chosen People and other essays.* Toronto, Canada: Inner City Books.

Knapp, B. (1984). *A Jungian approach to literature.* Carbondale: Southern IL University Press.

Knox, J. (1998). Transference and countertransference. In I. Alister & C. Hauke (Eds.), *Contemporary Jungian analysis: Post-Jungian perspectives from the Society of Analytic Psychology* (pp. 73–84). London: Routledge.

Koester, C. (2003). *Symbolism in the Fourth Gospel: Meaning, mystery, community* (2nd ed.). Minneapolis: Fortress Press.

Kohlberg, L. (1987). *Child psychology and childhood education: A cognitive-developmental view.* New York: Longman.

Kohut, H. (1978). *The search for self: Selected writings of Heinz Kohut: 1950–1978.* P. Ornstein (Ed.). Madison, CT: International Universities Press.

Kopp, S. (1972). *If you meet the Buddha on the road, kill him! The pilgrimage of psychotherapy patients.* Ben Lomond, CA: Science and Behavior Books.

Kornfield, J. (1993). *A path with heart: A guide through the perils and promises of spiritual life.* New York: Bantam.

Kuhn, T. (1970). *The structure of scientific revolutions.* Chicago: University of Chicago Press.

Laing, R. D. (1967). *The divided self.* New York: Penguin Books.

Lakoff, G. (1981). *Metaphors we live by.* Chicago: University of Chicago Press.

Lakoff, G. (1987). *Women, fire, and dangerous things: What categories reveal about the human mind.* Chicago: University of Chicago Press.

Lauter, E., & Rupprecht, C. (Eds.). (1985). *Feminist archetypal theory: Interdisciplinary revisions of Jungian thought.* Knoxville: University of Tennessee Press.

Luckmann, P. (1979/1995). The structural conditions of religious consciousness in modern societies. In S. Bruce (Ed.), *The sociology of religion* (pp. 636–646). Aldershot, UK: The International Library of Critical Writings in Sociology.

Lundquist, S. (1991). *The trickster: A transformation archetype.* San Francisco: Mellen Research University Press.

Maccoby, E. (1974). *The psychology of sex differences.* Stanford, CA: Stanford University Press.

Macdonald, J. (1995). *Theory as a prayerful act: The collected essays of James P. Macdonald.* B. Macdonald (Ed.). New York: Peter Lang.

Machtiger, H. (1995a). Countertransference. In M. Stein. (Ed.), *Jungian analysis* (pp. 210–237). Chicago: Open Court Publishing Co.

Machtiger, H. (1995b). Reflections on the transference/countertransference process with borderline patients. In N. Schwartz-Salant & M. Stein (Eds.), *Transference/countertransference* (pp. 119–146). Wilmette, IL: Chiron Publications

MacIntyre, A. (1985). *After virtue: A study in moral theory.* Notre Dame, IN: University of Notre Dame Press.

Madden, K. (2008). *Dark light of the soul.* Great Barrington, MA: Lindisfarne Books.

Main, R. (2004). *The rupture of time: Synchronicity and Jung's critique of modern Western culture.* New York: Brunner-Routledge.

Marshak, M. (1998). The intersubjective nature of analysis. In I. Alister & C. Hauke (Eds.), *Contemporary Jungian analysis: Post-Jungian perspectives from the Society of Analytic Psychology* (pp. 57–72). London: Routledge.

Martin, L. (1985). Jung as gnostic. In L. Martin & J. Goss (Eds.), *Essays on the study of Jung and religion.* Lanham, MD: University Press of America.

Martin, L., & Goss, J. (Eds.). (1985). *Essays on the study of Jung and religion.* Lanham, MD: University Press of America.

Marty, M. (1970). *Righteous empire: The Protestant experience in America.* New York: The Dial Press.

Marty, M. (1987). *Religion and republic: The American circumstance.* Boston: Beacon Press.

Marx, K., & Engels, F. (1978). *The Marx-Engels reader.* R. Tucker (Ed.). New York: W.W. Norton.

Maslow, A. (1968). *Toward a psychology of being* (2nd ed.). Princeton, NJ: D. Van Nostrand.

Maslow, A. (1970). *Religions, values, and peak-experiences.* New York: Penguin Books.

Mattoon, M. (1985). *Jungian psychology in perspective.* New York: The Free Press.

Mattoon, M. (1998). Dirty politics, clean voters. In M. Kittelson (Ed.), *The soul of popular culture: Looking at contemporary heroes, myths and monsters* (pp. 243–250). Chicago: Open Court.

Maurer, A. A. (1982). *Medieval philosophy.* Toronto: Pontifical Institute of Medieval Studies.

May, R. (1969). *Existential psychology.* New York: Random House.

May, R., & Yalom, I. (1995). Existential psychotherapy. In R. Corsini & D. Wedding (Eds.), *Current psychotherapies* (pp. 262–292). Itasca, IL: F.E. Peacock Publishers.

Mayes, C. (2001). A transpersonal developmental model for teacher reflectivity. *Journal of Curriculum Studies, 33*(4), 477–493.

Mayes, C. (2002a). Personal and archetypal aspects of transference and counter-transference in the classroom. *Encounter: Education for Meaning and Social Justice, 15*(2), 34–49.

Mayes, C. (2002b). The teacher as an archetype of spirit. *Journal of Curriculum Studies, 34*(6), 699–718.

Mayes, C. (2003). Foundations of an archetypal pedagogy. *Psychological Perspectives: A Semiannual Journal of Jungian Thought. C. G. Institute of Los Angeles, 46,* 104–116.

Mayes, C. (2004a). *Seven curricular landscapes: An approach to the holistic curriculum.* Lanham, MD: University Press of America.

Mayes, C. (2004b). *Teaching mysteries: Foundations of spiritual pedagogy.* Lanham, MD: University Press of America.

Mayes, C. (2005a). *Jung and education: Elements of an archetypal pedagogy.* Lanham, MD: Rowman & Littlefield Education Press.

Mayes, C. (2005b). Teaching and time: Foundations of a temporal pedagogy. *Teaching Education Quarterly, 32*(2), 143–160.

Mayes, C. (2007). *Inside education: Depth psychology in teaching and learning.* Madison, WI: Atwood Publishing.

Mayes, C. (2009a). *The archetypal hero's journey in teaching and learning: A study in Jungian pedagogy.* Madison, WI: Atwood Publishing.

Mayes, C. (2009b). The psychoanalytic view of education: 1922–2002. *Journal of Curriculum Studies. 49*(1), 539–567.

Mayes, C. (2016, in press). *Understanding the whole student: Holistic multicultural education.* Lanham, MD: Rowman & Littlefield Education Press.

Mayes, C., & Blackwell Mayes, P. (2002). The use of sandtray in a graduate educational leadership program. *The Journal of Sandplay Therapy: The C. G. Jung Institute of Los Angeles, 11*(2), 103–124.

Mayes, C., & Blackwell Mayes, P. (2006). Sandtray therapy with a 24-year-old woman in the residual phase of schizophrenia. *The International Journal of Play Therapy, 15*(1), 101–117.

Mayes, C., Cutri, R., Montero, F., & Rogers, C. (2010). *Understanding the whole student: Holistic multicultural education.* Lanham, MD: Rowman & Littlefield.

Mayes, C., & Ferrin, S. (2001). The beliefs of spiritually committed public school teachers regarding religious expression in the classroom. *Religion and Education, 28*(1), 75–94.

Mayes, C., & Williams, E. (2012). *Nurturing the whole student: Five dimensions of a nurturing pedagogy.* Lanham, MD: Rowman & Littlefield.

McLaren, P. (1998). *Life in schools: An introduction to critical pedagogy in the foundations of education.* (3rd ed.). New York: Longman.

Meissner, W. (1984). *Psychoanalysis and religious experience.* New Haven: Yale University Press.

Merton, T. (1947). *The seven storey mountain.* New York: Harcourt, Brace.

Merton, T. (1967). *Mystics and Zen masters.* New York: Dell Publishing Company.

Miller, A. (1978). *The drama of the gifted child: The search for the true self.* New York: Basic Books.

Miller, J. (2004). *The transcendent function: Jung's model of psychological growth through dialogue with the unconscious.* Albany: State University of New York Press.

Miller, J., & Seeler, W. (1985). *Curriculum: Perspectives and practices.* New York: Longman.

Mitroff, I., & Bennis, W. (Eds.). (1993). *The unreality industry: The deliberate manufacturing of falsehood and what it is doing to our lives.* New York: Oxford University Press.

Mocanin, R. (1986). *Jung's psychology and Tibetan Buddhism: Western and Eastern paths to the heart.* London: Wisdom Publications.

Moore, R., & Meckel, D. (Eds.). (1990). *Jung and Christianity in dialogue: Faith, feminism, and hermeneutics.* New York: Paulist Press.

Morrow, R., & Torres, C. (1995). *Social theory and education: A critique of theories of social and cultural reproduction.* Albany: State University of New York Press.

Mosak, H. (1995). Adlerian psychotherapy. In R. Corsini & D. Wedding (Eds.), *Current psychotherapies: Basics and beyond* (pp. 51–94). Itasca, IL: F.E. Peacock.

Nagy, M. (1991). *Philosophical issues in the psychology of C. G. Jung.* Albany: State University of New York Press.

Neumann, E. (1954). *The origins and history of consciousness* (vol. 1). New York: Harper Brothers.

Neumann, E. (1973). *Depth psychology and a new ethic.* New York: Harper and Row Publishers.

Noll, R. (1994). *The Jung cult: Origins of a charismatic movement.* Princeton, NJ: Princeton University Press.

Nord, W. (1995). *Religion and American education: Rethinking a national dilemma.* Chapel Hill: University of North Carolina Press.

O'Boyle, C. (2006). *History of psychology: A cultural perspective.* Mahwah, NJ: Lawrence Erlbaum.

Odajnyk, V. (1976). *Jung and politics: The political and social ideas of C. G. Jung.* New York: Harper and Row.

Odajnyk, V. (1993). *Gathering the light: A psychology of meditation.* Boston: Shambhala.

Orr, D. (1988). Transference and countertransference: A historical survey. In B. Wolstein (Ed.), *Essential papers on counter-transference* (pp. 91–110). New York: New York University Press.

Orwell, G. (1984). *1984.* New York: Harcourt, Brace, Jovanovich.

Otto, R. (1960). *The idea of the holy.* Middlesex, England: Penguin Books.

Owens, L. (2010). The hermeneutics of vision: C. G. Jung and *Liber novus. The Gnostic: A Journal of Gnosticism, Western Esotericism and Spirituality, 3,* 23–46.

Paden, L. (1985). Jung and the phenomenology of religion. In J. Martin & J. Goss (Eds.), *Essays on Jung and the study of religion.* Lanham, MD: University Press of America.

Pagels, E. (1992). *The Gnostic Paul: Gnostic exegeses of the Pauline letters.* Philadelphia, PA: Trinity Press International.

Palmer, M. (1995). *Freud and Jung on religion.* London: Routledge.

Palmer, P. (1983). *To know as we are known: A spirituality of education.* San Francisco: Harper Collins Publishers.

Palmer, P. (1990). "All the way down": A spirituality of public life. In J. Palmer, B. Wheeler, & J. Fowler (Eds.), *Caring for the commonweal: Education for religious and public life* (pp. 147–164). Macon, GA: Mercer University Press.

Palmer, P. (1997). The grace of great things: Reclaiming the sacred in knowing, teaching, and learning. *Holistic Education Review, 10*(3), 8–16.

Palmer, P. (1998). *The courage to teach: Exploring the inner landscape of a teacher's life.* San Francisco: Jossey-Bass Publishers.

Papadopoulos, R. (1991). Jung and the concept of the other. In R. Papadopoulos & G. Saayman (Eds.), *Jung in modern perspective: The master and his legacy* (pp. 54–88). Dorset, UK: Prism Press.

Pauli, W., & Jung, C. G. (2001). *Atom and archetype.* Princeton, NJ: Princeton University Press.

Pauson, M. (1988). *Jung the philosopher: Essays in Jungian thought.* New York: Peter Lang.

Peat, F. D. (1988). *Synchronicity: The bridge between mind and matter.* New York: Bantam.

Peller, L. (1978). The development of the child's self. In E. Plank (Ed.), *On development and education of young children: Selected papers* (pp. 55–88). New York: Philosophical Library.

Pfister, O. (1922). *Psychoanalysis in the service of education, being an introduction to psychoanalysis.* London: Henry Kimpton.

Philipson, M. (1994). *An outline of Jungian aesthetics.* Boston: Sigo Press.

Piaget, J. (1997). *The moral judgment of the child.* New York: Simon and Schuster.

Piaget, J., & Inhelder, B. (1969). *The psychology of the child.* New York: Basic Books.

Pintrich, P., Marx, R., & Boyle, R. (1993). Beyond cold conceptual change: The role of motivational beliefs and classroom contextual factors in the process of conceptual change. *Review of Educational Research, 63,* 167–199.

Progoff, I. (1959). *Depth psychology and modern man: A new view of the magnitude of human personality, its dimensions and resources.* New York: Julian Press.

Ravitch, D. (2000). *Left back: A century of failed school reforms.* New York: Simon and Schuster.

Redfearn, J. W. T. (1981). *My self: My many selves.* London: Academic Press.

Ricoeur, P. (1976). Introduction. In P. Ricoeur (Ed.), *Cultures and time* (pp. 13–33). Paris: UNESCO.

Ricoeur, P. (1991). *Freud and philosophy: An essay in interpretation.* New Haven: Yale University Press.

Rieff, P. (1961). *Freud: The mind of the moralist.* Garden City, NY: Doubleday and Company.

Riegel, K. (1979). *Foundations of dialectical psychology.* New York: Academic Press.

Ritzer, G. (2009). *The McDonaldization of society.* Los Angeles: Pine Forge Press.

Rizzuto, A-M. (1979). *The birth of the living God: A psychoanalytic study.* Chicago: University of Chicago Press.

Roberts, T. (Ed.). (1975). *Four psychologies applied to education: Freudian, Behavioral, Humanistic, Transpersonal.* Cambridge, MA: Schenkman.

Robertson, R. (1995). *Jungian archetypes: Jung, Godel, and the history of archetypes.* York Beach, ME: Nicolas-Hays.

Rogoff, B. (2003). *The cultural nature of human development.* New York: Oxford University Press.

Rowland, S. (2005). *Jung as a writer.* New York: Routledge.

Rowling, J. K. (2003). *Harry Potter and the order of the phoenix.* New York: Arthur A. Levine Books/Scholastic Press.

Rummelhart, D. (1980). Schemata: The building blocks of cognition. In R. Spiro, B. Bruce, & W. Brewer (Eds.), *Theoretical issues in reading comprehension* (pp. 125–167). Hillside, NJ: Lawrence Erlbaum Associates.

Salzberger-Wittenberg, I. (1989). *The emotional experience of learning and teaching.* London: Routledge and Kegan Paul.

Samuels, A. (1991). *Psychopathology: Contemporary Jungian perspectives.* London: The Guilford Press.

Samuels, A. (1997). *Jung and the post-Jungians.* London: Routledge.

Samuels, A. (2001). *Politics on the couch: Citizenship and the internal life.* London: Routledge.

Sandner, D. (1991). *Navaho symbols of healing: A Jungian exploration of ritual, image, and medicine.* Rochester, VT: Healing Arts Press.

Sanford, J. (1993). *Mystical Christianity: A psychological commentary on the Gospel of John.* New York: Crossroads.

San Roque, C. (2000). Arresting Orestes: Mythic events and the law. In T. Singer (Ed.), *Myth, politics, and psyche in the world* (pp. 105–121). London: Routledge.

Sardello, R., & Sanders, C. (1999). Care of the senses: A neglected dimension of education. In J. Kane (Ed.), *Education, information and transformation: Essays on learning and thinking* (pp. 226–237). Columbus, OH: Merrill/Prentice Hall.

Sartre, J. (1956). *Being and nothingness: An essay on phenomenological ontology.* New York: Philosophical Library.

Schafer, R. (1980). Narration in the psychoanalytic dialogue. *Critical Inquiry 7*(1): 29–54.

Schipani, D. (1988). *Religious education encounters liberation theology.* Birmingham, AL: Religious Education Press.

Schumpeter, J. (1975). *Capitalism, socialism and democracy.* New York: Harper and Row.

Schwartz-Salant, N. (1995). Archetypal factors underlying sexual acting-out in the transference/countertransference process. In N. Schwartz-Salant & M. Stein (Eds.), *Transference/countertransference* (pp. 1–30). Wilmette, IL: Chiron Publications.

Scotton, B., Chinen, A., & Battista, J. (1996). *Textbook of transpersonal psychiatry and psychology.* New York: Basic Books.

Segal, R. (1995). *The allure of Gnosticism: The Gnostic experience in Jungian psychology and contemporary culture.* Chicago: Open Court.

Shamdasani, S. (2003). *Jung and the making of modern psychology: The dream of a science.* Cambridge: Cambridge University Press.

Shamdasani, S. (2005). *Jung stripped bare by his biographers, even.* London: Karnac.

Sheldrake, R. (1981). *A new science of life: The hypothesis of formative causation.* Los Angeles: Jeremy P. Tarcher.

Singer, J. (2000). *Blake, Jung, and the collective unconscious: The conflict between reason and imagination.* York Beach, ME: Nicolas-Hays, Inc.

Singer, T. (Ed.). (2000). *The vision thing: Myth, politics and psyche in the world.* London: Routledge.

Skinner, B. F. (1971). *Beyond freedom and dignity.* New York: Knopf.

Slife, B. (1993). *Time and psychological explanation.* Albany: State University of New York Press.

Smith, C. (1990). *Jung's quest for wholeness: A religious and historical perspective.* Albany: State University of New York Press.

Smith, H. (1991). *The world's religions: Our great wisdom traditions.* San Francisco: Harper.

Snider, C. (1990). *The stuff that dreams are made on: A Jungian interpretation of literature.* Wilmette, IL: Chiron Publications.

Solomon, H. (1994). The transcendent function and Hegel's dialectical vision. *Journal of Analytical Psychology, 39*(1), 77–100.

Solso, R. (1998). *Cognitive psychology.* Boston: Allyn and Bacon.

Sovatsky, S. (1998). *Words from the soul: Time, East/West spirituality, and the psychotherapeutic narrative.* Albany: State University of New York Press.

Spiegelman, J. M., & Mansfeld, V. (1996). On the physics and psychology of the transference as an interactive field. In J. Spiegelman (Ed.), *Psychotherapy as a mutual process* (pp. 183–206). Tempe, AZ: New Falcon Publications.

Spiegelman, J. M., & Mokusen, M. (1984). *Buddhism and Jungian psychology.* Tempe, AZ: New Falcon Publications.

Spiegelman, J. M., & Vasavada, U. (1987). *Hinduism and Jungian psychology.* Tempe, AZ: New Falcon Publications.

Spindler, G., & Spindler, L. (1992). Cultural process and ethnography: An anthropological perspective. In M. LeCompte, W. Millroy, & J. Preissle (Eds.), *The handbook of qualitative research in education* (pp. 52–92). London: Academic Press.

Spring, J. (1976). *The sorting machine: National educational policy since 1945.* New York: David McKay Co., Inc.

Spring, J. (2000). *The intersection of cultures: Multicultural education in the United States and the global economy.* New York: McGraw Hill.

Stein, M. (Ed.). (1982). *Jungian analysis.* Boulder, CO: Shambhala Publications.

Stein, M. (1984). Jung's Green Christ: Jung's challenge to contemporary religion. In M. Stein & R. Moore (Eds.), *Jungian analysis.* Wilmette, IL: Chiron Publications.

Stein, M. (1990). C. G. Jung: Psychologist and theologian. In R. Moore & D. Meckel (Eds.), *Jung and Christianity in dialogue: Faith, feminism, and hermeneutics* (pp. 3–20). New York: Paulist Press.

Stein, M. (1995). Power, shamanism, and maieutics in the countertransference. In N. Schwartz-Salant & M. Stein (Eds.), *Transference/countertransference* (pp. 67–88). Wilmette, IL: Chiron Publications.

Stein, M. (2006). *The principle of individuation: Toward the development of human consciousness.* Wilmette, IL: Chiron Publications.

Stevens, A. (1999). *On Jung: An updated edition with a reply to Jung's critics* (2nd ed.). Princeton, NJ: Princeton University Press.

Stevens, A. (2000). *Archetype revisited: An updated natural history of the self.* London: Brunner-Routledge.

Stone, L. (1988). The transference-countertransference complex. In B. Wolstein (Ed.), *Essential papers on counter-transference* (pp. 270–281). New York: New York University Press.

Sugg, R. (1992). *Jungian literary criticism.* Evanston, IL: Northwestern University Press.

Suzuki, D. T. (1964). *An introduction to Zen Buddhism.* New York: Grove Press, Inc.

Swatos, W., Jr. (Ed.). (1987). *Religious sociology: Interfaces and boundaries.* New York: Greenwood Press.

Tacey, D. (2001). *Jung and the New Age.* Philadelphia, PA: Brunner Routledge.

Tarnas, R. (2011). *Cosmos and psyche: Intimations of a new worldview.* New York: Random House.

Taylor, C. (1992). *Sources of the self: The making of modern identity.* Cambridge, MA: Harvard University Press.

Tennyson, A. (2013). *Alfred, Lord Tennyson: An anthology*. Cambridge: Cambridge University Press.

Thoreau, H. D. (2008). *Civil disobedience and other essays*. New York: W.W. Norton.

Thoma, S. (1986). Estimating gender differences in the comprehension and preference of moral issues. *Developmental Review, 6*(2), 165–180.

Tillich, P. (1952). *The courage to be*. New Haven: Yale University Press.

Tillich, P. (1956). *The essential Tillich*. New York: Macmillan Publishing Co.

Tillich, P. (1959). *Theology of culture*. New York: Oxford University Press.

Tillich, P. (1987). *The essential Tillich: An anthology of the writings of Paul Tillich*. E. Church (Ed.). New York: Macmillan.

Tyack, D. (1974). *The one best system: A history of American urban education*. Cambridge, MA: Harvard University Press.

Ulanov, A. (1985). Image and Imago: Jung and the study of religion. In J. Martin & J. Goss (Eds.), *Essays on Jung and the study of religion*. Lanham, MD: University Press of America.

Ulanov, A. (1999). *Religion and the spiritual in Carl Jung*. New York: Paulist Press.

Ulanov, A. (2001). *Finding space: Winnicott, God, and psychic reality*. Louisville, KY: Westminster John Knox Press.

Ulasney, D. (2000). Cultural transition and spiritual transformation: From Alexander the Great to cyberspace. In T. Singer (Ed.), *The vision thing: Myth, politics and psyche in the modern world* (pp. 213–231). London: Routledge.

Underhill, E. (1961). *Mysticism: A study in the nature and development of man's spiritual consciousness*. New York: E.P. Dutton.

Van der Heydt, V. (1976). *Prospects for the soul: Soundings in Jungian psychology and religion*. London: Barton, Longman, and Todd.

Van der Post, L. (1975). *Jung and the story of our time*. New York: Pantheon Books.

Vaughan-Lee, L. (1998). *Catching the thread: Sufism, dreamwork, and Jungian psychology*. Inverness, CA: The Golden Sufi Center.

Vivas, E., & Krieger, M. (Eds.). (1953). *The problems of aesthetics*. New York: Reinhart.

Von Franz, M.-L. (1974). *Number and time: Reflections leading toward a unification of depth psychology and physics*. Evanston, IL: Northwestern University Press.

Von Franz, M.-L. (1981). *Puer aeternus*. Santa Monica, CA: Sigo Press.

Von Franz, M-L. (1991). Meeting and order: Concerning meeting points and differences between depth psychology and physics. In R. Papadopoulos & G. Saayman (Eds.), *Jung in modern perspective: The master and his legacy* (pp. 268–286). Dorset, UK: Prism Press.

Von Franz, M.-L. (1992). *Psyche and matter*. Boston: Shambhala.

Von Franz, M.-L. (1997). *Archetypal patterns in fairy tales*. Toronto: Inner City Press.

Vygotsky, L. (1986). *Mind in society: The development of higher psychological processes*. Cambridge, MA: Harvard University Press.

Wade, J. (1996). *Changes of mind: A holonomic theory of the evolution of consciousness*. Albany: State University of New York Press.

Walsh, R. (1990). *The spirit of shamanism*. Los Angeles: Jeremy P. Tarcher, Inc.

Washburn, M. (1995). *The ego and the dynamic ground: A transpersonal theory of human development*. Albany: State University of New York Press.

Watts, A. (1969). *The divided self: An existential study in sanity and madness*. New York: Penguin Books.

Wehr, G. (2002). *Jung and Steiner: The birth of a new psychology*. Great Barrington, MA: Anthroposophic Press.

Weinrib, E. (1983). *Images of the self*. Boston: Sigo Press.

Weisstub, E. (2000). Reflections from the backside of a dollar: Myth and the origins of diversity. In T. Singer (Ed.), *The vision thing: Myth, politics and psyche in the world*. London: Routledge.

Welch, J. (1982). *Spiritual pilgrims: Carl Jung and Teresa of Avila*. New York: Paulist Press.

Weston, J. (1957) *From ritual to romance*. Garden City, NY: Doubleday.

Wexler, P. (1996). *Holy sparks: Social theory, education and religion*. New York: St. Martin's Press.

Wheelwright, P. (1974). Poetry, myth, and reality. In W. Handy & M. Westbrook (Eds.), *Twentieth century criticism: The major statements* (pp. 252–266). New York: Macmillan.

White, M., & Epston, D. (1990). *Narrative means to therapeutic ends.* New York: W.W. Norton.

White, V. (1982). *God and the unconscious.* Dallas, TX: Spring Publications.

Whitehead, A. (1929). *Process and reality: An essay in cosmology.* New York: Macmillan Co.

Whitmore, D. (1986). *Psychosynthesis in education: A guide to the joy of learning.* Rochester, VT: Destiny Books.

Wickes, F. (1966). *The inner world of childhood.* Englewood Cliffs, NJ: Prentice Hall.

Wilber, K. (1983). *A sociable God: A brief introduction to a transcendental sociology.* New York: McGraw-Hill Book Company.

Wilber, K. (1996). *A brief history of everything.* Boston: Shambhala.

Wilber, K. (2000). *Integral psychology: Consciousness, spirit, psychology, therapy.* London: Shambhala.

Wilber, K. (2001). *Sex, ecology and spirituality: The spirit of evolution.* Boston: Shambhala.

Wilson, G. (1995). Behavior therapy. In R. Corsini & D. Wedding (Eds.), *Current psychotherapies: Basics and beyond* (pp. 229–261). Itasca, IL: F.E. Peacock.

Wilson, W. J. (1987). *The truly disadvantaged: The inner city, the underclass, and public policy.* Chicago: University of Chicago Press.

Winnicott, D. W. (1988). *Psychoanalytic explorations.* C. Winnicott, R. Shepherd, & M. Davis (Eds.). Cambridge, MA: Harvard University Press.

Winnicott, D. W. (1992). The mother-infant experience of mutuality. In C. Winnicott, R. Shepherd, & M. Davis (Eds.), *Psychoanalytic explorations* (pp. 251–260). Cambridge, MA: Harvard University Press.

Wittgenstein, L. (1953). *Philosophical investigations.* New York: Macmillan.

Wolstein, B. (Ed.). *Essential papers on counter-transference.* New York: New York University Press.

Woodman, M. (1990). *The ravaged bridegroom: Masculinity in women.* Toronto: Inner City Books.

Woodman, M. (1995). Transference and countertransference in analysis dealing with eating disorders. In N. Schwartz-Salant & M. Stein (Eds.), *Transference/countertransference* (pp. 53–66). Wilmette, IL: Chiron Publications.

Woods, P. (1992). Symbolic interactionism: Theory and method. In M. LeCompte, W. Millroy, & J. Preissle (Eds.), *The handbook of qualitative research in education* (pp. 337–404). London: Academic Press.

Wrightsman, L. (1994). *Adult personality development: Theories and concepts.* Thousand Oaks, CA: Sage Publications.

Wuthnow, R. (1994). *Producing the sacred: An essay on public religion.* Chicago: University of IL Press.

Yeats, W. B. (1971). *The collected poems of William Butler Yeats.* New York: Vintage Books.

Yogananda, Paramahansa. (1946). *Autobiography of a yogi.* Los Angeles: Self Realization Fellowship.

Young-Eisendrath, P. (1997). Gender and contrasexuality: Jung's contribution and beyond. In P. Young-Eisendrath & T. Dawson (Eds.), *The Cambridge companion to Jung* (pp. 223–239). Cambridge: Cambridge University Press.

Yutang, L. (1948). *The wisdom of Laotse.* New York: The Modern Library.

Zinn, H. (1990). *A people's history of the United States.* New York: Harper Perennial.

Zoja, L. (1998). Analysis and tragedy. In A. Casement (Ed.), *Post-Jungians today: Key papers in contemporary analytical psychology* (pp. 33–49). London: Routledge.

Index